AF766649

International Sanctions in Practice: An Interdisciplinary Perspective

Unilateral or plurilateral restrictive measures, commonly referred to as "sanctions", by States or regional organizations have been acquiring an enormous practical importance in the last decades, leading also to the institution of a European Union's sanctioning mechanism of its own. In addition to that, the war in Ukraine, triggered by the Russian aggression, has given them an unprecedented visibility, including in the mainstream media. The matter nevertheless remains particularly complex, given its diverse implications from a legal as well as from an economic-financial point of view, and not least in a political perspective.
This book follows up the workshop that was held at the University of Florence on 9-10 December 2021 and collects original contributions from promising or acclaimed/leading experts on sanctions. This book's aim is to address key aspects relating to the use of international sanctions by assembling contributions from different fields of expertise with a view to providing readers with an interdisciplinary perspective. Insofar as possible, each part of the book (devoted to three main themes: legality and legitimacy; extraterritorial implications; effectiveness) consists of a "dialogue" between experts coming from different fields.
What is the legal basis of sanctions but also how does this impact their legitimacy and the perception of their legitimacy? What are the complex implications of the extraterritorial effects that sanctions often produce or are even intended to produce? And last but not least, how effective are they and – most importantly – in relation to what underlying aims? It is hardly possible to tackle such key questions through a unique disciplinary lens. This book thus represents an invitation (to scholars, experts and decision-makers) to adopt an interdisciplinary approach that at this point can no longer be eluded.

Antonio Bultrini is associate professor at the University of Florence, where he teaches international law, human rights and the law of armed conflict. He formerly served at the Council of Europe, in Strasbourg, for over 13 years. As of 2020 he is a member of the Committee "Use of Force: Military Assistance on Request" of the International Law Association. His research currently deals with the use of armed force, also in relation to civil wars, international sanctions and the protection of human rights at universal level.

Mirko Sossai is associate professor of international law at the Law Department of the Roma Tre University, Italy, where he also teaches law of international organizations. He was co-rapporteur of the study group of the International Law Association on UN sanctions and international law. His research interests include the law of arms control, the history of international law, as well as the growing role of cities in international law.

Francesco Giumelli is an associate professor in international relations at the University of Groningen, specializing in international sanctions and illicit trade. His expertise extends to international security, European studies, foreign policy, and global governance. Dr. Giumelli employs diverse research methods to analyze complex dynamics within international sanctions and trade relations, with a focus on illicit trade and sanctions evasion. He has published three monographs and numerous articles in prestigious journals. Dr. Giumelli earned his Ph.D. at the University of Florence and has served as the deputy director of the IR department at the University of Groningen. He currently chairs the CA21133 – Globalization, Illicit Trade, Sustainability, and Security (GLITSS) and he is the Director of the theme "Development, Security and Justice" of the Rudolf Agricola School for Sustainable Development.

Clara Portela currently teaches political science at the Law School of the University of Valencia (Spain). Prior to that, she was a senior analyst with the Institute of Security Studies of the Eurpean Union and a professor at Singapore Management University. Her research focuses on multilateral sanctions, arms control and EU foreign policy. She holds a PhD from the European University Institute in Florence (Italy) and an MA from the Free University of Berlin (Germany). She is the author of the book "European Union Sanctions and Foreign Policy" (2010), for which she received the THESEUS Award for Promising Research on European Integration.

Antonio Bultrini, Francesco Giumelli,
Clara Portela and Mirko Sossai

International Sanctions in Practice: An Interdisciplinary Perspective

Routledge
Taylor & Francis Group
LONDON AND NEW YORK

G. Giappichelli Editore

First published 2025
by Routledge
4 Park Square, Milton Park, Abingdon, Oxon OX14 4RN

and by Routledge
605 Third Avenue, New York, NY 10158

Routledge is an imprint of the Taylor & Francis Group, an informa business

and by G. Giappichelli Editore
Via Po 21, Torino – Italia

British Library Cataloguing-in-Publication Data
A catalogue record for this book is available from the British Library

Names: Bultrini, Antonio, editor. | Giumelli, Francesco, editor. | Portela, Clara, editor. | Sossai, Mirko, editor.

Title: International sanctions in practice: an interdisciplinary perspective / Antonio Bultrini, Francesco Giumelli, Clara Portela, Mirko Sossai.

Description: Abingdon, Oxon [UK]; New York, NY: Routledge; Torino: G. Giappichelli Editore, 2024. | Series: Routledge-Giappichelli studies in law | Includes bibliographical references and index. | Identifiers: LCCN 2024015241 (print) | LCCN 2024015242 (ebook) | ISBN 9781032481302 (hardback) | ISBN 781032481340 (paperback) | ISBN 9781003387589 (ebook)

Subjects: LCSH: Sanctions (International law)--Congresses. | Economic sanctions--Congresses.

Classification: LCC KZ6373 .I575 2024 (print) | LCC KZ6373 (ebook) | DDC 327.1/17--dc23/eng/20240409

LC record available at https://lccn.loc.gov/2024015241
LC ebook record available at https://lccn.loc.gov/2024015242

ISBN: 978-1-032-48130-2 (hbk-Routledge)
ISBN: 978-1-003-38758-9 (ebk-Routledge)
ISBN: 978-1-032-48134-0 (pbk-Routledge)
ISBN: 979-12-211-0440-0 (hbk-Giappichelli)

Typeset in Simoncini Garamond
by G. Giappichelli Editore, Turin, Italy

The manuscript has been subjected to a peer review process prior to publication.

CONTENTS

LIST OF FIGURES AND TABLES

CONTRIBUTORS

The Editors

Antonio Bultrini is Associate Professor of International Law at the University of Florence, where he teaches International Law, Human Rights and the Law of Armed Conflict. He formerly served at the Council of Europe, in Strasbourg, for over 13 years. He also teaches International Humanitarian Law for the Italian Air Force and he is a visiting Professor at the Sant'Anna School, Pisa. As of 2020 he is a member of the Committee "Use of Force: Military Assistance on Request" of the International Law Association. His research currently deals with the use of armed force in international relations and civil wars, international sanctions and with the protection of human rights at universal level.

Francesco Giumelli is an Associate Professor in International Relations at the University of Groningen, specializing in international sanctions and illicit trade. His expertise extends to international security, European studies, foreign policy, and global governance. Dr. Giumelli employs diverse research methods to analyze complex dynamics within international sanctions and trade relations, with a focus on illicit trade and sanctions evasion. He has published three monographs and numerous articles in prestigious journals. Dr. Giumelli earned his Ph.D. at the University of Florence and has served as the deputy director of the IR department at the University of Groningen. He currently chairs the CA21133 – Globalization, Illicit Trade, Sustainability, and Security (GLITSS) and he is the Director of the theme "Development, Security and Justice" of the Rudolf Agricola School for Sustainable Development.

Clara Portela teaches Political Science at the Law School of the University of Valencia, having previously served as a Professor at Singapore Management University and as a Research Fellow with the European Union Institute for Security Studies of the (EUISS) in Paris. Her research focuses on multilateral sanctions, arms control and EU foreign policy. She holds a PhD from the European University Institute in Florence (Italy) and an

MA from the Free University of Berlin (Germany). She is the author of the book *European Union Sanctions and Foreign Policy* (Routledge, 2010), for which she received the THESEUS Award for Promising Research on European Integration. Clara Portela has been a Visiting Professor at the College of Europe, SciencesPo Grenoble, SciencesPo Lyon, SciencesPo Paris, the University of London and the University of Innsbruck, and has consulted for the European Commission, the Prime Minister Office of Finland, the Ministry of Foreign Affairs of Spain, and civil society organizations. She also serves as an advisor to the European Economic and Social Committee.

Mirko Sossai is Associate Professor of International Law at the Law Department of the Roma Tre University, Italy, where he also teaches Law of International Organizations. He received his PhD from the University of Siena and subsequently held a research position at the LUISS Guido Carli University in Rome. He was co-rapporteur of the study group of the International Law Association on UN sanctions and international law. His research interests include the law of arms control and the history of international law.

The Authors

Antonino Alì, Associate Professor of International Law, University of Trento.

Peter A.G. van Bergeijk, Full Professor of International Economics and Macroeconomics Erasmus University, International Institute of Social Studies.

Annalisa Ciampi, Full Professor, University of Verona; Ambassador of the European Network for Women Excellence.

Tiziana Corda, Postdoctoral Researcher, University of Milan.

Tabasom Djourabi-Asadabadi, Doctoral Researcher, University of Cologne; Legal Trainee at the Higher Regional Court of Cologne.

Sajjad Faraji Dizaji, Lecturer, Coventry University, School of Economics, Finance and Accounting & Associate Professor Tarbiat Modares University.

Alexandra Hofer, Assistant Professor, Utrecht University.

Erica Moret, Senior Researcher at the Graduate Institute Geneva, Global Governance Centre – IHEID & Geneva Centre of Humanitarian Studies – University of Geneva/IHEID.

Stefano Palestini, Assistant Professor in International Relations at the University of Trento, and Adjunct Professor at the Institute of Political Science, Pontificia Universidad Católica de Chile.

Keith Preble, Visiting Assistant Professor, Miami University of Ohio, USA and Postdoctoral Researcher at the Center for Policy Research at the University at Albany, SUNY, USA.

Felipe Rodriguez Silvestre, PhD Candidate at the Ghent Rolin-Jaequemyns International Law Institute of Ghent University.

Daniel Ventura, Associate Professor of Public Law, University Côte d'Azur.

Acknowledgements

The editors and the authors express their gratitude to the Department of Economics ("Dipartimento di Scienze per l'Economia e l'Impresa") of the University of Florence and to the Law Departement ("Dipartimento di Giurisprudenza") of the University Roma Tre for their financial support, without which this volume would not have been possible. We are truly grateful for their commitment to supporting cutting-edge and action-oriented research and to fostering academic growth.

FOREWORD

Antonio Bultrini

If I was asked to explain what led me to start dealing with what is commonly named "sanctions", be that properly speaking sanctions or plurilateral/unilateral restrictive measures, I would answer by referring to a more general issue: understanding what works in pushing States and other relevant actors of the international society to bring their behavior in line with international law. Of course, sanctions are nowadays about much more than finding ways to foster compliance with international law, and clearly also have wider political, economic and strategic implications: see Erika Moret's preface for an exemplification of the diverse goals for which sanctions may be adopted. Indeed, sanctions are not only functional to obtaining compliance with international law. Furthermore, part of the issues relate to sanctions *per se*, apart from their underlying purpose and legal basis, particularly whether, under which conditions and to what extent sanctions *work* – in relation to their target and to the intended aim. And even if sanctioning infringements of international law is the actual aim, the very violations that they are meant to respond to are not always clearly laid/spelled out, which would instead be highly desirable also in the case of sanctions targeting individuals.

The resort to plurilateral or unilateral "restrictive measures" or sanctions (economic, commercial, financial, targeted measures and so on), has at this point become a topical subject in the field of international relations. Its growing interest and relevance are also due to the fact that such measures, by States or regional organizations, are in the process of topping those decided by the Security Council of the United Nations. The institution, by the European Union, of a sanctioning mechanism of its own, and needless to say the unprecedented wave of packages of restrictive measures against Russia following its invasion of Ukraine, add to the topic's relevance. A bit like galaxies in outer Space ... sanctions too are expanding and accelerating at the same time.

The matter is however particularly complex, given the diverse issues that it raises from a legal point of view, from a socio-economic angle, concerning *inter alia* the collateral economic effects and the technical modalities, and last but not least in a political perspective, including such important questions as the concrete impact of sanctions, their effects, the expected results and those that are actually attained. The combined legal-political issue of their legitimacy closes the circle.

Are plurilateral or unilateral sanctioning regimes, in some cases, a mere form of punishment rather than – if that is the case – a means for obtaining compliance with international commitments? Is the proliferation of unilateral/plurilateral sanctions the consequence, or a side effect, of a certain decline of United Nations sanctioning regimes, or the opposite? Is the increasingly frequent resort to sanctions affecting the international economic-financial system and in what ways? With what costs, for whom and how does this impact on an overall cost-benefit analysis? And when we look for effective tools, for example to react to serious violations of international law, is the almost exclusive focus on sanctions leading us to neglect other useful tools, perhaps ancillary rather than frontal, particularly in institutional contexts? For example, appointments for top posts, hosting or including in major international events, and the like.

The matter is also fraught with a number of serious and tricky issues of a more fundamental character. Sanctions are clearly a direct expression of the international system being – as all international law textbooks put it – a decentralised system. On the other hand, to some extent they also express the growing failure to implement multilateral mechanisms, beginning with the United Nations collective security machinery. Furthermore, given their inherent "decentralised" nature, plurilateral and even more so unilateral sanctions tend to be the prerogative of powerful states or other international actors possessing a similar leverage. This carries with it the risk of double standards: fully justified sanctions against Russia by several States and the EU for – to begin with – its involvement in occupation of Ukrainian territory as of 2014, but no sanctions at all – so far – against Israel or Israeli natural or legal persons, by the EU and those very States, for the occupation of the Palestinian territories, now approaching its 57th year … (which issue is separate from and unrelated to the unjustified and brutal attacks waged by the Hamas movement against the South of Israel on 7th October 2023). There is also a clear need to proceed in a more orchestrated fashion, in order to avoid gaps that may well exist even within the same group of senders.

It is virtually impossible to try to gain a deeper understanding of such a complex and challenging reality without adopting a broader, holistic approach to sanctions, that is an interdisciplinary approach. And the list of issues that need to be tackled within each one of the relevant areas is impressive.

As to the law: the legal basis or justification for unilateral restrictive measures, especially when adopted "in the general interest"; legitimacy/legality issues with regard to "counter-sanctions"; the relationship with the Security Council's (properly speaking) sanctions; the new mechanism set up by the European Union, including its legal-institutional features and relevant aspects relating to its legitimacy under international law (special attention should also be paid to the formal motives/justifications underpinning specific decisions imposing restrictive measures); human rights implications of unilateral/plurilateral restrictive measures in relation to targeted individuals.

As to the economics: collateral economic effects, especially for the civilian population and key infrastructures and services; the actual economic/financial losses for the targeted State; the cost for the State resorting to restrictive measures and its economic actors (including the problem of "counter-sanctions"); the financial mechanisms that are used to impose restrictive measures; the latter's impact on companies from third States (including European Union member States), especially with regard to secondary sanctions; the measures aimed at mitigating adverse effects on companies from third States; whether the restrictive measures actually hit the targeted State or its assets and relevant actors.

As to the politics: nature and logic of restrictive measures as a foreign policy tool; profile of the States/organizations that most often resort to unilateral restrictive measures and related implications; political tool versus legal tool; actual effects of restrictive measures on the targeted State's behavior (and whether this is always a pertinent focus); whether restrictive measures actually hit the targeted State; whether the targeted State is invariably the right or the only right target; benefits in relation to costs; the problem of "counter-sanctions"; possible effects on the multilateral system resulting from the increased resort to unilateral/plurilateral restrictive measures; whether the latter are more or less effective compared to the Security Council's sanctions/sanctioning regimes.

This book originates from a workshop that was held in Florence on 12-13 December 2021. I am particularly grateful to all those who contributed to the success of the workshop as well as to those who then accepted to contribute to this volume, including some who had not been able to make it to the workshop. Interestingly, given the interdisciplinary approach that inspired it, the workshop was organised by a multidisciplinary team, including myself and the co-editors of this book as chairs of the three multidisciplinary sessions, and, not least, thanks to the funding of the Department of Economics of the University of Florence. Being myself an international lawyer and being fortunate enough to have my Department (of Economics) funding this book as well, together with the much appreciated financial support from the Law Department of RomaTre University, I can humbly say that our interdisciplinary experiment was not far-fetched after all. On the contrary, an interdisciplinary look now appears the more and more to be the only reasonable and fruitful way forward, at a time when "sanctions" and their rapidly developing ramifications are playing a significant part in re-shaping the dynamics of international relations.

PREFACE

Erica Moret

ABSTRACT: *Sanctions have become the policy instrument of choice for many governments and regional organizations around the world in addressing breaches of international norms. While their use in tackling global peace and security has plateaued in recent years at the United Nations Security Council, the use of autonomous or unilateral sanctions has been growing exponentially in recent decades in tackling global challenges and emerging threats. This trajectory looks set to continue in the years, and probably decades, to come. Twenty after targeted sanctions were first created so as to minimise harms on ordinary civilians, the growing complexity of the contemporary compliance landscape poses new ethical, legal and practical considerations, which are explored from a variety of academic disciplines in this book.*

I. Introduction

Sanctions have firmly entrenched themselves as a prominent tool of foreign and security policy in the contemporary political and economic landscape. Open any newspaper, or turn on any television news channel, and sanctions tend to figure centre stage on any given day. They impart an impact on almost every jurisdiction on earth. Most people originate from a country that either imposes sanctions, or has been the target of sanctions, at one point or another. Sanctions affect most sectors in significant ways – from international organizations (IOs), governments and law, to banks, private sector firms and non-governmental organizations (NGOs). Even areas that have long been immune to sanctions' reach on ethical grounds, such as sports and culture, are once again subject to their reach.[1] This ever popu-

---

[1] Reuters, *IOC stands by sanctions against Russia and Belarus over invasion of*

lar, yet fiercely contested, instrument, is clearly here to stay for the foreseeable future.

Reasons for sanctions' popularity are clear. They can help to encourage a shift in direction on the part of a target's behaviour or curtail its access to vital resources.[2] They allow for flexibility in showing displeasure at another's actions. They can stigmatise targets through their "naming and shaming" function. They can be applied in ways that are typically less costly than military action and can represent a useful alternative or complement to diplomacy. Sanctions can be combined with other policy instruments in a variety of ways to heighten their chances of success.[3] They can also be a useful leverage tool and a valuable way of showing solidarity with allies, as well as a means through which to demonstrate leadership in the global arena.[4] They can punish a target for its misdmeanors, while making it pay for its actions.

At the same time, debates over the legality, ethics and legitimacy of sanctions are prominent in both scholarship and public debates. Legal scholars tend to disagree on the legality of autonomous sanctions,[5] as well as the ways their use may affect International Humanitarian Law and Human Rights obligations. Others question whether they are compatible with states' obligations under the international treaties to which they subscribe (including the UN Charter as well as bilateral and multilateral trade agreements).[6] Sanctions regimes are increasingly subject to disinformation campaigns seeking to delegitimise the tool, particularly those stemming from Russia.[7] Also back in the spotlight are concerns over unintended humanitarian consequences – two decades after the creation of targeted sanctions that were intended to minimise negative impacts on civilians.[8]

Ukraine, 1 February 2023, available at https://www.theguardian.com/sport/2023/feb/01/ioc-stands-by-sanctions-against-russia-and-belarus-over-invasion-of-ukraine.

[2] Giumelli F., "New Analytical Categories for Assessing EU Sanctions", *The international Spectator: Italian Journal of International Affairs* (2010), 45, 3, 131-144.

[3] Biersteker T.J., Eckert S.E., Tourinho M. (eds.), *Targeted Sanctions: The Impacts and Effectiveness of United Nations Action*, Cambridge University Press, 2016.

[4] Taylor B., *Sanctions as Grand Strategy*, Routledge, 2010.

[5] See, for example, Van Aaken A., "Introduction to the Symposium on Unilateral Targeted Sanctions", *AJIL Unbound* (2019), 113, 130.

[6] De Vries A.W., Portela C., Guijarro-Usobiaga B., "Improving the Effectiveness of Sanctions: A Checklist for the EU", *CEPS Special Report* (2014), 95, November.

[7] Canetta T., Danko V., Dukach Y. "'Sanctions Do Not Work': Russian Disinformation Narratives About Sanctions in the EU, in Ukraine, and in Russia Itself", *euvsdisinfo.eu* (2023) available at https://euvsdisinfo.eu/sanctions-do-not-work-russian-disinfo/.

[8] Moret E., *Time to Act: Harmonizing Global Initiatives and Technology-Based Inno-*

II. Rising complexity and costs associated with sanctions

The rising complexity of sanctions and other regulations, results in a confusing, costly and complicated compliance environment, fuelled by a number of drivers. First, is the rise in numerous, intersecting sanctions regimes (with a current gap in knowledge on cumulative intended and unintended impacts). Second, is the move away from carefully targeted measures (such as travel bans, asset freezes and arms embargoes) over the past ten years, to broader, sweeping measures targeting some countries' strategically important sectors, such as finance and energy.

Third, is the fact that sanctions are typically adopted alongisde other related regulations, including counter-terrorism legislation, anti-money-laundering and countering the financing of terrorism (AML/ CFT) measures, Financial Action Task Force (FATF) listings, anti-corruption measures and export controls. Fourth, the dominance of the US Dollar (which is subject to US legislation the world over) in international finance further extends the reach of US sanctions. Fifth, is the US' use of extraterritorial measures (or secondary sanctions), which apply to individuals and entities outside of the US jurisdiction, even in the absence of any links to the country.

III. The global rise in autonomous sanctions use

Modern sanctions can take a number of forms, ranging from those adopted in the United Nations (UN) framework via a UN Security Council Resolution (UNSCR), to autonomous measures that supplement UN sanctions, to those adopted completely in their absence. The United Nations' use of sanctions has plateaued in recent years. In parallel, a number of countries have started employing autonomous restrictive measures with increased regularity: in an increasing variety of contexts; to tackle a growing number of challenges, and imposed against a mounting range of targets.[9] These shifts have come hand-in-hand with multilateralism's crisis of legitimacy, at

---

vations Addressing De-Risking at the Interfacing Sanctions-Counterterrorism-Humanitarian Nexus, in Lohmann S., Vorrath J. (eds.), *International Sanctions: Improving Implementation through Better Interface Management*, Stiftung Wissenschaft und Politik (SWP), 2021, 74-82, available at https://www.swp-berlin.org/publications/products/arbeitspapiere/WP_International_Sanctions.pdf.

[9] Moret E., *Unilateral and Extraterritorial Sanctions in Crisis: Implications of their Rising use and Misuse in Contemporary World Politics*, in Beaucillon C. (ed.), *The Research Handbook on Unilateral and Extraterritorial Sanctions*, Edward Elgar Publishing, 2021.

a time when cooperation across borders to tackle a broad range of international challenges has never been more pertinent.

Difficulties surrounding agreement on new multilateral sanctions regimes between the UNSC's Permanent members (P5), Russia, China, France, the United Kingdom (UK) and the United States (US), is a key reason for this rise in autonomous measures. Look no further than Russia's full-scale invasion of Ukraine in 2022, or the protracted crises in Syria and Venezuela, to see the weight placed on autonomous sanctions by wealthier, industrialised nations in addressing regional security challenges, conflicts and human rights abuses. Autonomous sanctions have been equally prominent in responses to resurgent threats like chemical weapons use (by Russia and Syria); emerging challenges like cyber security, or growing criminal enterprises, with dire human rights implications, such as modern slavery and human trafficking. [10]

The US is the most active and wide-ranging adopter of autonomous sanctions, which is amplified through the sizeable investigative and enforcement capabilities of the US Department of the Treasury's Office of Foreign Assets Control (OFAC). By the year 2020, the US was making use of more sanctions than the EU, UN and Canada combined; marked by some 70 sanctions programmes and the designation of around 10,000 persons (individuals, companies and other entities) around the world. [11]

A new US-EU-UK-Canada "sanctions quad" has emerged as the norm in autonomous sanctions practice, often with similar measures imposed by a G7+ grouping, that (depending on the target) can include Australia, Japan, New Zealand, South Korea, Switzerland and Singapore. In many of these countries, sanctions capacity and resourcing has been bolstered and new sanctions units have been created over the past five years. This has particularly been the case since the intensification of sanctions against Russia since 2022 – again, marking the weight that is now placed on sanctions being used outside the UN framework. Adding to the mix, non-EU European countries tend to closely align with the EU's restrictive measures through a formalised alignment process, including Norway, Lichtenstein, Iceland and Ukraine. [12] While there is some harmonisation between auton-

[10] Moret E., *What is the Role of Financial Sanctions in Tackling Modern Slavery and Human Trafficking?*, Finance Against Slavery and Trafficking Initiative (FAST), United Nations University Centre for Policy Research (UNU-CPR), 2022, available at http://collections.unu.edu/eserv/UNU:8896/UNU_FAST_FinancialSanctions.pdf.

[11] Demarais A., *Backfire: How Sanctions Reshape the World Against U.S. Interests*, Center on Global Energy Policy Series, 2022.

[12] Cardwell P.J., Moret E., "The EU, Sanctions and Regional Leadership", *European Security* (2022), June, available at https://www.tandfonline.com/doi/full/10.1080/09662839.2022.2085997.

omous this complicated web of sanctions laws and practices, major differences persist, which results in a raft of legal and regulatory risks for private sector actors and other organizations.

IV. Lower and middle income country use of autonomous sanctions

Regional organizations, such as the League of Arab States, the African Union, the Organization of American States (OAS), the Organization for Security Cooperation in Europe (OSCE) and the Economic Community of West African States (ECOWAS), have also made use of autonomous regional sanctions against their members in recent years.[13] Even the Association of Southeast Asian Nations (ASEAN), which has long opposed the use of sanctions, recently made use of restrictive measures against one of its members (Myanmar).[14] At the same time, a growing number of countries across Asia, Africa, the Middle East and Latin America are also starting to use (or have used) their own autonomous sanctions, some more transparently than others.[15]

Particularly notable is the regular use of sanctions by major non-Western economies that have historically opposed the use of autonomous sanctions. These include the cases of Russia (such as through halts to gas supplies and controls over agricultural trade with neighbouring countries)[16] and China (such as controls over leadership visits and trade deals, state-led consumer boycotts and preferential tariffs).[17] In 2019 and 2021, China went on to adopt legislation allowing for the use of Chinese autono-

[13] Charron A., Portela C., *The Relationship between United Nations Sanctions and Regional Sanctions Regimes*, in Eckert S., Weiss T. (eds.), *Targeted Sanctions: The Impacts and Effectiveness of United Nations Action*, Cambridge University Press, 2016, 101-118.

[14] Al Jazeera, "Myanmar Generals Banned from ASEAN until Peace Plan Progress", 6 August 2022, available at https://www.aljazeera.com/news/2022/8/6/myanmar-generals-banned-from-asean-until-peace-plan-progress.

[15] Eversheds Sutherland, "Global Sanctions Guide – Third Edition", (2023), available at https://ezine.eversheds-sutherland.com/global-sanctions-guide/.

[16] Moret E., Biersteker T., Giumelli F., Portela C., Veber M., Jarosz D., Bobocea C., *The New Deterrent? International Sanctions against Russia over the Ukraine Crisis: Impacts, Costs and Further Action*, Programme for the Study of International Governance, Graduate Institute, 2016, available at https://repository.graduateinstitute.ch/record/294704?ln=en.

[17] Reilly J., "China's Unilateral Sanctions", *The Washington Quarterly* (2012) 35:4:121-133, Fall.

mous sanctions and measures to protect Chinese business interests from the extraterritorial reach of US sanctions.[18]

V. Contested narratives

The use of autonomous sanctions is described by Russia, China and a number of heavily sanctioned countries using the politicised term "unilateral coercive measures".[19] When they use autonomous sanctions themselves, however, these states tend to term them "countermeasures" or avoid terming them as sanctions, per se... In spite of this, the term is out-dated does not adequately describe the reality of sanctions' contemporary use. With a few exceptions, very few sanctions regimes today are truly unilateral in nature.[20] Instead, autonomous sanctions use is increasingly "plurilateral" in nature (to borrow the term from the World Trade Organization or WTO) – often involving close coordination and alignment between 30 or more countries. The G7 also issued a statement in 2023 challenging the use of Economic Coercion used by other states.

VI. Effectiveness

Studies suggest that sanctions, when used strategically and judiciously, can sometimes play a useful role in addressing areas such as armed conflict, human rights abuses, the proliferation of weapons of mass destruction and respect for democracy.[21] Particularly important is the way in which they are combined with other policy instruments, such as diplomacy, trade, defence and referrals to legal tribunals.[22] Another important factor is collaboration between international partners: to close evasion routes; reduce cir-

---

[18] ICLG, *Sanctions China 2023*, 2023, available at https://iclg.com/practice-areas/sanctions/china.

[19] The same terminology is used in the mandate of the UN's Special Rapporteur on Unilateral Coercive Measures, adopted on 26 September 2014 by the Human Rights Council through resolution 27/21 and Corr.1 on human rights and unilateral coercive measures and renewed on October 2020, through HRC resolution 45/5.

[20] Which, according to the Cambridge Dictionary, describes "the process or fact of deciding a policy or action without involving another group or country". See, "Unilateralism", (2022), available at https://dictionary.cambridge.org/dictionary/english/unilateralism.

[21] See, for example, assessments on UN sanctions effectiveness, in the UN Sanctions App (www.unsanctionsapp.org).

[22] *Ibidem*.

cumvention, and coordinate new listings. The degree to which a given sanctions regime is targeted is another important consideration in how effective they are. Recent studies show that a single type of sanction on its own is never effective, nor is a full-blown embargo.[23] Instead, the optimal level appears to sit at three to four measures, which include some sectoral bans, excluding those on a country's energy sector.[24] At a time of increased sanctions adoption, most states and organizations do not yet have a way to systematically monitor or assess the impacts and efficacy of their sanctions regimes, including those imposed collectively.

VII. Unintended consequences

A rise in concern over unintended humanitarian consequences is another feature of the contemporary sanctions' scene. This is in spite of the best efforts of policymakers to mitigate such risks through various policy interventions and progress made since December 2022, with the creation of humanitarian carveouts across all UN sanctions regimes and many of an autonomous nature.[25] In parallel to these landmark steps forward on humanitarian exemptions, further attention is needed to curb and mitigate financial sector derisking and wider private sector over-compliance. This refers to mounting reluctance experienced among banks and other firms in providing services to the private and non-for-profit sectors seeking to operate in, or trade with, heavily sanctioned jurisdictions, due to a combination of compliance and reputational risks, lack of financial incentives and untenable resourcing burdens.

Banking derisking, in particular, places a range of constraints on humanitarian actors, such as in Syria and Afghanistan,[26] including increased bureaucracy, costs, delays and difficulty accessing functioning banking channels or accounts.[27] Furthermore, it can contribute to financial exclu-

---

[23] *Ibidem.*

[24] *Ibidem.*

[25] UNSCR 2664, available at http://unscr.com/en/resolutions/2664, and introductions of General Licences across US autonomous sanctions available at https://home.treasury.gov/policy-issues/financial-sanctions/recent-actions/20221220, with further details in FAQs 1105 to 1108, available at https://home.treasury.gov/policy-issues/financial-sanctions/faqs/added/2022-12-20.

[26] Moret E., *Life and Death: NGO access to financial services in Afghanistan*, Norwegian Refugee Council, January 2022, available at https://www.nrc.no/globalassets/pdf/reports/life-and-death/financial-access-in-afghanistan_nrc_jan-2022.pdf.

[27] Dahler J., Moret E., *Invisible Sanctions: How Over-compliance Limits Humanitari-*

sion and the weakening of resilience among vulnerable communities,[28] including through constraints on the sending of diaspora remittances.[29] It can also contribute to a rise in inflationary pressures, which in turn can reduce purchasing power and push up the cost of basic goods.[30] The phenomenon of de-risking has been recognised as such a fast-growing problem that organizations such as the International Monetary Fund (IMF), World Bank, Financial Stability Board (FSB) and FATF have called for urgent, new measures to tackle the problem.[31]

VIII. Conclusion

The increasing complexity of legislative frameworks governing autonomous sanctions use presents novel legal, normative and compliance challenges. The explosion in plurilateral autonomous sanctions use means there is a heightened need for thinking on how best to apply, enforce and lift[32] sanctions as a concerted and harmonised strategy, as well as finding collective ways to better avoid unintended consequences. This is particularly the case with measures that are of a broad, sectoral nature or when multiple autonomous and multilateral sanctions regimes overlap with one another, and withrelated regulations, with (as yet) poorly understood consequences. An added risk is

---

an Work on Syria, IMPACT, 2020, available at https://www.impact-csrd.org/invisible-sanctions/; Walker J., "Risk Management Principles Guide for Sending Humanitarian Funds into Syria and Similar High-risk Jurisdictions", 2020, available at https://www.graduateinstitute.ch/index.php/communications/news/compliance-dialogue-syria-related-humanitarian-payments.

[28] Pelter Z., Teixeira C., Moret E., "Sanctions and their Impact on Children", UNICEF, February 2022, available at https://www.unicef.org/globalinsight/media/2531/file/%20UNICEF-Global-Insight-Sanctions-and-Children-2022.pdf.

[29] Moret E., "A lifeline under threat? Syrian household remittances in light of sanctions, de-risking, the Covid-19 pandemic & regional developments", UN-ESCWA, National Agenda for the Future of Syria (NAFS) Phase II, 2022, available at https://nafs.unescwa.org/sites/default/files/2023-02/A%20Lifeline-under-Threat-EN-Web.pdf.

[30] Batmanghelidj E., "The Inflation Weapon: How American Sanctions Harm Iranian Households", Fourth Freedom Forum, 2022, available at https://sanctionsandsecurity.org/wp-content/uploads/2022/01/2022-January-Iran-Case_Batmanghelidj.pdf.

[31] Moret E., "More Civilian Pain than Political Gain (Again?): The Demise of Targeted Sanctions and Associated Humanitarian Impacts", in Charron A., Portela C. (eds.), *Multilateral Sanctions Revisited: Lessons Learned from Margaret Doxey*, McGill Queen's University Press, 2022.

[32] Hudáková Z., Biersteker T., Moret E., "Sanctions Relaxation and Conflict Resolution: Lessons from Past Sanctions Regimes", Carter Center, October 2021, available at https://www.cartercenter.org/resources/pdfs/peace/conflict_resolution/sanctions-relaxation-10-2021.pdf.

that sanctions between the world's two economic powerhouses, the US and China, are likely to become a new battleground of economic statecraft in the years to come. Additional risks are associated with the creation of altnerative financial systems, payment pathways and a rise in retaliatory countermeasures.[33]

With over 20 years having passed since the Bonn-Berlin, Interlaken and Stockholm Process of the early 2000s, which led to the creation of targeted sanctions, careful reflection is vital on how the UN, states and regional organizations can continue using sanctions in the decades to come in a way that adapts – judiciously and ethically – to technological, financial and geopolitical change.[34] Also fundamental are assessments on the intended and unintended impacts of sanctions by those who make use of them, to allow for risks and negative consequences to be minimised and mitigated, not only reactively but also preventatively. Academia can contribute to this process. The far-reaching and multi-faceted nature of sanctions lends them to be studied from a multiplicity of academic angles – from political science and international relations, to economics and history, to human geography and environmental science, and to social anthropology and public health. It is for this reason that this book, which approaches sanctions legality and effectiveness from a variety of academic perspectives, marks an important and timely contribution to the literature.

---

[33] Demarais A., *Backfire: How Sanctions Reshape the World Against U.S. Interests*, Center on Global Energy Policy Series, 2022.

[34] This is the focus of a new international stakeholder engagement at Wilton Park, UK: "Advancing Humanitarianism through Sanctions Refinement or AHSR", launched in 2022, available at https://sanctionsreformproject.org/about/.

Chapter 1

'COMMUNITY INTERESTS' AS AN APPROPRIATE LEGAL BASIS FOR THE IMPLEMENTATION OF UNILATERAL TARGETED MEASURES

Daniel Ventura

ABSTRACT: *This contribution aims at questioning the validity under international law of unilateral targeted measures justified by the 'interests of the international community'. Based upon the inadequacy of the legal qualification of 'countermeasures', it postulates that a particular set of targeted measures could be considered prima facie lawful and contributing to the emergence of an international public order.*

1.1. Introductory remarks

The interest of the international community has become a convenient – not to say, trendy – argument raised by a growing number of States to justify the implementation of 'confrontational means' of enforcement of international human rights and fundamental principles of international law.[1] Such 'confrontational means' include unilateral measures targeting foreign individuals, waivers of jurisdictional immunity of State officials, or domestic judicial proceedings based on a universal or quasi-universal title of jurisdic-

---

[1] See: Wolfrum R., "Solidarity and Community Interests: Driving Forces For the Interpretation and Development of International Law", *Collected Courses of the Hague Academy of International Law* (2021), 416, 386.

tion. Each of these measures contribute to the progressive 'consolidation of peremptory norms of *jus cogens*, with the corresponding obligations *erga omnes* of protection'.[2] They eventually pave the way for the creation of a decentralized international public order based upon the observance of international human rights by accountable entities.

This ambition is rooted in the belief that the minimalist bilateral model of international rights and duties, which is grounded in a reciprocity-based framework, can be overcome.[3] From this perspective, it is in line with a certain conception of 'global constitutionalism' that seeks to 'humanise' State sovereignty by considering that its *telos* – its ultimate end – rests in the protection of human interests.[4] This approach does not require to endow the international legal order with a formalized international Constitution arranging the powers of institutionalized bodies. Rather, it seeks to constitutionalize the fragmentation of international law by preserving its horizontal distribution of powers and competences, while at the same time placing universal values at the heart of the international society.[5]

It is not the purpose of this contribution to venture into a risky attempt to systematise the notion of international public order and its interplay with that of 'community interests'. Its specific content, as well as the responsibility regime and precise means of enforcement, are the subject of heated debates, with respect to not only the law on immunities but also State jurisdiction and the content of *jus cogens* norms. Nor is it the aim of the chapter to assess the validity of so called 'unilateral coercive measures' in international law.[6] It is indeed doubtful, to say the least, that this catch-all catego-

---

[2] *Legal Consequences of the Separation of the Chagos Archipelago from Mauritius in 1965*, Advisory Opinion, ICJ Reports 2019, 95, sep. op. Cançado Trindade [120].

[3] Simma B., "From Bilateralism to Community Interest", *Coll. Courses of the Hague Academy of International Law* (1994), 250, 217.

[4] Peters A., "Humanity as the A and Ω of Sovereignty", *EJIL* (2009), 20:3, 513.

[5] See de Frouville O., "Une théorie non constitutionnaliste de la Constitution internationale", *Jus Politicum* (2018), 19; Peters A., *Fragmentation and Constitutionalization*, in Orford A., Hoffmann F. (eds.), *The Oxford Handbook of the Theory of International Law*, OUP, 2016, 1011.

[6] For vivid critics on the legality of such measures in international law, see e.g.: Ronzitti N., *Sanctions as Instruments of Coercive Diplomacy: An International Law Perspective*, in Ronzitti N., *Coercive Diplomacy, Sanctions and International Law* , Brill, 2016, 1; Hofer A., *Chapter 11 – Unilateral Sanctions as a Challenge to the Law of State Responsibility*, in Beaucillon C. (ed.), *Research Handbook on Unilateral and Extraterritorial Sanctions*, EE Elgar, 2021, 186; Dawidowicz M., *Chapter 19 – Third-party countermeasures: observations on a controversial concept*, in Chinkin C., Baetens F. (eds.), *Sovereignty, Statehood and State Responsibility, Essays in Honours of James Crawford*, CUP, 2015, 340.

ry may be of any relevance when it comes to assess whether such measures can be qualified as wholly lawful or unlawful under international law.[7] This '*terra incognita*', as Alain Pellet called it, is the breeding ground for a myriad of decentralized measures of enforcement, each with its own particularities, scope, and therefore, legal regime.[8] Despite this observation, 'unilateral coercive measures' have been understood as a homogeneous phenomenon for the past fifteen years through the work of the UN General assembly,[9] the UN Human Rights Council[10] and its Special Rapporteur on the topic.[11] These bodies were able to unambiguously assert that 'unilateral coercive measures' are 'contrary to international law, international humanitarian law, the Charter of the United Nations and the norms and principles governing peaceful relations among States'.[12] Relying upon this finding, the vast majority of doctrinal debates revolve around whether countermeasures or so-called 'third-party countermeasures' may preclude the alleged inherent wrongful-

---

On the assumption that some of these measures might be inherently lawful, see e.g., Alland D., "Les mesures de reaction à l'illicite prises par l'Union européenne motif pris d'un certain intérêt general", *Rivista di Diritto Internazionale* (2022), 105:2, 369; Sossai M., *Sanzioni delle nazioni unite e organizzani regionali*, Tre Press, 2020, 160-170; Ruys T., *Sanctions, Retorsions and Countermeasures: Concepts and International Legal Framework*, in van den Herik L. (ed.), *Research Handbook on UN Sanctions and International Law*, EE Publishing, 2017, 709-710; Gaja G, *Obligations Erga Omnes, International Crimes and Jus Cogens: A Tentative Analysis of Three Related Concepts*, in Weiler J.H.H., Cassese A., Spinedi M. (eds.), *International Crimes of States. A Critical Analysis of the ILC's Draft Article 19 of State Responsibility*, de Gruyter, 1989, 151, 158; Simma B., *Peace through Law: The Role of the ILC*, in Nolte G. (ed.), *Peace through International Law*, Springer, 2009, 189; Tams C., *Individual States as Guardians of Community Interests*, in Fastenrath U., et al., (eds.), *From Bilateralism to Community Interest. Essays in Honour of Bruno Simma*, OUP, 2011, 379, 390-392, 399. See also, Ventura D., "Le gel des avoirs d'individus dans l'ordre juridique international: Caractérisation et qualification d'une voie d'exécution en mutation", *Revue Générale de Droit International Public* (2022), 2, 247.

[7] On this topic, see e.g. Prezas I., *From Targeted States to Affected Populations: Exploring Accountability for the Negative Impact of Comprehensive Universal Sanctions on Human Rights*, in Beaucillon C. (ed.), *Research Handbook*, cit., 385.

[8] Pellet A., "Memorandum from Alain Pellet: Unilateral Sanctions and International Law", *AIDI* (2015), 76, 723-736, 726.

[9] See Resolution 71/193 adopted on 19 December 2016, A/RES/71/193.

[10] Under the 'Human rights and unilateral coercive measures' agenda of the HRC, see e.g., Resolution 6/7, 28 September 2007; Resolution 34/13, 7 April 2017.

[11] See e.g. the first report of Special Rapporteur Alena Douhan, "Negative impact of unilateral coercive measures: priorities and road map", A/HRC/45/7, 21 July 2020. See also the fifth annual report submitted to the HRC by the former Special Rapporteur Idriss Jazairy, A/HRC/42/46, 5 July 2019.

[12] As recalled in every document quoted above.

ness of unilateral measures taken as a whole. In other words, the law of international responsibility of States has still been perceived as the main legal framework to assess the validity of unilateral coercive measures.

Against this background, it is our understanding that a particular set of 'unilateral coercive measures' – in this instance, targeted individual measures – may be singled out as a coherent legal phenomenon, whose purpose is not to implement State responsibility and even less so to enforce 'countermeasures' but to secure the implementation of fundamental values of the international legal order, as a matter of universal concern and through the exercise of specific public powers.[13] More precisely and to avoid any confusion, targeted individual measures, that are implemented by non-injured States in defence of 'community interests', may be considered – when and where appropriate – to implement the international public order in a decentralized yet lawful manner. In that respect, the European Union has been reacting to violations of international humanitarian law as well as 'serious human rights violations and abuses worldwide'.[14] Other jurisdictions, such as the United States (US) or Canada, have extended the reach of 'community interests' to economic damages to the rule of law, such as acts of corruption or embezzlement of public funds. The so-called '*Magnitsky acts*' are flourishing in this regard and enable States to freeze the assets of allegedly corrupt leaders, which are stored within their territory.[15] All these normative bases share the assumption that the implementation of a specific set of international norms calls for a specific set of enforcement measures, beside the centralized mechanisms provided by universal organisations and jurisdictions.

Assessing the validity of decentralized individual measures on the basis

---

[13] Simma B., "From Bilateralism to Community Interest", cit., 233. See also, Tams C.J., *Individual States as Guardians of Community Interests*, in Fastenrath U., et al. (eds.), *From Bilateralism to Community Interest. Essays in Honour of Bruno Simma*, OUP, 2011, 379, 379-380; Feichtner I., *Community Interest*, in Wolfrum R. (ed.), *Max Planck Encyclopedia of Public International Law*, Oxford University Press, online ed.

[14] EU Council Decision 2020/1999 of 7 December 2020, OJ L 410I, 7.12.2020, 13.

[15] See for instance the US *Global Magnitski Human Rights Accountability Act*, 18 April 2016, Sec 3 'Authorization of imposition of sanctions' (a) (3) available at https://www.congress.gov/bill/114th-congress/senate-bill/284/text.

The UK *Global Anti-Corruption Sanctions Regulations 2021*, 23 April 2021, SI 2021 No. 488, available at https://www.legislation.gov.uk/uksi/2021/488/contents/made.

The Canadian *Justice for Victims of Corrupt Foreign Officials Act (Sergei Magnitsky Law)*, 18 October 2017, SC 2017, C 21; see also the Resolution of the EU parliament of 8 July 2021 on the *EU Global Human Rights Sanctions Regime (EU Magnistky Act)*, calling to include acts of corruption as a ground for EU autonomous sanctions: available at https://www.europarl.europa.eu/doceo/document/TA-9-2021-0349_EN.html.

of 'community interests' requires, in the first place, identifying their peculiarities. On the one hand, what needs to be done is to deconstruct the idea that the law of State responsibility is necessarily the appropriate tool to apprehend their validity (**1.2.**). On the other hand, it is our purpose to demonstrate that these measures are not necessarily *prima facie* illegal, anarchic or 'unpolite'. In the absence of a clear conventional legal regime, their validity can be assessed either in light of general principles of international law or, in an axiological perspective, in light of ethics, as the main criterion of the emerging international public order (**1.3.**).

1.2. Assessing the peculiarity of targeted individual measures adopted in the name of 'community interests'

The validity of targeted individual measures under international law cannot, for the time being, be established by reference to any *ad hoc* legal regime. In this context, a common view is to consider their validity through the notion of 'countermeasures' which proves to be a misleading legal justification in many cases (**1.2.1.**). To say the least, protecting 'community interests' through targeted individual measures is a spontaneous and remedial phenomenon of international law whose validity cannot be excluded. The current lack of *ad hoc* regimes does not mean that these measures operate in a legal vacuum but only that their legal regime still needs to be sophisticated and systematized (**1.2.2.**).

1.2.1. 'Countermeasures' as a misleading legal justification

A countermeasure, as a response to the continuing international wrongful act of a responsible State, is aimed at inducing it to comply with its international obligations to either cease the violation of a primary obligation or to provide reparation to the injured State (or to the international community in the case of so-called 'third-party countermeasures'). 'Countermeasures' can be invoked as a legal defence only if the relevant acts are inherently unlawful, and most importantly, if they actually fit their core requirements. Yet, there are at least three reasons why 'countermeasures' may be irrelevant to assess the validity of targeted individual measures adopted in the name of 'community interests'.

First, such measures may be directed against individuals who simply do not hold an official status and whose acts are in no way attributable to a State. For instance, acts of corruption, embezzlement of State funds and money laundering are acts which cannot – or in any way *should not* – be attributed to a State insofar as they are not accomplished 'in an official capacity' but rather 'under the cover' of State functions and at the expense of the State. As such, they are deemed to be '*detachable*' from the exercise of official functions and fall beyond the scope of the law of international responsibility of States. [16] Asset freezing measures against former Tunisian, [17] Egyptian [18] and Ukrainian [19] leaders illustrate this finding. These leaders were listed by the EU shortly after their flight or removal from office, based on alleged misappropriation of State funds and at the request of all three States, to help their ongoing or imminent judicial proceedings and prevent the flight of assets. In such cases, asset freezing measures have exactly the same effects as judicial measures of attachment of assets, pending trial.

In the same manner, both the *UK Global Human Rights Sanctions Regulations 2020* [20] as well as the *UK Global Anti-Corruption Sanctions Regulations 2021* [21] provide for financial restrictions and travel bans in response to continuing or past activities performed at the expense of a State. Notably, in April 2021, the UK Foreign Secretary froze the assets of the Gupta brothers, accused of serious corruption with the former South African government of Jacob Zuma and misappropriating hundreds of millions of dollars until 2018. These measures were taken in the context of the ongoing investigations by the National Prosecuting Authority of South Africa in an attempt to get INTERPOL to issue Red Notices against them. [22]

Second, it is not because targeted measures may respond to acts which are inherently attributable to a State (such as grave violations of humanitarian law or human rights committed in the exercise of official functions) that the analytical template of 'countermeasures' is *ipso facto* relevant to assess their legality. Notably, some targeted measures are not meant to induce an illegitimate and tyrannical regime to comply with its obligations; rather, they are aimed at putting pressure on it, while taking steps to help the civilian population to empower itself and obtain a democratic transition process. In Belarus, for instance, the resumption of EU targeted sanctions

---

[16] See for instance the position of Pr. Mathias Forteau at the ILC: *Provisional summary record of the 3275th meeting*, 22 July 2015, A/CN.4/SR.3275.

[17] Council Decision 2011/72/CFSP of 31 January 2011.

[18] Council Decision 2011/172/CFSP of 21 March 2011.

[19] Council Decision 2014/119/CFSP of 5 March 2011.

[20] SI 2020 No. 680.

[21] SI 2021 No. 488.

[22] See the press release following the media statement issued by the NPA of South Africa the 5 July 2021: available at https://www.reuters.com/world/africa/south-africa-says-interpol-issued-red-notices-guptas-associates-2021-07-05/.

against the regime, in the wake of the fraudulous presidential elections of August 2020, was in line with the EU's 'full support for Belarus' sovereignty and independence'.[23] While promoting a 'peaceful democratic transition', the EU Commission decided to 'scale down bilateral cooperation with the Belarusian authorities at central level, recalibrate EU financial assistance to Belarus in order to ensure it benefits the population at large by directing it to the maximum possible extent away from central authorities, while increasing its support for the Belarusian people and civil society'.[24] It is not convincing that such measures against individuals could qualify as countermeasures insofar as they do not implement the responsibility of a State but that of usurpers.

The same logic underlies the measures against the Venezuelan regime which the EU member States do not recognize. These sanctions are coupled with calls for a credible, democratic transition process, in parallel with a humanitarian support and assistance to the civil society.[25] The 'Lima Group', which is composed of 13 American States who do not recognize the Maduro regime, goes along the same line.[26] Targeted measures against the Burmese regime, in the wake of the *coup d'État* of February 2021, follow the same path as well.[27] These examples demonstrate that democratic infringements to the rule of law can be made at the expense of the State and may result in distinguishing the recalcitrant regime on the one hand and the interests of the State taken in the name of its civil society on the other.

Finally, the third and perhaps most important argument lies in the fact that countermeasures were not designed 'as a form of punishment for wrongful conduct, but as an instrument for achieving compliance'.[28] Yet, although targeted measures are administrative in nature, their inner and

---

[23] EU Council Conclusions on Belarus, 12 October 2020, para 3.

[24] Annex of the Commission Implementing Decision on the special measure 2020 in favour of Belarus, 4, available at https://ec.europa.eu/neighbourhood-enlargement/commission-implementing-decision-special-measure-favour-republic-belarus-2020_en.

[25] See the Council Conclusions on Venezuela, 25 January 2021. See also Council Decisions (CFSP) 2017/2074 of 13 November 2017 and 2021/276 of 22 February 2021.

[26] *Lima Group declaration of 10 January 2019*, available at https://www.international.gc.ca/world-monde/international_relations-relations_internationales/latin_america-amerique_latine/2019-01-04-lima_group-groupe_lima.aspx?lang=eng.

[27] See the EU Council Conclusions on Burma, 22 February 2021, § 2: 'The EU stands in solidarity with all those citizens of Myanmar/Burma who exercise their fundamental right to peaceful assembly in support of the legitimate civilian government and parliament, and their choice for a democratic future'. See also the Statement of the US Secretary of State Blinken, 11 February 2021, available at https://www.state.gov/designating-officials-and-entities-in-connection-with-the-military-coup-in-burma/.

[28] (2001)II Part two *YILC* 130, para 1.

acknowledged intent is increasingly to retribute an individual for his wrongful conduct. Put differently, such measures seem to pertain, substantially, to the sphere of criminal matter, and to carry an accusation for criminal conduct.[29]

This retributive character has been noticed in the stigmatising effects of targeted measures.[30] Yet, the purpose of ensuring accountability is first and foremost apparent in the statutes themselves: the UK *Global Human Rights Sanctions Regulations 2020* does not hide the fact that its purpose is 'to deter, and *provide accountability* for, activities falling within [its scope]'.[31] In the same vein, the US Executive order 13818 '*Blocking the Property of Persons Involved in Serious Human Rights Abuse or Corruption*' provides that 'the United States seeks to impose tangible and significant consequences on those who commit serious human rights abuse or engage in corruption'.[32] The preamble of the Canadian Magnitsky Act also very clearly states that 'all violators of internationally recognized human rights should be treated and sanctioned equally throughout the world'.[33] Finally, the EU Council Decision 2020/1999 of 7 December 2020 distinguishes its scope – i.e. 'a framework for targeted restrictive measures to address serious human rights violations and abuses worldwide' – from other regimes of restrictive measures which are taken 'in view of the situation in certain third countries'.[34] The former relates to a strictly individual responsibility when the latter may concern the responsibility of a State.

That being said, it is crucial to note that if an asset freezing measure contributes to the retribution for a wrongful conduct, it is not in itself a penalty or a 'sanction' insofar as it is always reversible, as opposed to a confiscation order which is a definitive deprivation of property comparable to an expropriation without compensation. In this respect, targeted measures resemble more and more provisional measures in criminal or civil matters insofar as they secure the ability of the *forum* State or any other competent jurisdiction to adjudicate the targeted individuals.

---

[29] This minority opinion is not isolated. See for instance Godinho J., "When Worlds Collide: Enforcing United Nations Security Council Asset Freezes in the EU Legal Order", *EJIL* (2010), 16:1, 76.

[30] See, notably, Giumelli F., *The purposes of Targeted Sanctions*, in Biersteker T., Eckert S., Tourinho M. (eds.), *Targeted Sanctions: The Impacts and Effectiveness of United Nations Action*, CUP, 2016, 47-48.

[31] Regulation 1(4)(1).

[32] E.O. 13818 of Dec 20, 2017.

[33] *Supra* (n. 15).

[34] *Supra* (n. 14), preamble, para 4.

As an illustration, the US *Global Magnitsky Act* states that the President may terminate the application of the measures if he determines that 'the person has been prosecuted appropriately for the activity for which sanctions (*sic*) were imposed'.[35] Similarly, the UK *Sanctions and Anti-Money Laundering Act 2018* gives to the appropriate Minister who made a designation the power to revoke it 'at any time' if the designation is not appropriate anymore.[36] In the same vein, the European Court of Justice has stressed on numerous occasions that the EU restrictive measures, their maintenance, or withdrawal may depend on the decision of a judicial authority of a third State, which is competent to initiate and conduct criminal investigation.[37]

It follows that the targeted measures analysed in this subparagraph participate to the accountability of individuals rather than that of States. They implement a certain conception of the international public order which cannot be captured by the misleading dialectic of the law of international responsibility of States. Targeted individual measures have emerged spontaneously as a remedial phenomenon in international law, governing the status of individuals rather than States.

1.2.2. The protection of 'community interests' as a spontaneous and remedial phenomenon of international law

The swift development of decentralized targeted measures is not disconnected from the incredibly low development of centralized mechanisms for enforcing binding international human rights. Put differently, decentralized targeted measures are the result of the endogenous shortcomings of enforcement mechanisms in international law, especially those of the UN Security Council and the International Criminal Court. The latter suffers from a very limited jurisdiction *ratione materiae* – it cannot adjudicate grave violations of human rights or acts of corruption and embezzlement of public funds – coupled with a systemic lack of efficiency. The former is hampered by its repeated paralyses and its powers are not designed to provide individual accountability but to address threats or breaches to international peace and security.

One might wonder whether the flaws of the international legal order are satisfactory justifications for the willingness of some western States to sub-

---

[35] As quoted in (n. 15), Section 3 (g)(2).

[36] UK Public General Acts, 2018 c. 13, Section 22.

[37] E.g. C-530/17P *Azarov v. Council* ECLI:EU:C:2018:1031, para 25.

stitute themselves to centralized mechanisms? To say the least, Scelle's theory of 'role splitting' in international law (*dédoublement fonctionnel*) very adequately illustrate the aspiration of some countries to enforce 'community interests' through decentralized measures.[38] As Cassese observed as early as 1990, 'momentous normative trends have emerged in the world community which aim at imposing respect for a set of fundamental values that conspicuously restrain State sovereignty'.[39] In the absence of international bodies to perform this mission, State organs may use the powers conferred on them in the domestic legal order to ensure the effectiveness of the fundamental values of the international legal order.[40]

This aspiration of States to enforce international norms through their own means of coercion is also reflective of the '*modèle du réseau*', theorized by Ost and Van de Kerchove. Twenty years ago, these two authors questioned the pyramidal paradigm of law, imbued with the legal dogmatism inherent in centralized systems. Against this background, they discussed the validity of a paradigm composed of several vanishing points, generating 'a network of entangled worlds that is not synonymous with chaos'.[41] As such, they accurately demonstrated the multiplication of law-making sources; the progressive reduction of the *domaine reservé* of States; the entanglement of normative systems as well as the diversification of the criterion of validity of norms.[42] From that perspective, the grey areas surrounding the *formal* validity of decentralized measures of enforcement could be balanced on account of their effects and legitimacy.

Undoubtedly, unilateral measures seeking to impose 'values' in the name of the interests of the international community can be a source of grave abuses. Decentralized actions could drive to circumvent the ban on the use of armed force, under article 2(4) of the UN Charter, on the basis of so-called humanitarian grounds, or it could lead a State to pursue its own interest through extraterritorial measures or 'secondary sanctions'. The above-mentioned work of the Human Rights Council on the matter speaks for itself. Be that as it may, unilateral actions are an inherent feature of the international legal order. Targeted individual measures emerged in

---

[38] See Cassese A., "Remarks on Scelle's Theory of Role Splitting (dédoublement fonctionnel) in International Law", *EJIL* (1990), 210.

[39] *Ivi*, 227.

[40] See Scelle G., *Le phénomène juridique du dédoublement fonctionnel*, in Schätzel W., Schlochauer H.J. (eds.), *Rechtsfragen der Internationalen Organisation - Festschrift fur H. Wehberg*, Klostermann, 1956, 331.

[41] Ost F., Van de Kerchove M., *De la pyramide au réseau? Pour une théorie dialectique du droit*, Publication des Facultés Universitaires Saint-Louis, 2002, 9.

[42] *Ivi*, 494.

the shadows of the inaction of the UN Security Council and operate as a proxy for a universal standing in criminal and civil matters. They respond to violations of *erga omnes* norms without prejudice to either the ability of competent States to exercise their jurisdiction to adjudicate targeted individuals, or the primary responsibility of the UN Security Council to maintain peace and security. As such, they do not involve competing and potentially overlapping competences but complementary ones. They constitute one means among others to remedy the imperfections of the international legal system. Rather than reflecting an 'unpolite international society', they reflect a spontaneous construction whose validity cannot be excluded. Indeed, the current lack of *ad hoc* regimes does not mean that these measures operate in a legal vacuum but only that their legal regime still needs to be sophisticated and systematized.

1.3. 'Community interests' measures as *prima facie* lawful measures?

Several arguments have been advanced to disqualify the validity of unilateral measures justified by 'community interests'. Each of them deserves an in-depth analysis that cannot be carried out exhaustively in this contribution. We will simply contend that their most salient features primarily represent a risk rather than an essential cause of invalidity (**1.3.1.**). In the absence of *ad hoc* legal regime, general principles of law should be deemed to provide suitable safeguards against a disproportionate recourse to these measures (**1.3.2.**).

1.3.1. Debunking certain preconceptions

The principles of sovereign equality of States and non-intervention in internal affairs are the main legal grounds invoked to challenge 'unilateral coercive measures' as a whole[43] (**1.3.1.1.**). Procedural safeguards are also advanced to criticize targeted individual measures such as immunities of State officials or international standards governing the due process of law (**1.3.1.2.**).

---

[43] See e.g. *The Declaration of the People's Republic of China and the Russian Federation on the Promotion of International Law*, 26 June 2016, available at https://www.fmprc.gov.cn/mfa_eng/wjdt_665385/2649_665393/201608/t20160801_679466.html.

1.3.1.1. Sovereign equality, non-intervention, and the protection of 'community interests'

In order to defend the validity of targeted individual measures justified by 'community interests', three distinct and at the same time intertwined perspectives are relevant: that of State jurisdiction first; that of the interference caused in the '*vie privée étatique*' then, and finally, that of the legal regime of *erga omnes* norms.

As far as State jurisdiction is concerned, unilateral targeted measures do not in principle extend the prescriptive jurisdiction of a State in a disproportionate way. Indeed, except for the highly contested US 'secondary sanctions', domestic legislations or regulations providing for targeted measures do not subject any actors beyond the undisputed territorial or personal principles of jurisdiction. What is questionable then is not the process through which the measures are enforced but their purpose, which is linked to their effects: travel bans and asset freezing measures are meant to produce effects abroad, in such a way that they could interfere with the territorial sovereignty of a foreign State. The issue is not whether the measures under consideration contravene international rules of State jurisdiction but whether their extraterritorial *effects* constitute a prohibited intervention in the State's internal affairs.

From this second perspective, it is understood that an intervention in the internal affairs of a State is prohibited insofar as it bears 'on matters in which each State is permitted, by the principle of State sovereignty, to decide freely'.[44] It follows that a mere interference in a State's internal affairs could be deemed lawful if a State has indeed assumed international obligations restraining this 'sphere of freedom' (*vie privée étatique*), and if this interference does not violate other international obligations.[45] It is therefore crucial to consider the national margin of appreciation of the targeted State when interpreting these international obligations. Targeted measures could be deemed to interfere disproportionately with the internal affairs of a State if they deny or limit this margin in a disproportionate way. In this case, the scope of the *problématique* shifts again: does the interference created by targeted individual measures operate within or without its sphere of *vie privée étatique*?

Certainly, the question is irrelevant whenever the measures are called

---

[44] *Military and Paramilitary Activities in and against Nicaragua (Nicaragua v United States of America) (Merits)* [1986] ICJ Rep 14 (Nicaragua) 114 [241].

[45] On the concept of '*vie privée étatique*', see Verhoeven J., *Non-intervention, 'affaires intérieures' ou 'vie privée'?*, in *Le droit international au service de la paix, de la justice et du développement. Mélanges Michel Virally*, Pedone, 1991, 493.

for by the – then improperly called – targeted State insofar as it waived any potential barrier to an intervention (as in the case of Tunisia, Egypt, or Ukraine…). Whenever the targeted measures are unsolicited, the nature of the charges against the individuals involved is then crucial. In the context of Venezuela, for instance, the Office of the Prosecutor of the ICC concluded in 2020 that there was a reasonable basis to believe that crimes against humanity, particularly in the context of detention, had been committed since at least April 2017. The same office concluded on 11 December 2020 that there was a reasonable basis to believe that war crimes and crimes against humanity were committed in Ukraine.[46] Other regimes of measures are based on grave violations of the right to life (e.g., Sergueï Magnitky and Jamal Khashoggi's death); the right to be free from torture (Belarus; Gambia; China; Russia…); or the right to be free from slavery (North Korea).

All these regimes of targeted measures respond to serious violations of internationally recognized human rights that can be qualified as *erga omnes* norms for more than fifty years.[47] This *erga omnes* nature confirms the interest of the international community to react to such violations. Yet, critics may still assert that decentralized targeted measures overestimate the content of the reactions that *erga omnes* rules involve. In any event, we are not convinced that the effects of decentralized targeted measures may be disputed from the standpoint of either the titles of jurisdiction or the principle of non-intervention in internal affairs. It remains to be seen whether they could be in breach of procedural rules of international law, namely, immunities, and international standards governing the due process of law.

1.3.1.2. Procedural safeguards and the protection of 'community interests'

The invalidity of targeted measures may stem from the procedural rights owed to the targeted individuals. This might be the case of sovereign immunities (**1.3.1.2.1.**). This is certainly the case with due process standards (**1.3.1.2.2.**).

[46] Following the Russian invasion of Ukraine in February 2022, the Prosecutor of the ICC decided to open an investigation into this Situation. available at https://www.icc-cpi.int/Pages/item.aspx?name=20220228-prosecutor-statement-ukraine.

[47] *Barcelona Traction, Light and Power Company, Limited* (Belgium v Spain) (Judgment) [1970] ICJ Rep 3 [33].

1.3.1.2.1. *Immunities as an unlikely legal defence*

As for the law on immunity, it is worth noting that its weight remains speculative, due to a lack of adequate precedent on the matter. The two branches of the following alternative can be considered. On the one side, if we consider asset freezing measures as mere administrative measures, the assets could only be 'sanctuarized' through the inviolability of the foreign official. As Ruys demonstrated, such a defence would be of very limited use, notably for diplomatic agents and members of special missions, including senior State officials but only for the duration of the mission. [48] By contrast, if we consider that asset freezing measures are comparable to judicial precautionary measures, then a foreign official could theoretically claim the benefit of jurisdictional immunities and be entitled to immunity from execution measures. In that case, we may consider (at best) that only individuals who enjoy immunity *ratione personae* may claim to be immune from execution measures against their personal assets. [49] On the contrary, if the foreign official only benefits from an immunity *ratione materiae*, we do not see why and how could his personal property be protected in any way, giving due regard to the nature of the acts that led to the asset freezing measure.

The scope of the customary exceptions to the immunity *ratione materiae* remains uncertain. Yet, draft article 7 of the ILC articles on the 'immunity of State officials from foreign criminal jurisdiction' is an evolutive provision whose scope can only expand through the progressive development of law. [50] From a strictly positivist point of view, insufficient State practice maybe at odds with this finding. Yet again, as the late Judge Cançado Trindade pointed out so eloquently, the empirical factual exercise consisting in identifying opposing practices is 'over-attentive to facts and oblivious of values' and leads to 'the fossilization of international law,

[48] Ruys (n6) 708.

[49] See in this regard the opinion of the Special Rapporteur of the ILC on immunity of State officials from foreign criminal jurisdiction, Concepción Escobar Hernández, in her sixth report, A/CN.4/722, 12 June 2018, [93]-[94]. It is worth adding that even where an individual may claim the benefit of an immunity *ratione personae*, there is much to think that, as exemplified by the Institute of International Law, taking provisional measures with respect to assets is lawful 'for the maintenance of control over [the property] while the legality of the appropriation remains insufficiently established'. See Article 4, § 2 of the 2001 resolution of the IIL on the 'Immunities from Jurisdiction and Execution of Heads of State and of Government in International Law'.

[50] The exceptions provided for in Article 7 are currently limited to (a) crime of genocide; (b) crimes against humanity; (c) war crimes; (d) crime of apartheid; (e) torture; (f) enforced disappearance. Article adopted at the 3378th meeting of the ILC, A/CN.4/SR.3378, 18 August 2017.

and [...] persistent underdevelopment, rather than its progressive development'.[51]

1.3.1.2.2. *The shortcomings of due process standards as a valid defence*

A last and undoubtedly more pertinent cause of invalidity lies in the probable inadequacy of the review mechanisms offered to targeted individuals when it comes to challenging the validity of measures under both domestic and international law.[52] Such mechanisms implement the right to an effective remedy which is guaranteed, for instance, by Article 2(3) ICCPR and article 13 ECHR.

Whenever an asset freezing measure responds to past behaviours rather than continuing acts and is not lifted until the targeted person has been properly convicted, such measure is comparable to a provisional seizure in criminal matters, based on an allegation that a criminal offense has been committed. Why should the procedural safeguards attached to the right to a fair trial in criminal matters not be deemed applicable in this scenario? The right to a fair trial does not concern exclusively the trial and sentencing phase; it applies to the entire procedure once the person has been 'charged with a criminal offence'.[53] Moreover, the concept of a 'criminal charge' bears an autonomous meaning, that is independent of the categorisations employed by the national legal system of the States parties.[54] As a result, the right to a fair trial should not be excluded on the mere basis that asset freezing is not a criminal penalty. Listed persons have been arguing in vain that being included in the lists of targeted measures of the EU was tantamount to being 'charged with a criminal offence', as interpreted in a 'material' and not a 'formal' manner by the ECtHR.[55]

From this perspective, the granting of an appropriate level of procedural rights may not only dispel any criticism regarding the implementation of targeted individual measures, but also confirm that they should be envisioned, where appropriate, as provisional measures in criminal matters.

---

[51] Diss. op., *Jurisdictional immunities of the State (Germany v. Italy)* [2012] ICJ Rep 99, 284 [293].

[52] On this matter, see notably A/HRC/45/7 (n 12) [61].

[53] See HRC, General comment No. 32, CCPR/C/GC/32, 23 August 2007 [31].

[54] HRC, *Osiyuk v. Belarus*, views, Communication No. 1311/2004, 30 July 2009 [7.3]-[7.5].

[55] See T-47/03 *Sison v Council* ECLI:EU:T:2007:207,[115]-[116].

1.3.2. General principles of law as a transient (and suitable) legal regime

At this stage of the analysis, it seems interesting, if not necessary, to reassess our understanding of the validity of decentralized unilateral measures. Since they are neither inherently illegal nor specifically governed by *ad hoc* rules of international law, it is important to establish the significant role that general principles of law may provide as a valid yet transient legal regime. General principles of law, as enshrined in Article 38(1)(c) of the ICJ Statute, constitute an autonomous and legitimate source of international law whose purpose and constitutive elements are tailored to emerging phenomena of international law. Such principles ensure substantive coherence between sectoral rules and potentially diverging practices, thus encouraging the progressive development of more specific and binding international standards.

In this quest for substantive coherence, the overarching general principles of legality, necessity, proportionality as well as the prohibition of the abuse of rights already operate as binding safeguards against an unreasonable use of unilateral targeted measures. Such principles are not only grounded in every domestic legal system implementing targeted measures but also in a number of international human rights instruments and branches of customary international law, notably international humanitarian law.

The principle of legality, for instance, as a general protection of individuals against State arbitrariness lie at the intersection of international criminal law, international human rights and humanitarian law so as to prevent unforeseeable depravations of liberties and violations of due process of law. When combined with the principle of necessity, which refers to the legitimacy of the aims pursued by the measure in a democratic society, both principles dictate that clear, precise, and comprehensive legislations specify the purposes for which a targeted measure could be deemed 'necessary'.

Finally, the general principle of 'proportionality' designates a relationship of adequacy between the legitimate objective pursued by a State and the means that it uses to reach that objective. This meta-principle is essential for assessing the validity of unilateral measures, notably to determine the limits of the discretionary power of States to implement domestic policies having extraterritorial effects.[56] US 'secondary sanctions' may for instance be distinguished from EU targeted sanctions in this regard. As Enzo Cannizzaro perfectly noted, the proportionality review, in combination

[56] See Kolb R., *La Proportionnalité dans le Cadre des Contre-mesures et des Sanctions – Essai de Clarification Conceptuelle*, in Picchio Forlati L., Sicilianos L.-A., *Economic Sanctions in International Law*, Brill, 2004, 379.

with the margin of appreciation review enabled the ICJ, in the *Whaling in the Antarctic* case,[57] to shape the contours of the international control of discretionary powers.[58] We do not see why such an assessment may not be applied to targeted individual measures.

1.4. Concluding remarks

The absence of *ad hoc* legal regime governing targeted individual measures protecting 'community interests' gives room to an extraordinary laboratory of propositions. It is an opportunity to methodically analyse the positions of States and determine the true content of the legal controversy. Legal doctrine cannot overcome the antagonism between States as to the validity of these measures. However, it can unravel the conditions for useful dialogue. This involves assessing the rationale behind this legal phenomenon.

Indeed, due to the lack of clear conventional or merely codified rule, an axiological lecture of these measures is also possible. Law and ethics come together and lie at the very heart of the emerging international public order. There is no doubt that 'community interests' might be subject to abuses. Inevitably, the self-entitlement to enforce international norms based on a subjective appreciation of a breach of the law necessarily raises concerns. Yet, this issue is not specific to measures enforcing 'community interests'. This subjectivity is inherent, by definition, to any 'decentralized' mechanism. Invoking and implementing State responsibility in the absence of a prior judicial assessment of the existence of a wrongful act is inherently subjective and yet not necessarily abusive. The same applies to countermeasures and the implementation of universal jurisdiction in criminal matters. Current practice tends to demonstrate that general principles of law can (for the time being) adequately limit the willingness of States to implement the international public order through unilateral measures targeting foreign officials.

---

[57] ICJ Reports (2014) 226, Judgment, 31 March 2014.

[58] Cannizzaro E., "Proportionality and Margin of Appreciation in the Whaling Case: Reconciling Antithetical Doctrines?", *EJIL* (2017), 27, 4, 1061.

Chapter 2

EXAMINING THE LEGALITY OF EU RESTRICTIVE MEASURES ON THE RUSSIAN FEDERATION: THE INFORMATION GATHERING PROCESS IN SANCTION IMPOSITION

Antonino Alì

ABSTRACT: *Given the complex nature of restrictive measures, it's crucial to carry out a comprehensive analysis of their legal basis, as well as the potential consequences that may result from their application. This review process is necessary to ensure their alignment with international law, European Union law, and more generally, the principle of the rule of law. It ensures that while punitive measures are taken to maintain international order, they are carried out within the limits of the law in order to safeguard the rights of all individuals and entities involved.*

2.1. EU restrictive measures on the Russian Federation: a legal analysis (2014-2023)

Between 2014 and 2021, the European Union, mainly in partnership with the United States (US), implemented a series of restrictive measures against the Russian Federation. These actions were in response to Russia's illegal annexation of Crimea and Sevastopol and violation of Ukraine's sovereignty and territorial integrity. These sanctions encompassed a range of measures such as the freezing of assets freezes and travel bans imposed on certain individuals. Additionally, economic sanctions were introduced, targeting critical sectors such as finance, energy, and defence. The implementation of these sanctions has always sparked ongoing discourse and legal disputes, raising questions about their effectiveness, legitimacy, and the resulting consequences for both the Russian Federation and the sanctioning states.

Given the complex nature of these sanctions, a thorough examination of their legal basis and the potential impact of their implementation is necessary. This analysis will focus on their compliance with international law, EU law, and the rule of law in general.

The situation further escalated in February 2022 when the restrictive measures were extended and intensified due to the invasion of Ukraine. On one hand, they targeted a larger number of companies and individuals. On the other hand, they extended to even wider sectors in a pervasive manner, striking at the political, economic, and military foundations that underpin the Russian leadership, which decided on and supported the conflict against Ukraine.

Indeed, the fundamental objective of sanctions is to bring about a change in the policy or behaviour of the targeted entity. A clear and coherent link between the target of the sanction and the overarching foreign policy objective is essential. Sanctions against the Russian economy are designed to raise the costs [1] associated with the actions of the Russian Federation, with the aim of ending the state of war and violations of international humanitarian law that often result from such conflicts. [2] This objective is consistent with a key public interest of the international community, which is the preservation of peace and respect for humanitarian law. [3]

Although massive and considerably broader than those adopted between 2014 and 2022, sanctions against Russia, starting from February 2022 onwards continue to mainly target those who are directly responsible for the undesirable policies or actions. Recently there has been a gradual widening of the categories of individuals considered to be even remotely responsible for the conflict or for supporting the Russian regime. It is true that the intensity of the sanctions packages adopted has had a significant impact on wider sectors of the economy of the Russian Federation.

The potential global impact of such measures on the entire population could inevitably led to the same critical objections that have been raised against the imposition of (non-targeted) global sanctions, as seen in previous cases such as the sanctions imposed on Iraq in the 1990s.

---

[1] CJEU, 17 September 2020, *Rosneft*, C-732/18 P, ECLI:EU:C:2020:727, § 92.

[2] GC, 27 July 2022, *RT France*, T-125/22, ECLI:EU:T:2022:483, § 166.

[3] CJEU, *Bosphorus*, 30 July 1996, C-84/95, ECLI:EU:C:1996:312, § 26.

2.2. Rule of law and EU sanctioning policies

The adoption of EU sanctions against the Russian Federation raises important questions as to their legality and compliance with the rule of law. Article 19 of the Treaty on the European Union (TEU) entrusts the Court of Justice of the European Union with the task of ensuring that the law is observed in the interpretation and application of the Treaties. In accordance with this provision, the EU Courts have the role of safeguarding the rule of law within the European Union and and the responsibility to exercise their review powers fully.

The Court of Justice plays a fundamental role especially when in cases involving international security. As General Poiares Maduro argued in the famous Kadi case, considering restrictive measures as a 'political question' where any form of judicial interference would be inappropriate is untenable. The necessity of a measure for international peace and security should not be used to silence the general principles of EU law or deprive individuals of their fundamental rights. The Courts have the responsibility to assess the legality of measures, acting as a safeguard against political expediency. In matters of public security, the political process may prioritize immediate concerns over the rights of a few individuals. It is the courts' responsibility to intervene and ensure that political imperatives do not become legal realities in the future. The courts have a duty to ensure that what may be politically expedient is consistent with the rule of law which is essential for the long-term prosperity of a democratic society. [4]

Over the past twenty years, the Court of Justice has delivered a number of judgments which have had a significant impact on the development of the European Union's sanctions policy and the promotion of the rule of law within its framework. These rulings have played a crucial role in providing clarity regarding the legal prerequisites for implementing restrictive measures. They have also underlined the importance of basing sanctions on solid evidence and of maintaining a commitment to respect fundamental rights and procedural safeguards throughout the entire sanctions process. [5]

---

[4] Opinion of Advocate General Poiares Maduro, 16 January 2008, *Kadi v. Council* and Commission, ECLI:EU:C:2008:11, §§ 34-45.

[5] Poli S., "*The right to effective judicial protection with respect to acts imposing restrictive measures and its transformative force for the Common Foreign and Security Policy*", *CMLR* (2022), 1045-1080; Lenaerts K., "The Kadi Saga and the Rule of Law within the EU", *SMU L. Rev.* (2014), 707-715.

2.3. Judicial review of EU restrictive measures: scope and intensity

In reviewing the Council's decision on restrictive measures, the Court of Justice of the European Union (CJEU) has a fundamental responsibility to carry out a full review of legality.[6] As underlined in the Kadi II case (para. 97) the EU courts "must [...] ensure the review, in principle, the full review, of the lawfulness of all Union acts in the light of the fundamental rights forming an integral part of the European Union".

By adopting this approach, the Court has established a broad scope of review of restrictive measures, in contrast to the stance encouraged by Advocate General Bot, who argued for a narrower focus on external legality and limited internal legality review.[7] In summary, Advocate General Bot's position suggests that the EU judge's review of the internal legality of Union acts implementing decisions by the UN sanctions committee should not generally involve questioning the validity of the listing, unless the procedure within the Union in relation to that listing has revealed a manifest error in determining the facts, their legal classification, or the assessment of proportionality.

Ate the same time, in the Kadi II case, the Court, referring to its own precedent in ZZ,[8] underlined the importance of striking a delicate balance between respect for procedural rights of the person concerned party and the protection of security interests when considering the disclosure of information or evidence elements in cases concering the security of the Union or its Member States. The judge is not bound by secrecy or confidentiality and must assess the validity of the reasons given by the Union authority for opposing disclosure. If the reasons do not preclude disclosure, the EU authority may proceed with the communication. If they do, however, a careful balance must be struck between ensuring effective judicial protection and addressing security concerns. The judge will then assess the legality of the contested act on the basis of the elements communicated.

---

[6] Eckes C., "EU restrictive measures against natural and legal persons: from counterterrorist to third country sanctions", *CMLR* (2020), 869-905; Triart N., "Portée et intensité du contrôle de légalité des mesures restrictives de l'Union européenne par le juge de l'Union", *ERA Forum* (2020), 637-658.

[7] See Opinion of Advocate General Bot, 19 March 2013, Joined Cases C-584/10 P, C-593/ 10 P, and C-595/10 P, *European Commission, Council of the European Union, United Kingdom of Great Britain and Northern Ireland v Yassin Abdullah Kadi*, ECLI:EU:C:2013:176, §§ 53-110.

[8] Court of Justice, 4 June 2013, C-200/11, *ZZ v. Secretary of State for the Home Department*, ECLI:EU:C:2013:363.

2.4. Legal challenges to restrictive measures in the EU courts (2014-2022)

From 2014 to 2022, a significant body of case law was developed before the Tribunal and the Court of Justice on the legality of the restrictive measures adopted. The restrictive measures imposed in 2014 against the pro-Russian Ukrainian leadership, including asset freezes, were renewed annually. Many of these measures were subsequently been lifted, resulting in the de-listing of individuals. The freezing of funds and economic resources targeted those responsible for the misappropriation of Ukrainian state funds and human rights violations, with the aim of supporting the rule of law and human rights in Ukraine. The number of cases related to former President Viktor Yanukovych and his entourage posed the most significant legal challenges. The Council could only freeze assets on the basis of evidence provided by the Ukrainian judicial authorities. The reasoning behind the adoption of sanctions was found to be weak.

Sectoral sanctions have faced fewer legal challenges compared to the “Ukrainian cases”. Illustrative in this regard was the case of Andriy Portnov (T-290/14) which exemplifies the challenges of imposing sanctions for the misappropriation of state funds. The statement of reasons for these restrictive measures taken against the former adviser to the President of Ukraine reads: “Person subject to criminal proceedings in Ukraine to investigate crimes in connection with the embezzlement of Ukrainian State funds and their illegal transfer outside Ukraine”. The General Court (GC) annulled the part of the regulation concerning Mr. Portnov on the grounds that it lacked specific details of the facts alleged against him. It could be argued that the EU judicial system has shown a willingness to highlight the shortcomings of targeted sanctions against the Yanukovych regime. However, it is worth noting that the lifting of these restrictive measures often occurred immediately after their annual renewal, resulting in many cases where the lifting had symbolic value but no significant impact on the situation.

Despite the significant number of sanctions that have been annulled since 2014, particularly in the context of the “Ukrainian cases,” the Court of Justice has refrained from challenging the broader foreign policy choices regarding the extensive use of economic sanctions against Russia. While the Court has played a crucial role in scrutinizing individual cases and safeguarding the fundamental rights of those affected by the sanctions, it has recognized the wide discretion that EU institutions possess in making political, economic, and social decisions. Thus, the Court’s focus has primarily been on ensuring the legality of specific measures rather than challenging the overall foreign policy approach of imposing economic sanctions on Russia.

2.5. Evidence standards in EU restrictive measures cases

In cases concerning restrictive measures, the evidentiary standards applied by the EU Courts involve careful allocation of the burden of proof and the determination of the required standard of proof required to establish a fact. This task requires careful consideration as the Courts seek to strike a delicate balance between the discretionary powers held by EU institutions and the protection of due process and fundamental rights. When it comes to the burden of proof, the primary responsibility rests with the EU authority to establish the validity of the alleged reasons against the individuals concerned. However, the EU Courts retain the power to request additional information or evidence and to intervene in the process of evidence gathering or supplementing evidence in order to ensure a fair and comprehensive assessment.

In litigation concerning EU restrictive measures, the standard of proof requires a thorough assessment of the evidence in order to establish facts convincingly beyond a minimum threshold of evidence quality and quantity. Guided by the principle of the "unfettered evaluation of evidence",[9] the EU Courts exercise discretion in assessing the reliability and credibility of the evidence presented. While the concept of the standard of proof is not extensively developed in EU law, the EU Courts favour decisions based on a solid factual basis. Factors such as the source, manner of acquisition, and overall reliability of the evidence are taken into account. This principle allows flexibility in the assessment of evidence, and empowers EU Courts to independently judge its value and weight in each case.

2.6. Challenges in EU's evidence gathering and investigative processes

When the Council presented evidence from its file during court proceedings, it often relied on evidence obtained from the relevant national authorities. The Council often presents "open source" evidence, which consists of information gathered from internet searches and press articles about the individuals or entities under scrutiny. However, the lack of clarity about the source, reliability, and relevance of this evidence.

This change reflects an effort to provide at least some material to support a designation, which is seen as an improvement over no evidence at

---

[9] See Filpo F., "Evidence standards in the judicial review of restrictive measures", *ERA Forum* (2019), 619-621.

all. The use of open-source evidence in the sanction's justification process is viewed as a step towards fairness, as it provides a basis for reviewing and assessing the validity of a designation. The existence of some material in support of a designation provides a degree of transparency and accountability and gives the Court an opportunity to review the reasons for the Council's decision and to determine whether the information provided is sufficient to maintain the designation. In cases where the disclosed open-source material contains relevant details, such as information on the ownership structure of the company, it may strengthen the case for maintaining the designation. There are several concerns about the use of open-source material as evidence in the Courts. As has been highlighted, material accepted as "evidence" by the court may not meet the appropriate evidentiary thresholds that would be required in a national court. [10] Open-source material, such as press articles and websites, often contains opinions from non-objective sources and unreliable information that hasn't been adequately verified. Relying solely on such material raises concerns about fairness and the strength of the evidence, as it may not meet the rigorous legal standards expected in court proceedings. While this type of evidence provides some information and different perspectives, it may lack the necessary depth, reliability and conclusive facts. Press articles may be influenced by bias, while internet searches may not be rigorously verified. Presenting such material as evidence without additional robust sources undermines both the reliability and credibility needed to support the imposition of sanctions. Another problem relates to the fact that Member states are reluctant to share sensitive intelligence information due to security concerns.

The rules of the General Court of the European Union and the Court of Justice provide for the possibility of allowing confidential documents to be produced by one of the parties. This is particularly evident in the light of the "Kadi II" case [11] and subsequent amendments made to the rules of procedure of both Courts. [12] These rules serve as a framework for the effective-

---

[10] On this subject, see the insightful observations on the legality of the EU sanctions process, House of Lords, EU Justice Sub-Committee, Written evidence (EUS0001) from Maya Lester QC, Brick Court Chambers 10 October 2016, available at https://committees.parliament.uk/writtenevidence/73703/pdf/ and Supplementary written evidence (EUS0002), available at https://committees.parliament.uk/writtenevidence/75039/pdf/.

[11] CJEU, 18 July 18 2013, "Kadi II", §§ 125-129.

[12] See Article 105 (*Treatment of information or material pertaining to the security of the Union or that of one or more of its Member States or to the conduct of their international relations*) of the Rules of Procedure of the General Court, and Article 190a

ly handling of confidential or sensitive information throughout the entirety of the proceedings. The overall objective of the Courts is to strike a delicate balance between transparency and confidentiality. As part of this effort, the Courts establish comprehensive procedures for the submission, examination, and handling of classified documents and implement various measures to ensure the utmost confidentiality while upholding the fundamental principles of fairness and transparency within the judicial process. It is essential to emphasize that the decision to admit or exclude secret documents depends on the specific circumstances of each individual case, as well as the courts' careful evaluation of the relevance and necessity of such documents. Ultimately, the decision to admit or to exclude secret documents will depend on the specific circumstances of each case and careful assessment by the courts of the relevance and necessity of such confidential material.

However, it is important to recognize that there is a wide range of evidence that could be considered, ranging from highly sensitive intelligence to other forms of reliable and tested information.

While it is understandable that certain information cannot be disclosed, it should not justify a complete absence of evidence beyond internet searches and listing proposals. This is particularly relevant in cases involving the EU's "misappropriation" regimes, where relying solely on an open letter from a state prosecutor stating an ongoing investigation for corruption may not provide a fair and solid basis for imposing EU-wide asset freezes.

It is possible that the Council faces limitations in conducting thorough investigations and providing robust evidence. The Council is in a better position to comment on the specific challenges it faces in gathering and presenting evidence. There has been a notable shift in the use of evidence in the sanctions process towards the inclusion of open-source material. [13]

2.7. Analyzing legal challenges in post-February 2022 EU restrictive measures

The sanctions imposed on Russia in 2022 were part of an overarching sanctions structure. This structure took root in March of 2014 and underwent numerous modifications over the course of the following year. These changes culminated in a multifaceted set of strategies, deliberately designed

---

(*Treatment of information or material produced before the General Court in accordance with Article 105 of its Rules of Procedure*).

[13] House of Lords, European Union Committee, *The legality of EU sanctions*, 11th Report of Session 2016-17, HL Paper 102, 2 February 2017.

to pressure key sectors of the Russian economy as well as its power brokers. Similar punitive measures have been extended to Belarus and Iran for their involvement in the Russia-Ukraine conflict. Some sixty legal cases related to these sanctions are currently awaiting a decision by the General Court.

Concerted action is needed to ensure the effective application of these sanctions and to thwart any attempts to circumvent them. This requires a renewed commitment to align measures and to close possible loopholes in the system. It should be noted that the preliminary rulings of General Court are of considerable importance. As a result, our attention will focus to a selection of the most pertinent cases.

The implementation of targeted sanctions has seen a significant increase in the number of individuals and entities subject to such measures. The numbers have soared, surging from just a few hundred to a staggering total of more than 1,500 individuals and 200 entities. These measures are particularly notable as they not only target high-profile figures such as Russia's President Putin and Minister of Foreign Affairs Lavrov but also extend to encompass the wider economic and political support network that reinforces the power structure in Russia. This includes individuals associated with various branches of the Russian government, high-ranking officials, military personnel, businesspeople, oligarchs, and propagandists.

Coordinating bodies have been set up to ensure the effective enforcement of these sanctions. One notable example is the European Commission's "Freeze and Seize" Task Force, which aims to streamline coordination among EU member states in implementing sanctions against designated Russian and Belarusian oligarchs. This task force works in conjunction with the newly formed 'Russian Elites, Proxies, and Oligarchs (REPO)' Task Force, which facilitates cooperation between the EU and G7 countries, including Canada, France, Germany, Italy, Japan, the United Kingdom, and the US, as well as Australia.

The impact of these measures on Russian oligarchs and businesspeople is significant, as it considerably affects the assets held by large corporations. In many cases, the consequences have also extended to their family members.[14] It is not always an easy task to establish a clear link between family members and the economic activities of the main targets of the sanctions.

---

[14] It is worth noting the parallel with another situation concerning the Syrian regime, where similar measures have been taken. In the case of Syria, the Council found that Mrs Al-Assad, the sister of President Bashar Al-Assad and the former wife of a key regime figure, benefited from her close personal and financial ties to the regime. As a result, she was added to the list of persons subject to restrictive measures, resulting in the freezing of her funds in the EU and a ban on her entry into EU Member States. See

2.8. Asset freezing sanctions: targeting individuals and beneficial owners in the EU

Navigating the intricate web of family relationships and economic activities in the context of the Russian Federation, particularly in the context of sanctions, is often a daunting task. It becomes even more difficult when the available evidence is insufficient to establish a clear link between family members and the primary target of sanctions.

This conundrum was recently brought to the forefront in the General Court through the case known as Prigozina (Case T-212/22), adjudicated on March 8, 2023.[15] The case underscored the necessity of robust intelligence activities in substantiating the grounds for imposing sanctions and brought into focus the hurdles faced in establishing a direct linkage between the primary targets of sanctions and their familial relations.

The Prigozina case underscores the importance of diligent fact-gathering and intelligence analysis in the enforcement of sanctions. It underscores the importance of intelligence operations as the backbone for establishing the rationale for the implementation of these sanctions.

In October 2020, the Council of the European Union, acting in accordance with its authority and mandate, imposed a series of restrictive measures against Mr. Yevgeniy Viktorovich Prigozhin. It should be noted that Mr. Prigozhin, a Russian businessman, has established close links and connections with an entity known as the Wagner Group, which has recently been involved in military operations carried out in Libya and subsequently in Ukraine during the period spanning from 2022 to 2023. On June 1, 2022, the Court of Justice rejected the application for annulment of these measures.

In accordance with the provision of Article 2 of Regulation 2069/2014, the imposition of freezing measures on funds and economic resources is applicable to both natural and legal persons, as well as entities or bodies that exhibit an association with individuals or entities explicitly identified in Annex I of the regulation. The Council included Violetta Prigozhina within the said list. The basis for her inclusion stems from her status as the mother of Mr. Yevgeniy Viktorovich Prigozhin, and and also takes into account her ownership stake in Concord Management and Consulting LLC. It is worth noting that this particular entity, previously affiliated with the

General Court, 12 March 2014, T-202/12, *Bouchra Al Assad v Council of the European Union*, ECLI:EU:T:2014:113.

[15] See General Court, 8 March 2023, T-212/22, Violetta Prigozhina v Council, ECLI:EU:T:2023:104.

Concord Group, was founded by and under the ownership of Mr. Prigozhin until the year 2019. Ms. Prigozhina was also associated with other companies owned by her son. This association links her to an individual responsible for deploying Wagner Group mercenaries in Ukraine and benefiting from lucrative public contracts with the Russian Ministry of Defense following the illegal annexation of Crimea and the occupation of eastern Ukraine. The Council contended that her actions and support undermined Ukraine's territorial integrity, sovereignty, and independence. In response, Ms. Prigozhina has requested that her inclusion on the list be annulled and has challenged the Council's decision.

According to established case law, the imposition of restrictive measures solely on the basis of family ties with individuals associated with leaders of a third country, irrespective of the personal conduct of the family members, is contrary to the principles upheld by the Court. This requirement ensures a sufficient link between the persons subject to the the measures and the third country against which the measures are directed. The Council's decision to include the applicant, Ms. Prigozhina, on the contested lists was solely based on her family relationship at the time of the adoption of the contested acts. Consequently, that relationship was considered insufficient to justify the applicant's inclusion in the lists.

Furthermore, the Council failed to prove that Ms. Prigozhina was involved in her son's activities. During the proceedings, the Council argued that the association criteria created a risk of circumvention. According to the General Court, the criteria of association normally apply to any entity that is in any way connected to another entity that supports the targeted government, as long as there is a non-negligible risk that this connection could be exploited by the supporting entity to bypass the imposed sanctions. if an entity's funds are frozen, there is a non-negligible risk that it will seek to exert pressure on the entities it owns or controls in order to circumvent the effect of the measures taken against it. However, in the specific case of Ms. Prigozhina, the association link between the parties through companies was not established, and the connection between them was based solely on family ties. In summary, the General Court held that the risk of circumvention of the association criteria cannot be invoked on the basis of family ties alone, without additional evidence demonstrating a genuine risk of circumvention. The Council should have established a direct link between the individuals and the sanctioned activities in order to justify their inclusion in the sanctions list, rather than relying solely on their family relationship with sanctioned individuals.

Furthermore, the Council failed to prove the mother's actual involvement in her son's activities in the specific case mentioned. The General

Court emphasized that association criteria should apply to entities that have a connection with entities providing support to the targeted government, but only when there is a non-negligible risk of exploitation to evade the imposed mesures. In this case, the connection between the parties was exclusively based on family ties, and the association link through companies was not established. Therefore, the General Court ruled that the risk of circumvention through association criteria cannot be invoked solely based on family ties without additional evidence demonstrating a real risk.

The evolving approach to sanctions criteria has led to a trend towards including family members in the scope of targeted measures. Expanding the criteria to include family members in sanctions regimes aims to close potential loopholes and ensure a more comprehensive impact. This broader approach recognizes that family members may indirectly benefit from or support the actions of the designated individuals. By including them in the scope of sanctions, it aims to strengthen the effectiveness and impact of these measures. However, this approach raises legal issues regarding the accountability of family members. One concern is whether it is fair and just to consider close relatives as possible tools for circumventing sanctions through clandestine transfers. It raises questions about the degree of responsibility that should be attributed to these family members. Treating them as equally responsible as the primary designated individual can be a complex matter. Determining the responsibility of family members for the actions or benefits derived from the activities of the designated individual requires careful examination. It is essential to establish a clear and evidence-based connection between the actions of the designated individual and the involvement or complicity of their family members. Holding family members accountable solely on the basis of their family relationship without adequate evidence and legal review could raise issues of fairness and due process. Therefore, while the inclusion of family members in sanctions regimes may be intended to enhance the effectiveness of these measures, it is crucial to strike the right balance between accountability and the protection of individual rights. This requires a thorough assessment of each case to ensure that the responsibility attributed to family members is based on clear evidence and legal principles, and not solely on their family ties.

In a recent development, the Council has expanded the range of the sanction's regime concerning Russia and Ukraine (Council Regulation, Council Decision) in order to minimize efforts aimed at evading the imposed measures by allowing for the direct identification of both family members and other individuals who reap the benefits from Russian business people. The amendment made to article 3(1)(g) of Regulation (EU)

No. 269/2014 now allows the identification of prominent individuals engaged in business activities in Russia, as well as their immediate family members, other individuals who reap the benefits from them, and business people engaged in economic sectors that generate significant revenue for the Russian Government. This amendment was introduced with the explicit goal of thwarting any attempts made by these business people to conceal their assets and ensuring transparency and accountability.

Countering the pervasive practices of circumvention within the EU requires the involvement of various actors, including Member States, financial operators, and the European Commission. [16] The fundamental aspect is to promote in fostering cooperation and dialogue between these stakeholders, as it is through their concerted efforts that compliance with the EU's restrictive measures can be ensured. The seriousness of the threat posed by circumvention becomes clear when considering its potential to undermine the effectiveness and overarching objectives of these measures. By enabling designated persons to avoid the full impact of the imposed sanctions, circumvention jeopardizes the effectiveness of the EU's efforts. The anti-circumvention clause therefore has a crucial role to play in preventing and countering such insidious practices, which is the very essence of its mission.

Inadequate evidence provided by the Council to substantiate the reason for listing an individual or entity is a critical concern when it comes to the imposition of sanctions. In order to ensure a fair and lawful process, it is essential that the Council provides robust evidence to justify the inclusion of an entity on the sanctions list. This evidence should clearly demonstrate the link between the targeted individual or company and the alleged activities or policies that justify the imposition of sanctions. Failure to provide sufficient evidence undermines the integrity and effectiveness of the sanction's regime, as it may lead to arbitrary or unjustified designations that violate the rights of those affected. Upholding the rule of law requires that decisions to impose sanctions be based on credible and substantiated evidence, allow for proper scrutiny and ensure the protection of fundamental rights and due process.

2.9. Restricting media broadcasts: the 'RT France' Case and freedom of information

The European Union Council imposed a series of restrictions on 1 March

---

[16] On this topic, see Finelli F., "Countering circumvention of restrictive measures: the EU response", *CMLR* (2023), 733-762.

2022 including a ban on certain media channels, such as RT France, preventing them from broadcasting.[17]

The Council pointed the finger at the Russian Federation for using to propaganda methods to justify its acts of aggression against Ukraine. It claimed that selected media channels were involved in spreading falsified information and twisting the narrative around the invasion of Ukraine. This was allegedly done with the intention to destabilize neighbouring countries and the European Union. As a countermeasure, the European Union imposed sanctions on media outlets and individuals involved in the spreading this false information. As a result, the Council stopped to the broadcasting of Sputnik and RT/Russia Today, either within or directed towards the EU.[18]

On March 24, 2022, RT France brought an action for annulment before the General Court, requesting urgent measures to suspend actions affecting its operations. The President of the Court dismissed the application for interim measures request on March 30 but expedited the proceedings due to the exceptional nature of the case. In its judgment of July 27, the Grand Chamber of the General Court recognized the Council's broad discretion in determining the objectives of the EU's restrictive measures under the Common Foreign and Security Policy.[19] The temporary ban on the broadcasting of content by certain Russian state-funded media outlets was considered a necessary response to the serious threat to peace on Europe's borders and the violation of international law resulting from their support for Russia's military aggression against Ukraine.

With regard to the alleged violation of the freedom of expression and

---

[17] While these measures were originally put into effect until July, they were later extended. On this topic see Cabrera Blázquez F.J., *The implementation of EU sanctions against RT and Sputnik*, European Audiovisual Observatory (Council of Europe), 2022, available at https://rm.coe.int/note-rt-sputnik/1680a5dd5d; Madiega T., "Russia's war on Ukraine: The digital dimension", *European Parliamentary Research Service* (2022); Andriukaitis L., Kalensky J., Kargar S., Panchulidze E., Smetek J., Vangeli A., *The misuse of social media platforms and other communication channels by authoritarian regimes: Lessons learned*, European Parliament, Inge Commission, December 2021, available at www.europarl.europa.eu/thinktank/en/document/EXPO_IDA(2021)653658.

[18] Previously, the Council had imposed restrictive measures on the management of RT, including editor-in-chief Simonyan, and Kiselev, the head of the news agency Rossiya Segodnya. In 2017, the EU Court of Justice rejected Kiselev's appeal. The court ruled that these measures were taken because Kiselev had spread propaganda in support of the Russian government's actions to destabilise Ukraine and did not unreasonably restrict his freedom of expression. See General Court, 15 June 2017, T-262/15, *Kiselev v Council*, ECLI:EU:T:2017:392.

[19] See General Court, 27 July 2022, T-125/2, RT France v Council, ECLI:EU:T:2022:483.

information, the General Court confirmed that the Council may impose restrictive measures limiting RT France's freedom of expression if certain conditions are met and, in particular, that the restrictions on freedom of expression must be laid down by law, and that the scope and duration of the temporary prohibition must be compatible with the nature of freedom of expression.

The Court found that the Council pursued the general interest objective of safeguarding the Union's public order and security while using restrictive measures to pressure the Russian authorities to stop their military aggression against Ukraine. The Council presented substantial evidence demonstrating RT France's support for Russia's aggression against Ukraine. Therefore, the restrictions on RT France's freedom of expression resulting from the restrictive measures were considered proportionate, appropriate, and necessary to achieve the objectives pursued. The temporary prohibition at issue preserved the essential content of freedom of expression without undermining it entirely. Consequently, the General Court dismissed RT France's action.

It is important to underline is that the Court's ruling confirms the line taken by the (EU) Council in the recitals (5-11) of its decision of 1st March 2022, the media are essential and instrumental in the implementation and support of the aggression against Ukraine and for the destabilization of neighbouring countries.[20] In view of the gravity of the situation and in response to Russia's actions destabilizing the situation in Ukraine, the (EU) Council has introduced additional restrictive measures to urgently suspend the broadcasting activities of these media (outlets) in or to the Union.

2.10. Concluding remarks on the EU sanctions on Russia and their legal implications

In a way, the analysis of the effectiveness of the measures taken against the Russian Federation is somewhat simpler than that of some political scientists or economists, who try to disentangle the political and economic effects of the sanctions from other events (such as the deterioration of the economic situation in Russia) and to understand the effects (or the correlation between them) and the effectiveness of the sanctions. From a legal point of view, it appears that the restrictive measures against Russia have been upheld by the Court of Justice, in particular the economic measures

[20] Council Decision (CFSP) 2022/346 of 1 March 2022 amending Decision 2014/512/CFSP concerning restrictive measures in view of Russia's actions destabilising the situation in Ukraine, OJ L 63, 2.3.2022, 5-7.

which have had a significant impact on Russia. These measures, which are not of an individual nature, may not even be subject to judicial review due to the limitations set out in Article 275 of the Treaty on the Functioning of the European Union (TFEU).

However, when it comes to sanctions against individuals, concerns have been raised about the lack of solid evidence. It is suggested that the European Union (EU) should consider the importance of obtaining first-hand information rather than relying solely on the internet or information provided by Member States to justify its actions. This raises the broader question of how the EU ensures its security and what mechanisms or bodies it needs to improve its capabilities.

Chapter 3

THE ELEPHANT IN THE ROOM: LEGITIMACY AND (DE)LEGITIMATION OF INTERNATIONAL SANCTIONS

Stefano Palestini

ABSTRACT: *The chapter advocates for placing the politics of legitimation and delegitimization at the center of the study of international sanctions. It argues that the politics of (de)legitimation flow from three distinct and constitutive legitimacy problems of contemporary international sanctions: what is the status of the international norm that has been violated? (The legitimacy of the norm); who has the right to impose a material deprivation against a state? (The legitimacy of the enforcer); is the measure adopted the right action? (The legitimacy of the measure). By drawing examples from two dissimilar sanction episodes – against Venezuela between 2014 and 2019, and against Russia after the invasion of Ukraine in 2022 –, the chapter shows intra-case and inter-case variation in the politics of (de)legitimation. Whereas the legitimacy of enforcers was the most contested issue in the case of Venezuela, the legitimacy of the measures has been, hitherto, the most salient object of contestation in the case of Russia. The chapter concludes by shedding light on the connections between the legitimacy and the effectiveness of sanctions.*

3.1. Introduction: the legitimacy problems of sanctions

> *Sanctions must become harsher. This is the time to move forward. Those against dictatorship should unite … we must starve the regime financially … that makes it necessary of course to target oil production, it makes it necessary to target the family of the dictators, it makes it necessary to target money-laundering.*
>
> (General Secretary of the Organization of American States, February 2018)

> *Unilateral coercive measures are a planned and deliberate violation of human rights and the right to food […] Those*

> *measures are part of a hostile strategy that applies maximum pressure and is aimed at the economic suffocation and international isolation of States.*
>
> (Brazilian representative at the United Nations Security Council, March 2022)

Statements as those above are all but uncommon. In the first statement, the Secretary General of the Organization of American States calls for harsher sanctions against the regime of Nicolás Maduro in Venezuela. In the second, the representative of a member of the UN Security Council makes a forceful condemnation of unilateral sanctions in a discussion about the sanctions against Russia. Although made under completely different circumstances in two different multilateral forums and notwithstanding advancing utterly opposite claims, the two statements have in common an underlying concern for legitimacy. While the former legitimizes the use of sanctions to force change in an autocratic regime, the second delegitimize sanctions as an act of aggression with pernicious consequences.

Curiously, despite the ubiquitousness of this type of legitimation struggles, legitimacy and (de)legitimation are the "elephant in the room" in the contemporary academic discussion about sanctions. In international law, the issue of legitimacy is often subsumed or conflated with the discussion about the legality of sanctions. Yet, legitimacy is a broader category than legality. The conformity with law – i.e., legality – is only one possible source from which agents can claim legitimacy for their authority and actions. In the words of Margaret Doxey "to be legitimized, an authority structure must be valued for itself; to be legal, it need only be in accordance with the law which it may have promulgated itself". [1] In International Relations we find a renewed interest in the legitimacy of international organizations, besides long-standing debates about the legitimacy of the use of force. But sanctions have been left out of these discussions. Furthermore, in these bodies of IR literature legitimacy usually gets entangled with the language of justice, morality, trust, and ethics. [2]

Early students of sanctions did pay some attention to issues related to the legitimacy of sanctions. Johan Galtung, for instance, argued that sanctions could have effect on the legitimacy of targeted regimes as well as on

[1] Doxey M., *International Sanctions in Contemporary Perspective*, Macmillan Publishers, 1987, 530.

[2] For a critique see Reus-Smit C., "International crises of legitimacy", *International Politics* (2007), 44(2-3), 157-174; Hurd, I., "Legitimacy and contestation in global governance: Revisiting the folk theory of international institutions", *Review of International Organizations* (2019), 14(4), 717-729.

their domestic opposition.[3] The 'rally round the flag' effect described how international sanctions could have the unintended effect of boosting the domestic legitimacy of the targeted regime. Two decades later, Margaret Doxey contended that powerful states can use international organizations, in order to enhance the legitimacy of their own sanctions.[4] These early insights could have led to a more systematic study of the legitimacy of sanctions. Nevertheless, the discussion on sanctions in the 1990s and 2000s swiftly moved towards the seemingly more policy-relevant issue of effectiveness. Even though, as Galtung's discussion of the 'rally round the flag' effect shows, the issues of legitimacy and effectiveness are not fully disconnected.[5]

In this contribution, I seek to bring the issue of legitimacy and (de)legitimation back into the discussion on international sanctions. While different understandings exist, most scholars accept a conception of legitimacy that emphasizes its subjective and socially constructed character. Legitimacy is a belief in the rightful use of authority by an agent or institution. Legitimacy makes appear an action as desirable, proper, or appropriate within some socially constructed system of meaning, values, and beliefs.[6] Closely related, the concept of legitimation refers to an active effort by agents to convince others about the legitimacy of their own actions and exercise of authority; delegitimization – its opposite – refers to the active effort by agents to contest and resist the legitimacy claims made by actors and institutions.[7]

Against this backdrop, I contend that international sanctions – under-

---

[3] Galtung J., "On the Effects of International Economic Sanctions: With Examples from the Case of Rhodesia", *World Politics* (1967), 19, 3, 378-416; Lindsay J.M., "Trade Sanctions As Policy Instruments: A Re-Examination", *International Studies Quarterly* (1986), 30, 2, 153-173.

[4] Doxey M., *International Sanctions in Contemporary Perspective*, Macmillan Publishers, 1987.

[5] Grauvogel J., von Soest C., "Claims to legitimacy count: Why sanctions fail to instigate democratisation in authoritarian regimes", *European Journal of Political Research* (2014), 53, 4, 635-653.

[6] Hurd I., "Legitimacy and contestation in global governance: Revisiting the folk theory of international institutions", *Review of International Organizations* (2019), 14, 4, 717-729; Reus-Smit C., "International crises of legitimacy", *International Politics* (2007), 44, 2-3, 157-174; Suchman M., "Managing Legitimacy: Strategic and Institutional Approaches", *The Academy of Management Review* (1995), 20, 3, 571-610; Weber M., *Economy and Society. A New Translation*, ed. by Tribe K., Harvard University Press, 2019 [1919].

[7] Tallberg J., Zürn M., "The legitimacy and legitimation of international organizations: introduction and framework", *Review of International Organizations* (2019), 14, 4, 581-606; Lenz T., Söderbaum F., "The origins of legitimation strategies in international organizations: agents, audiences and environments" *International Affairs* (2023), 99, 3, 899-920.

stood as material deprivations imposed against a norm-violator – face a constitutive legitimacy problem and therefore efforts at legitimation and delegitimization stand at the center of any discussion on sanctions.[8] The constitutive legitimacy problem of sanctions can be disaggregated into three questions:

- The legitimacy of the *norm*: What is the status of the international norm that has been violated?
- The legitimacy of the *enforcer*: Who has the right to impose a material deprivation against a state?
- The legitimacy of the *measure*: Is the measure adopted the right action?

These three questions or problems – the legitimacy of the norm, the legitimacy of the enforcer, and the legitimacy of the measure – are closely interlinked, and agents involved in a sanction episode (either in the position of a sender, a target, or different kinds of audiences and bystanders) might look at these problems in an undifferentiated way. I think, nonetheless, that it makes sense to analytically separate them in order to better understand the politics of the (de)legitimation of sanctions and its relevance.

In the remainder of the chapter, I will illustrate these three legitimacy problems and the ensued (de)legitimation politics, drawing on two very different recent cases of sanctions episodes: Venezuela between 2015 and 2019 and Russia in the aftermath of the invasion of Ukraine in 2022.

In the case of Venezuela, sanctions were triggered by the violation of democratic governance norms. After the death of Hugo Chávez – a populist leader who governed the country from 1999 to 2013 – his right hand and former minister Nicolás Maduro was elected in what was widely considered a rigged electoral process. Since Maduro came to power, a process of increasing autocratization transformed a troubled democracy into an electoral autocracy if not an outright closed autocracy. An important peak in this process was the shutdown of the National Assembly in 2017, and Maduro's irregular reelection in 2018. Between 2014 and 2019, 17 sanction regimes were imposed, including targeted sanctions against individuals and organizations and economic sectors, and the suspension from regional international organizations. Venezuela is a medium-size country in South America, its economic collapse – provoked by the regime's mismanagement and arguably worsened by sanctions, especially those with a higher level of

---

[8] Hofer A., "The developed/developing divide on unilateral coercive measures: Legitimate enforcement or illegitimate intervention?", *Chinese Journal of International Law* (2017), 16, 2, 175-214; Hellquist E., Palestini S., "Regional sanctions and the struggle for democracy: Introduction to the special issue", *International Political Science Review* (2021), 42, 4, 437-450.

comprehensiveness – has produced a massive outflow of migrants mostly absorbed by other South American countries.

In the case of Russia, sanctions were first enacted in the aftermath of the annexation of Crimea in 2014 and then new packages of sanctions have been imposed after the invasion of Ukraine in February 2022. Here we focus on this last episode of sanctions defined by a larger number of senders and the wide scope of the measures imposed. Different senders have imposed sanctions against Russia, several single states, more prominently the United States (US), but also states that had never enforced sanctions before, for example South Korea and Singapore, and international organizations such as the EU and the Council of Europe, who expelled Russia in March 2022. The measures have included targeted sanctions to individuals and organizations, embargoes to oil exports, freezing assets of the Central Bank and all major commercial banks, as well as bans to investment in Russia.[9]

3.2. The legitimacy of the norm

All international sanctions are linked to the violation of an international norm; but not all international norms have the same status within shared normative frameworks. Compare for instance the norm that prohibits aggression with the norm that obliges states to pay their financial commitments with an organization. Undoubtedly the former has a higher status than the latter and yet both can trigger sanctions when violated. Theorists have proposed different parameters to account for these differences of status among norms. Franck, for instance, suggests four indicators: pedigree, determinacy, coherence and adherence.[10] Pedigree refers to how deep are the historical roots of the norm; determinacy refers to the precision of the norm's content; coherence and adherence refer to the internal consistency and connectedness with other norms. While coherence underlines the lateral connectedness with similar norms, adherence refers to the vertical connectedness in a normative hierarchy.

Franck uses these indicators to evaluate the legitimacy of different international norms. However, the link between the legitimacy of a norm (in terms of pedigree, determinacy, coherence and adherence) and the (de)legitimation of the sanctions that seek to enforce those norms has not yet been made explicit. My theoretical expectation is that the higher the legit-

---

[9] Timofeev I.N., "Sanctions on Russia: A New Chapter", *Russia in Global Affairs* (2022), 20, 4, 103-119.

[10] Franck T., "The Emerging Right to Democratic Governance", *American Journal of International Law* (1992), 86, 1, 46-91.

imacy or status of a norm that is being violated by an international actor, the easier it is to legitimate (and therefore, harder to contest) the sanctions imposed to enforce that norm.

In the case of Russia and Venezuela, both sanction episodes differ greatly in terms of the legitimacy of the norm violated. By invading Ukraine, Putin's regime violated the norms with the highest pedigree, determinacy, coherence an adherence in the inter-state legal system. Norms such as international peace, self-determination and state sovereignty stand as bedrock pillars of international law. *Prima facie*, the norm breached by Maduro's regime – democratic governance – rests on less firm bases. Since democratic governance (the way in which government is carried out) has been traditionally understood as an internal affair of states, its enforcement through sanctions can be subject to delegitimization based on claims of non-intervention and state sovereignty. On these grounds, one could expect that the sanctions against Venezuela should be object of higher contestation than those against Russia.

Yet, this is only partially the case. It is true that the status of the norms violated by Russia's invasion of Ukraine has been out of the public discussion. The high status of the norms violated by Putin's military actions shield sanctions against Russia from common arguments about unlawfulness and intervention. For the case of Venezuela, however, these arguments did not play a salient role either in the contestation of the sanctions. Only at the outset of the crisis between 2014 and 2016, we find states representatives claiming that the problems in Venezuela were part of the internal-affairs and therefore there were no grounds for sanctions. But rapidly this argument lost traction, and especially after the shutdown of the National Assembly in 2017 few actors besides the Venezuelan regime and the representatives of Maduro's closest allies (Nicaragua and Bolivia) continued arguing that democratic governance was strictly a matter of the internal affairs of the Venezuelan state.

The fact that very few actors disputed the legitimacy of the norm violated by Maduro, suggests that democratic governance has indeed become an established norm in the Americas. All international organizations in the Americas have assumed collective commitments to protecting and promoting representative democracy and many have included sanctions to enforce such commitments.[11] In short, the delegitimization of the sanctions against Venezuela had less to do with disputing Maduro's wrongdoings

[11] Palestini S., Martinelli E., "Enforcing peoples' right to democracy: transnational activism and regional powers in contemporary Inter-American relations", *European Journal of International Relations* (2022), 29, 3, 780-805.

(e.g. the autocratization of his regime in a region that defines itself as a community of democracies) than with the legitimacy of the enforcers and measures.

3.3. The legitimacy of the enforcer

The legitimacy of the enforcer (or sender, to employ the most common jargon among sanction scholars), is very important in the politics of (de)legitimation. Most of the arguments used by states in the UN General Assembly Resolutions to condemn "unilateral coercive measures" have to do with the legitimacy of *who* enforces these measures [12]. What these Resolutions contest is the authority of a state (or coalition of states) to *unilaterally* impose a material deprivation against another state, in the context of an international order based on the principles of the formal equality among states, state sovereignty, and non-intervention. Unilateral senders must convince others about their right to punish wrongdoings perpetrated by equals, and therefore they must justify and legitimize their sanction policies. In other words, senders must *convincingly* take international sanctions outside the realm of *Realpolitik* and make the case that their sanctions are indeed based on collectively shared norms (e.g. the right to impose counter-measures) and interests.

In the contemporary international order, there is no monopoly of the legitimate use of sanctions and, accordingly, there is no single centralized sender. Three classes of agents frequently enforce international norms through sanctions: the United Nations Security Council (as the executive body of the United Nations), international organization (mostly regional organizations), and states acting alone or in coalitions. [13] Each of these classes of senders face the constitutive legitimacy problem described above, but they experience it with specific challenges.

Prima facie, the United Nations Security Council (UNSC) can claim legitimacy for its sanctions based on the Chapter VII of the UN Charter. The *legality* of UNSC is undisputed and, as we will see, oftentimes those who condemn unilateral coercive measures taken by single states argue that *only* UNSC sanctions are *legal* under international law. Yet, the *legitimacy* of

[12] Hofer, A., "The developed/developing divide on unilateral coercive measures: Legitimate enforcement or illegitimate intervention?", *Chinese Journal of International Law*, (2017), 16, 2, 175-214.

[13] Sossai M., *UN sanctions and regional organizations: An analytical framework*, in Van den Herik L. (ed.), *Research Handbook on UN Sanctions and International Law*, Edward Elgar, 2017, 395-417.

UNSC sanctions becomes object of contestation when they depart from the core of the UNSC mandate as established in Chapter VII, that is maintaining or restoring international peace and security. Since the end of the Cold War, the UNSC has indeed interpreted this mandate in a broader way and in fact expanded the use of sanctions to multiple and oftentimes overlapping purposes. [14] While this practice does not *per se* undermines the legitimacy of UNSC sanctions, it does compel the UNSC to engage in processes of legitimation. What is more, the UNSC membership and decision-making procedures (especially the veto of the permanent members), makes it very susceptible to accusations of political motivation and, therefore, delegitimization of the intent behind the imposition (or not imposition) of sanctions. [15] The absence of UNSC sanctions against Russia in the aftermath of the invasion to Ukraine has once again put this problem – and the need for justification – in evidence.

The legitimacy of international organizations (IOs) presents different challenges. Not all IOs impose sanctions or even have sanction provisions in their constitutive treaties. Many of those treaties have provisions that limit the use of sanction for violation by member states of operative rules, such as the nonpayment of financial commitments with the organization. Some IOs, especially regional IOs, go beyond this practice and have adopted provisions that authorize them to impose sanctions (including suspensions or expulsions) for the violation of international norms that are deemed constitutive principles of those organizations, such as regional security, the respect of democracy and the rule of law, or human rights. [16] Regional IOs can claim legitimacy for their sanctions by invoking the contractual relation they have with their members. In other words, member states have consented to – and therefore obliged themselves to abide by – the norms of the organization. This claim of legitimacy is less obvious for the European Union which stands not only as the most active sanction sender among regional IOs, but also as the only one that routinely sanctions states

[14] Biersteker T.J., Tourinho M., Eckert S.E., *Thinking about United nations targeted sanctions*, in Biersteker T.J., Eckert S.E., Tourinho M. (eds.), *Targeted Sanctions: The Impacts and Effectiveness of United Nations Action*, Cambridge University Press, 2016, 11-37.

[15] Doxey M.P., "Sanctions through the Looking Glass the Spectrum of Goals and Achievements" *International Journal: Canada's Journal of Global Policy Analysis* (2000), 55(2), 207-223; Hurd I., "The strategic use of liberal internationalism: Libya and the UN sanctions, 1992-2003", *International Organization* (2005), Vol. 59.

[16] Hellquist E., Palestini S., "Regional sanctions and the struggle for democracy: Introduction to the special issue", *International Political Science Review* (2021), 42, 4, 437-450; Charron A., Portela C., "The UN, regional sanctions and Africa", *International Affairs* (2015), 91, 6, 1369-1385.

which are non-members based on its Common Foreign Policy and Security framework. [17]

Among the three classes of senders, single states (acting alone or in coalitions) face the most pressing version of the legitimacy problem due to the fact both "the sender" and "the target" of sanctions are two independent and formally equal sovereign states. Following the Hobbesian formula, the distinction between "punishment" and "hostility" is hard to withstand when a state unilaterally imposes a sanction on another. For there is no contractual relationship between the sender and the target, it is harder for a state "sanctioning" another state than for an IO sanctioning a *member* state to claim that its sanctions "are appropriate" in accordance with a shared normative framework. Unilateral sanctions appear as intimately linked to the "national interest" of the sender and therefore claims of the universality or at least the collective character of the norm violated are less credible than similar claims made by the UNSC or a regional IO. The procedures that enable foreign policy sanctions are only valid within the jurisdictions of the sender and are normally opaque for the target and audiences outside the sender's national boundaries. Furthermore, as Brzoska has pointed out, the relationship between the state that acts as sender (normally a global power) and the state that acts as target (normally a state in the global South) is frequently characterised by a power asymmetry in favour of the former. [18]

The question about who has the right to impose sanctions has been quite more salient for the case of Venezuela than for the case of Russia. In Venezuela it could be said, it has been the core issue of the politics of (de)legitimation throughout the entire crisis and it has been mostly concerned with the legitimacy of the US as a sender.

Many Latin American governments, including governments that held a negative position regarding Maduro's regime, concur that the United State was not a legitimate sender. Underlying this evaluation there were concerns about the intentions behind Washington's sanctions perceived as ideologically or even geopolitically motivated. The Latin American contestation of US sanctions were evident since the first package of measures implemented by the Obama's administration back in 2015. Governments from left to right not only contested the opportunity of the measures – that could back-

---

[17] Giumelli F., Hoffmann F., Książczaková A., "The when, what, where and why of European Union sanctions", *European Security* (2021), 30(1), 1-23; Hellquist E., "Ostracism and the EU's contradictory approach to sanctions at home and abroad", *Contemporary Politics* (2019), 25, 4, 393-418.

[18] Brzoska M., "International sanctions before and beyond UN sanctions", *International Affairs* (2015), 91, 6, 1339-1349.

fire, radicalizing and polarizing a crisis that could have still been managed through diplomatic actions – but especially the fact the Washington framed Venezuela as a threat to US national security.[19]

In comparison with US sanctions, the legitimacy of other potential enforcers was much less contested. It was widely understood – especially with the increasing deterioration of the political and economic situation of Venezuela – that Maduro was violating international commitments upheld by regional organizations such as OAS and MERCOSUR and that, therefore, these organizations had the right to impose some sort of sanction. For instance, the opposition of Caribbean states within the OAS to impose sanctions was rather grounded on procedures and on the perceived inappropriate leverage of the US in the organization than on the legitimacy of the OAS and its Inter-American Democratic Charter.[20] Similarly, when MERCOSUR activated its democracy clause (the Protocol of Ushuiaia) and suspended Venezuela, it was widely understood that the organization had the right to do so, but the political intent behind the governments of Argentina and Brazil – the largest MERCOSUR members – was contested by other states and even by MERCOSUR's parliamentary assembly.[21]

The need of senders to legitimize themselves has been less prominent in the case of the sanctions against Russia. The distinction between more and less legitimate senders, apparent in the case of the sanctions against Venezuela does not exist for the case of Russia. In fact, an argument for the delegitimization of unilateral sanctions is that unilateral coercive measures undermine the authority of the UNSC. We do not find this argument in the resolutions and declaration about the sanctions against Russia, probably because Russia is a permanent member of the UNSC with veto power and therefore, it is understood that the target itself rather than the senders is undermining the UNSC authority.

3.4. The legitimacy of the measure

Finally, the measure itself (the material deprivation or harm) can be object of (de)legitimation. Two issues are particularly relevant in order to assert or to challenge the legitimacy of specific measures. First, the proportionality of the measures. Sanctions can vary a great deal in terms of the deprivation im-

[19] IANS, "OAS calls for dialogue between US, Venezuela", *IANS*, 20 March 2015.

[20] Sanders R., "World View: OAS compromised on Venezuela by its Secretary General", *The Tribune*, 22 May 2017.

[21] La Diaria, "Paralsur no acatará decisión de suspender a Venezuela", *La Diaria*, 21 February 2017.

posed, ranging from travel bans that affect the ability to move of specific individuals to core economic sectors embargoes that compromise an entire national economy. Audiences and bystanders – as well as other potential senders – will evaluate whether the measure imposed is proportionate to the violation that intends to address. Second, sanctions can have – and normally do have – serious unintended consequences that can pass the costs from those actors who are the intended targets to third parties, such as the population of the country or even third states and their respective population.

These two issues of proportionality and negative effect are entangled and normally manifest through (de)legitimation disputes about the level of comprehensiveness of the sanctions: do they affect an entire national economy or are they targeted enough to affect only those individuals or organizations who are direct responsible for the norm-violation? While the negative effects on the population of comprehensive sanctions – those that affect the entire economy of a state – are evident, targeted sanctions may also entail serious economic effect and potential humanitarian consequences through mechanisms such as de-risking and over-compliance[22]. Targeted sanctions are implemented mostly by private market actors who monitor blacklists of sanctioned individuals and organizations and, following cost-benefit calculations, will likely avoid commercial and financial operations in countries that figure to prominently in those blacklists[23].

The legitimacy of the measures has been central in the contestation of the sanctions against Russia, while less prominent for the case of Venezuela. The entire delegitimization discourse on sanctions against Russia is based on the nature of the measures and their effects. The core argument used by China, Brazil as well as African states such as Kenya and South Africa within the UNSC sessions since Russia's invasion, is that sanctions against Russia carry negative humanitarian effects on third countries, because they damage international economic relations (open markets and the multilateral trade system) and thereby affect global food security.

Delegitimization of sanctions based on humanitarian effects are not new. They are present in the UNGA resolutions against unilateral coercive measures.[24] It is interesting, however, that whereas those resolutions are

---

[22] Moret, E., "Time to act: Harmonizing global initiatives and technology-based innovations addressing de-risking at the interfacing sanctions-counterterrorism-humanitarian nexus", *SWP Working Paper* (2021). 01.

[23] Giumelli, F., Onderco, M., "States, firms, and security: How private actors implement sanctions, lessons learned from the Netherlands", *European Journal of International Security* (2021), 6, 2, 190-209.

[24] UNGA (1994). Unilateral coercive measures as a means of political and economic coercion against developing countries. United Nations General Assembly, Resolution

concerned with the humanitarian effects on the target's population, in the delegitimization discourse of the sanctions against Russia the concern is not about the humanitarian consequences on Russian citizens, but about those on third countries (especially, least developed countries) and on the potential global effects of the measures. Accordingly, legitimation efforts by the US and the EU have focused on claiming that global economic and humanitarian negative consequences are related to the effects of the war (therefore, responsibility of Russia) and not to sanctions.

In the case of Venezuela, the discussion about the legitimacy of measures and its effects has been less prominent. Even when in 2018, the Trump administration assumed a "maximum pressure" approach with Venezuela and imposed quasi-comprehensive bans to oil exports (the main Venezuelan commodity and source of income), few voices apart of Maduro's closest allies contested the proportionality of the measures. This can be related to three factors. First, the increased comprehensiveness of sanctions went somewhat in parallel – thus, proportionate – with an accelerated autocratization of Maduro's regime as demonstrated by the shutdown of the National Assembly in 2017 and the rigged presidential elections in 2018. Second, humanitarian concerns – mostly related to the massive outflow of migrants – was directly attributed to Maduro's economic mismanagement rather than to the sanctions. In other words, senders credibly disentangled their sanctions from the humanitarian situation in Venezuela. Third, and perhaps most importantly, Trump's threat of the use of force to bring about regime change in Venezuela made public in 2017, rendered sanctions a more appropriate measure in the eyes of international audiences and bystanders.[25] These three factors put in evidence the dynamic nature of sanction episodes in which agents constantly evaluate the measures vis-à-vis the situation on the ground in the targeted state as well as alternative policy options.

Due to the gravity of Putin's violations, contestation based on proportionality has been absent for the case of Russia. Mediation has been discussed in parallel to and not instead of sanctions. By 2023, only China had proposed the lifting of sanctions as condition for diplomatic mediation and peace talks, a proposal that has been widely considered unacceptable.[26]

48/168; UNGA (1997). Human rights and unilateral coercive measures. United Nations General Assembly, Resolution 51/103.

[25] The Washington Post, "Pence is Trump's global translator, spinning his pronouncements to soothe allies", *The Washington Post*, 16 August 2017.

[26] The Guardian, "Putin welcomes China's controversial proposals for peace in Ukraine", *The Guardian*, 21 March 2023.

3.5. Combined sanction regimes and the complexity of contemporary sanctions

The cases of Russia and Venezuela are illustrative of yet another important aspect of contemporary sanctions. Most contemporary episodes of sanctions consist of combined sanction regimes in which more than one sender imposes sanctions. Table 3.1 shows the sanction senders that have enforced sanctions against the Putin's and the Maduro's regimes.

Table 3.1. Combined sanction regimes against Russia and Venezuela

Targets / Senders	Russia	Venezuela
States (single, coalitions)	US; UK; Canada; Australia; Switzerland; Singapore; Japan; South Korea; Taiwan.	US; UK; Canada; Switzerland; Panama.
International Organizations	EU; Council of Europe; European Bank for Reconstruction and Development; World Bank; European Investment Bank	EU; MERCOSUR; OAS (Inter-American Treaty of Reciprocal Assistance); Inter-American Development Bank.

Source: authors' compilation.

Taking stock of this reality, students of sanctions should move from focusing on the sender-target relation towards conceiving the entire governance environment in which diverse senders, audiences, intermediaries, and targets are embedded. Such an analytical move would help us to better grasp the politics of (de)legitimation of sanctions. As I have argued elsewhere,[27] sanction senders observe and react to the legitimacy claims of others, constructing their own legitimation discourses either through *emulation* (taking other's legitimacy claims as templates), or through *differentiation* (distancing their own measures from others').

The case of Venezuela provides us with some interesting examples of how these dynamics play out. When Washington imposed its first package of sanctions against Venezuela claiming that the South American state was a national security threat, representatives of Latin American states and international organizations differentiated themselves from the US, contested the sanctions, and advocated instead for an approach based on diplomatic mediation. A senior adviser to the White House had to clarify that 'the US does not believe that Venezuela poses some threat to our national securi-

[27] Palestini S., "The politics of legitimation in combined sanction regimes: the case of Venezuela", *International Affairs* (2023), 99, 3, 1087-1107.

ty'[28] while President Obama himself responded to Latin American criticism by claiming: 'these sanctions are not intended to undermine the Venezuelan government or to promote instability in Venezuela'.[29]

Sometimes the differentiation of legitimation discourses underlies what *prima facie* resembles collaboration and alignment between senders.[30] In November 2017, the EU imposed its first package of restrictive measures against the Maduro's regime, joining the US which was the sanctions initiator. However, when looking at the legitimation discourses of EU actors – most prominently the High Representative for Foreign Affairs and Security Policy – it becomes apparent the efforts to differentiate EU sanctions from US sanctions.[31]

For instance, while US sanctions under the Trump administration became quasi-comprehensive affecting the oil industry and thus producing systemic effects on the entire national economy, the EU emphasized the targeted and selective character of its own measures. Furthermore, while the US dismissed any possible mediation or diplomatic effort, the EU continued justifying a mixed approach that combined targeted sanctions with multilateral mediation initiatives in tandem with Mexico, Uruguay and willing Latin American partners.

3.6. Conclusions

The distinction of the three legitimacy problems (the legitimacy of the norm, the legitimacy of the enforcer, and the legitimacy of the measure) allows us to carry out more systematic and nuanced analyses of the politics of the(de)legitimation of sanctions. Table 3.2 gives us an idea of how such an analysis could look like for the cases of the combined sanction regimes against Venezuela and Russia.

First, Table 3.2 shows us that the efforts at delegitimization can be directed to specific aspects of the sanctions. While admitting the fact that the

[28] EFE News Service, "US explains it doesn't consider Venezuela a "threat" to its security", *EFE News Service*, 7 April 2015.

[29] EFE New Service, "Obama: region cannot "remain silent" about situation in Venezuela", *EFE News Service*, 9 April 2015.

[30] von Borzyskowski I., Portela C., *Sanctions cooperation and regional organisations*, in Aris S., Snetkov A., Wenger A. (eds.), *Inter-organizational relations in International Security*, Routledge, 2018.

[31] For a similar pattern in the EU sanctions against Myanmar see Portela C., *The European Union, Human Rights and Bruma/Myanmar: Stakeholders' Perceptions in Southeast Asia*, in Holland M., Chaban N. (eds.), *Europe and Asia: Perceptions from Afar*, Nomos-Bloomsbury, 2015.

targeted state has violated international norms (thus, admitting that sanctions are required), states can still contest who is the legitimate enforcer or which are the right measures. In different degrees, this has been the case of the delegitimization made by governments of third states of the sanctions against both Maduro's and Putin's regimes. Identifying what exactly is being contested is, I believe, an important task that should precede any judgement about the motivations of those who contest sanctions. Oftentimes, sanction senders and the Western media portray state and non-state actors who engage in the contestation of sanctions as cynical as if contesting sanctions immediately imply to be the violator's accomplice. These evaluations overlook, however, that there may be good reasons for considering certain enforcers or measures as less legitimate. Listening to these voices could help to widen the debate on sanctions and perhaps even contribute to boost their legitimacy.

The politics of (de)legitimation not only vary according to the specific legitimacy problems, but also across concrete sanction episodes. Table 3.2 shows that legitimation and delegitimization unfolded differently for the cases of Venezuela and Russia. For instance, the contestation of unilateral senders (particularly the US) has been more prominent in the case of Venezuela than for the case of Russia. Conversely, the contestation of measures has been the most relevant issue in the delegitimization of sanctions against Russia, while almost totally absent in the case of Venezuela.

A more systematic explanation of this variation goes beyond the scope of the chapter. However, one could conjecture that at least part of the variation is due to the position of the respective targeted states in international hierarchies, measured not only in terms of relative power, but also in terms of authority and status. Venezuela – as any other Latin American state – is embedded in a highly asymmetrical regional order in which the United State stands out as a regional power with undisputed leverage on the other states both in bilateral relations as well as within multilateral forums, such as the OAS. Russia, instead, stands out as a regional power for parts of Eastern Europe as well as for the Caucasus and Central Asia (the so-called post-Soviet space). As a permanent member of the UNSC, the Russian state has the privileged position to veto measures taken under Chapter VII. Furthermore, in the context of the invasion of Ukraine, asymmetries of power play grossly out in favor of Russia. These different positions of the Venezuelan and the Russian states in international hierarchies probably explain differences in terms of the politics of (de)legitimation. Other possible explanations may be related to differences in the magnitude of the disruption in the global political economy associated to the different size of targeted states' economies. While the potential negative consequences of measures against Venezuela are bounded to the immediate neighbourhood (e.g. migration flows to South American countries), those associated to sanctions against Russia are potentially global in scope.

Table 3.2. (De)legitimation politics in two combined-sanction regimes

Legitimacy problem		Venezuela (2014-2019)	Russia (2022 -)
(violated) Norm	Legitimation	– based on the regional commitments to democratic governance	– almost no need to legitimate. The legitimacy of the violated norms was uncontested
	Delegitimization	– limited contestation, based on the principle of non-intervention. **Agents**: allied governments of Venezuela	– no contestation
Enforcer	Legitimation	– based on the regional commitments to democratic governance	– almost no need to legitimate the enforcers
	Delegitimization	– contestation of US unilateral sanctions on grounds of unlawfulness, and political intent. Limited contestation of other senders. **Agents**: several Latin American governments; allied governments of Venezuela	– almost no contestation of enforcers. No distinction between legitimate and illegitimate senders
Measure	Legitimation	– based on the increasing autocratization of the target, the need to curb the humanitarian crisis, and as an alternative to the use of force	– claims about the limited non-intended consequences of sanctions
	Delegitimization	– limited contestation of measures	– contestation of the effects of sanctions on the multilateral trade system and ensuing humanitarian effects on third countries. **Agents**: Some African and Latin American states; China

Source: author's compilation.

The chapter has hopefully shown the centrality of the issue of legitimacy and the politics of (de)legitimation in the discussion of international sanctions. But the question remains: why should we care about it? As said, the effectiveness of sanctions – broadly understood as the achievement of senders' intended objectives – seems a much more policy-relevant issue than legitimacy, at least from the senders' perspective. Yet, even those concerned with the effectiveness of sanctions and how to improve it, could benefit from the analysis of (de)legitimation, since states will be more willing to cooperate and to align themselves with senders that are seen as legitimate. Furthermore, the state and non-state actors that implement sanctions will probably feel more compelled to comply with measures that are widely seen as legitimate by relevant audiences. Broadly stated: sanctions that are perceived as more legitimate have better chances to be effective.

The legitimacy of sanctions is mostly case-specific. However, our triple distinction between legitimacy of the norm, the enforcer, and the measure, can provide some general guidance for rendering sanctions more legitimate. In particular, the legitimacy of the enforcer and the legitimacy of the measure are two dimensions that should be carefully factored in the sanctions' design. In principle, sanctions should be enforced by those senders who are perceived as more legitimate. This means that unilateral senders – widely seen as illegitimate by wide audiences – should refrain from being the initiators and limit themselves to be the followers of multilateral senders, either the UNSC or, if not possible, regional IOs. Measures should be designed based not only on the proportionality regarding the violation, but also considering the potential effects on third countries. At a more general level, policy makers should be very attentive to the politics of delegitimization and identify which are the claims – and the underlying motives – of those opposing sanctions.

Chapter 4

UNILATERAL SANCTIONS AS A CHALLENGE TO THE INTERNATIONAL LEGAL ORDER

Alexandra Hofer

ABSTRACT: *Unilateral sanctions are often framed as an appropriate tool to respond to grave breaches of international law. In fact, they are often seen as the only enforcement tool that is available. Yet, there are multiple drawbacks to their use that may outweigh their benefit as an enforcement mechanism. The justness of these tools is questionable when one considers that states and international organizations are inconsistent in adopting sanctions and that, when employed, these measures can have grave repercussions on the civilian population of targeted states. While sanctions are a means to impose punishment on a wrongdoer, it is precisely because sanctions are punitive that they are ill-adapted to the horizontal and decentralized legal order. Rather than focus on sanctions, research in psychology demonstrates that a more appropriate approach to changing behaviour should be grounded on empathy, where the other is viewed not only as human, but also as an equal.*

4.1. Introduction

Individual states and the European Union frequently rely on unilateral sanctions, which are the imposition of social or material costs in response to (perceived) wrongdoing, to enforce international norms. Though it is often unclear what the precise objectives of sanctions are, a topic that is heavily debated in political science scholarship, [1] they are "routinely legitimised by reference to the need to defend international norms, which are typically presented as being in the general interest, rather than expressing the particular interests of senders". [2] From an international law perspective, sanctions are repeatedly seen as a means to coerce a change in behaviour, signal commitment to norms or punish wrongdoing. In the wake of Russia's ag-

---

[1] Jones L., Portela C., "Evaluating the success of international sanctions: a new research agenda", *Revista CIDOB d'Afers Internacionals* (2020), 125, 39-60.

[2] *Ivi*, 51.

gression against Ukraine in February 2022, Professor Mary Ellen O'Connell called for states to "cut financial, trade and commercial ties with Russia [and] cut oil and gas purchases" in "support [of] Ukraine and the rules-based order founded on the prohibition of force".[3] Another commentator noted: "Sanctions are a necessary step in holding Russia accountable for its actions."[4] Josep Borrell, the EU's High Representative for Foreign Affairs and Security Policy, announced the EU was adopting sanctions alongside its allies (notably the US, the UK, Canada, Australia, Japan and other aligning countries) "to defend the peace order, international law and the rules based system".[5] Following reports of Russian war crimes, French President Emmanuel Macron advocated for further sanctions, "especially on coal and oil, which we know are particularly painful."[6] Concerned that the EU was not doing enough, there were calls to reduce its gas dependency on Russia to impose harsher measures.[7] Europeans were asked to lower the thermostat and take shorter showers to make Putin pay.[8] Such appeals were made with little understanding of how these measures shape state behaviour or indeed support international norms.[9]

This chapter argues that because of how they are adopted and imple-

---

[3] O'Connell M.E., "Opinion: How the world can make Putin pay for invading Ukraine", *CNN.com,* 24 February 2022, available at https://edition.cnn.com/2022/02/24/opinions/russia-repercussions-for-invading-ukraine-oconnell/index.html.

[4] Stanley M., "Why sanctions on Russia are necessary", *ResponsibleStatecraft.org*, 25 February 2022, available at https://responsiblestatecraft.org/2022/02/25/why-sanctions-on-russia-are-necessary/?highlight=sanctions.

[5] Council of the EU, Press Release, *Russia's military aggression against Ukraine*, 25 February 2022, available at https://www.consilium.europa.eu/en/press/press-releases/2022/02/25/russia-s-military-aggression-against-ukraine-eu-imposes-sanctions-against-president-putin-and-foreign-minister-lavrov-and-adopts-wide-ranging-individual-and-economic-sanctions/.

[6] "Macron calls for more Energy Sanctions as Ukraine Accuses Russia of War Crimes", *Politico*, 4 April 2022, available at https://www.politico.eu/article/emmanuel-macron-call-more-energy-sanction-ukraine-russia-war-crime/.

[7] "Full Embargo on Oil Could Stop War – ex Putin Aide", *BBC.com*, 10 April 2022, available at https://www.bbc.com/news/business-61040424; Dempsy J., "Judy Asks: Are Europeans Ready to Pay the Price for Ukraine's Sovereignty?", *Carnegie Europe*, 24 March 2022, available at: https://carnegieeurope.eu/strategiceurope/86722.

[8] "Phasing out Russian Oil: How UK Consumers can Help the War Effort", *The Guardian.com*, 10 March 2022, available at https://www.theguardian.com/environment/2022/mar/10/phasing-out-russian-oil-how-uk-consumers-can-help-the-war-effort.

[9] Jones L., Portela C., *op. cit.*, 53: "The extent to which a single sanctions regime contributes to the maintenance of a particular norm, for example, is virtually impossible to verify. We can only make counterfactual judgements about success here, by asking what might happen in the absence of sanctions regimes."

mented unilateral sanctions are not an appropriate enforcement mechanism in the international system. Unlike multilateral sanctions, unilateral sanctions are not based on a multilateral treaty whereby states grant the organ of an international organization (such as the United Nations Security Council) or a regional organization with the authority to adopt sanctions. Instead, unilateral sanctions are adopted by states pursuant to their own national or executive powers, or by an organization against non-member states. Because its focus is on unilateral sanctions as a tool of enforcement, the chapter is concerned with unilateral sanctions' coercive function where the goal (at least the one proclaimed by the sanction sender) is to change behaviour. [10] The discussion is also centred on targeted 'sectoral' sanctions, which are directed against specific economic and financial sectors (such as oil production or banking systems). [11]

It is first argued that, though sanctions seek to achieve justice, they are deeply unjust tools (section 4.2). This is because their adoption is inconsistent and selective (section 4.2.1) and they can have humanitarian consequences that perpetuate injustice upon the civilian population of the targeted state (section 4.2.2). Additionally, sanctions are inherently punitive (section 4.3). While this may be a good thing, after all sanctions are frequently adopted to punish wrongdoers, punishment is not suitable in the horizontal, decentralized structure of the 'international order'. This is mainly because it is a hierarchical practice that triggers resentment in those that are punished. To illustrate these issues, this chapter focuses on the sanctions implemented against Russia following its aggressive war against Ukraine in February 2022, in breach of international law. After this critique of sanctions as a tool of enforcement, it is argued that if we truly aspire to enforce international law, it is worth investing in an approach that is based on empathy and treating the other as an equal, which could be more constructive than coercion and the imposition of pressure (section 4.4).

4.2. An unjust tool

"[A] just man must take care to treat like cases alike", writes Lucas. [12] Justice encapsulates the idea that the law should be respected and that there

---

[10] On the other purposes of sanctions see *ibidem*, as well as Giumelli F., *The Success of Sanctions: Lessons Learned from the EU Experience*, Taylor and Francis, 2016.

[11] Targeted sanctions can also be directed against individuals and, in this case, consist of asset freezes and travels bans. These measures are not covered in this Chapter.

[12] Lucas J.R., "Justice", *Philosophy* (1972), 47, 181, 229-248, 229.

should be a response in case of a breach. A 'just response' must restore a balance between the one who has been injured and the wrongdoer; it should therefore be proportionate and limited to the perpetrator. Justice is closely related to fairness. [13] As argued in this section, the manner in which sanctions are imposed results in them failing to meet these criteria. Sanctions are rife with double-standards and, although they are supposed to be targeted and only be directed at those responsible for the wrongful policy, [14] they can have broad, harmful impacts on those who are not responsible for behaviour the sender aspires to change.

4.2.1. Inconsistencies and double standards

One of the key issues that undermines sanctions fairness is their ad hoc and arbitrary adoption. [15] After all, these tools are politically and economically costly and their adoption is not always convenient. [16] Sanctioners' inconsistent behaviour can undermine their normative objectives. For instance, when the US announced an embargo on Russian oil it turned to the Venezuelan and Saudi Arabian markets. Venezuela has been under US sanctions since 2015 for human rights violations. [17] The US had even gone as far as not acknowledging Nicolás Maduro as Venezuela's head of state and recognizing Juan Guaidó instead. [18] In an interview with CNN, John Bolton, former security advisor under President Trump, acknowledged that he had tried to orchestrate a *coup* against Maduro and that part of the sanctions' objectives was to cause regime change. [19] While campaigning for the 2024

---

[13] Kokaz N., "Theorizing International Fairness", *Metaphilosophy* (2005), 36, 1-2, 68-92.

[14] In being targeted, these measures were meant to reduce sanctions' humanitarian impact. See generally: Cortright D., et al. (dir.), *Smart Sanctions: Targeting Economic Statecraft*, Rowman and Littlefield, 2002.

[15] Chayes A., Handler Chayes A., *The New Sovereignty, Compliance with International Regulatory Agreements*, Harvard University Press, 1996, 2-3.

[16] On the costs of sanctions for senders see: Giumelli F., "The Redistributive Impact of Restrictive Measures on EU Members: Winners and Losers from Imposing Sanctions on Russia", *Journal of Common Market Studies* (2017), 55, 5, 1062-1080.

[17] Executive Order 13692 of March 8, 2015, Blocking Property and Suspending Entry of Certain Persons Contributing to the Situation in Venezuela.

[18] US Department of State, Press Release, *U.S. Recognition of Venezuela's 2015 National Assembly and Interim President Guaidó*, 4 January 2022, available at https://www.state.gov/u-s-recognition-of-venezuelas-2015-national-assembly-and-interim-president-guaido/.

[19] "Tapper and Bolton debate Trump's ability to plan a coup", *CNN.com*, 12 July

US Presidential election, Trump boasted that during his presidency Venezuela was on the brink of collapse and that the US almost had access to "all that oil". [20] Venezuela was one of the few countries to have voted against UNGA Resolution ES-11/1 [21] and to have legally supported Russia's intervention in Ukraine. Saudi Arabia also did not fully condemn Russia for its invasion of Ukraine. US-Saudi relations were rather cold during the first years of Joe Biden's presidency because, amongst other disagreements, Biden was reluctant to continue US support for the Saudi-led intervention in Yemen, [22] which has caused a humanitarian crisis. [23] Ultimately, however, the defense of international norms against Russia came at the cost of defending them in Venezuela and Saudi Arabia as the US sought alternatives to afford the imposition of costs on Russia.

Furthermore, sanctions that are intended to defend the 'rules-based international order' should be supported by the majority of the international community. However, when it comes to enforcing international norms, unilateral sanctions are only adopted by a select few of the international community, undermining their legitimacy. [24] In February 2022, while the sanctioners demonstrated "unmatched levels of coordination" [25] against Russia they struggled to garner additional international sup-

2022, available at https://edition.cnn.com/videos/politics/2022/07/12/jake-tapper-john-bolton-debate-january-6-coup-attempt-sot-lead-vpx.cnn.

[20] Norten B., "Trump boasts he wanted to take Venezuela's oil after overthrowing its government", *Geopoliticaleconomy.com*, 12 June 2023, available at https://geopoliticaleconomy.com/2023/06/12/trump-venezuela-oil-coup/.

[21] UNGA Resolution adopted by the General Assembly on 2 March 2022, Aggression against Ukraine (18 March 2022) UN Doc A/RES/ES-11/1. The resolution was adopted by a majority of 141; 5 states voted against and 35 abstained, it condemned Russia's 'Special Military Operation' as an act of aggression against Ukraine, in violation of the UN Charter.

[22] "Are Russia and Gulf States Trading Support for Wars in Ukraine and Yemen?", *Middle East Eye*, 28 March 2022, available at https://www.middleeasteye.net/opinion/russia-gulf-ukraine-yemen-trading-support.

[23] "Yemen: Why is the World's Worst Humanitarian Crisis Ignored?", *AlJazeera.com*, 28 March 2022, available at https://www.aljazeera.com/program/the-stream/2022/3/28/yemen-why-is-the-worlds-worst-humanitarian-crisis-ignored.

[24] It is certainly true that China and Russia adopt unilateral sanctions while they themselves condemn these measures, but unlike the US and the EU they don't adopt them to enforce norms and/or values. See: Congyan C., *China's Position and Practice Concerning Unilateral Sanctions*, and Timofeev I.N., *Unilateral and Extraterritorial Sanctions Policy: The Russian Dimension*, both in Beaucillon C. (ed.), *Research handbook on unilateral and extraterritorial sanctions*, Edward Elgar Publishing, 2021.

[25] Szép V., "Unmatched Levels of Sanctions Coordination", 25 March 2022, available at https://verfassungsblog.de/unmatched-levels-of-sanctions-coordination/.

port.[26] While the vast majority of states have condemned Russia's invasion as unlawful,[27] not all have adopted sanctions. Important economic players, such Turkey, Brazil, India, China, South Africa, have refrained from imposing restrictions, preferring to maintain a neutral position.[28] As commented upon by Trita Parsi, the West's failure to acknowledge its own disregard of international rules helps explain why non-Western states, particularly those that have been on the receiving end of Western unilateralism, did not rally to sanction Russia in 2022.[29] This illustrates how the lack of consistency in enforcing international norms and double standards can backfire.

The question of legitimacy is also relevant when taking into account how the target will respond to the sanctions. When conceptualized as an enforcement mechanism, sanctions are based on a rational choice approach to state decision-making. The reasoning is that these policy tools are able to shape behaviour by increasing the costs of wrongful behaviour, thereby manipulating the wrongdoer's cost-benefit analysis so that it chooses the less costly alternative. This however omits other factors that influence decision-making.[30] At its core, enforcement of international law is a question of shaping behaviour through inter-state interaction and peer pressure.[31] In

---

[26] "Russia Sidesteps Western Punishments, With Help From Friends", *NYTimes.com*, 31 January 2023, available at https://www.nytimes.com/2023/01/31/business/economy/russia-sanctions-trade-china-turkey.html.

[27] "Russian Invasion of Ukraine Draws Widespread – but Not Universal – Condemnation", *American Journal of International Law* (2022), 116, 3, 605-614.

[28] "The West v Russia: Why the Global South isn't Taking Sides", *The Guardian*, 28 March 2022, available at https://www.theguardian.com/commentisfree/2022/mar/10/russia-ukraine-west-global-south-sanctions-war.

[29] Parsi T., "Why non-West Countries Tend to see Russia's War Very, Very Differently", *MSNBC.com*, 12 April 2022, available at https://www.msnbc.com/opinion/msnbc-opinion/ukraine-russia-war-looks-very-different-outside-west-n1294280.

[30] Chesterman S., Pouligny B., "Are Sanctions Meant to Work – The Politics of Creating and Implementing Sanctions through the United Nations", *Global Governance* (2003), vol. 9, 503-518, 510: "The psychological dimensions of sanctions are central to understanding how both the ruling elite and the general population experience the sanctions regime, and how sanctions might affect decision-making.".

See also: Fukuyama F., "Identity: Contemporary Identity Politics and the Struggle for Recognition", *Profile Books* (2018), 32: "we have to expand our understanding of human motivation beyond this simple economic model that so dominates much of our discourse. No one contests that human beings are capable of rational behavior, or that they are self-interested individuals who seek greater wealth and resources. But human psychology is much more complex than the rather simpleminded economic model suggests".

[31] Hirsch M., *Invitation to the Sociology of International Law*, Oxford University

social interactions, how an actor perceives other actors and their behaviour matters. As Jervis puts it: "actors need to estimate what others will do and how they will react to alternative kinds of behavior on the part of the actor." [32] Consequently, how the target of sanctions perceives the senders' intentions is important as this will shape how it will respond to the measures. For example, it needs to trust that the sanctioner will lift the measures. [33] Furthermore, if the target views the measures as unfair or illegitimate it will be less inclined to comply with the sanctioners' demands. [34] According to Tyler, a psychologist whose research pioneered procedural justice: "People in social settings do not act simply as self-interested actors, pursuing individual or group gains and losses. Rather their feelings, thoughts and behaviors are shaped by their judgments concerning that is appropriate and fair". [35] Perceived illegitimacy can thus be counterproductive to the efficacy of coercive sanctions. Inconsistent policies provide Russian leaders and politicians ammunition to claim that the goal of the sanctions is not international justice but rather to weaken their state. If Russia believes the sanctions' purpose is to weaken it, then it will not trust that the sanctioners will lift the measures – further decreasing the likelihood it will comply with their demands.

Defining the sanctions as economic warfare, Vladimir Putin said they would have been imposed on Russia regardless and has sought to prepare the country to live with them in the long term, [36] thus suggesting he doubts

---

Press, 2015; Brunnée J., Troope S., *Legitimacy and Legality in International Law: An Interactional Account*, Cambridge University Press, 2010; Guzman A., "Reputation and International Law", *UC Berkeley Public Law Research Paper* (2008), 1112064.

[32] Robert J., *How Statesmen Think, The Psychology of International Politics,* Princeton University Press, 2017, 150.

[33] Demarais A., *Backfire: How Sanctions Reshape the World Against US Interests* Columbia University Press, 2022.

[34] Falk A., Fehr E., Fischbacher U., *Testing Theories of Fairness: Intentions Matter*, Institute for Empirical Research in Economics, University of Zurich, Working Paper Series, 2008. Hurd has argued that the assessment of legitimacy is subjective, see Hurd I., "Legitimacy and Authority in International Politics", *International Organization* (1999), 53, 2, 579-408. His study focuses on actor's subjective belief about a norm's legitimacy and whether it should be complied with, however to a large extent this reasoning can be applied to practices that are implemented to enforce norms. See also Tyler T.R., *Why People Obey the Law*, Princeton University Press, 2006, arguing that people abide by rules because they are legitimate, not because they fear punishment.

[35] Tyler T.R., *Justice Theory,* in Van Lange P.A.M, et al. (eds.), *Handbook of Theories of Social Psychology*, vol. 2, Sage Publications, 2012, 359.

[36] "Putin says Russia will emerge stronger, sanctions will rebound", *AlJazeera.com,* 10 March 2022, available at https://www.aljazeera.com/news/2022/3/10/putin-says-russia-will-emerge-stronger-sanctions-will-rebound.

the West is willing to lift the measures. Furthermore, while Putin's 2023 presidential address barely mentioned the sanctions, he did state:

> *[the West is] seeking to fight us on the economic front [...] the sanctions against Russia are merely a means, while the aim as declared by the Western leaders, to quote them, is to make us suffer. [...] They want to make our people suffer, which is designed to destabilise our society from within.*[37]

The senders would undoubtedly reject Putin's framing of the sanctions. Yet, they have made it clear that their objective is to, *inter alia*, "cripple the Kremlin's ability to finance the war" and "diminish its economic base" so as to prevent it from funding the war,[38] and thus proceeded to adopt unprecedented sanctions against Russia.[39] Given the breadth and scope of the measures it would be natural for the effects to be felt by Russian society. As Chachko and Heath note: "The pain that could be borne by ordinary Russians [...] is well-known and familiar from experiences in Iran, Iraq, and Cuba, among others."[40] This brings us to sanctions' potential negative humanitarian consequences and their disproportionate effects.

4.2.2. Humanitarian consequences and disproportionate effects

When it comes to the humanitarian impact of autonomous sectoral sanctions an important discussion point is causation. It is often disputed whether sanctions are responsible for a country's worsened social-economic situation. How can one make the distinction between the impact of a conflict (be it an international or non-international armed conflict) or a domestic political and economic crisis, and the consequences of the sanctions? Syria has been ravaged by a civil war since 2011 that has drastically lowered living standards. Venezuela has been in a severe social, economic and political crisis since before the first US sanctions were adopted in 2015. Nonetheless, even if the

---

[37] *Presidential Address to Federal Assembly*, 21 February 2023, available at http://en.kremlin.ru/events/president/news/70565.

[38] European Commission, *EU Sanctions Against Russia*, available at https://ec.europa.eu/info/strategy/priorities-2019-2024/stronger-europe-world/eu-solidarity-ukraine/eu-sanctions-against-russia-following-invasion-ukraine_en.

[39] Mulder N., "The Toll of Economic War: How sanctions on Russia will upend the global order", *Foreign Affairs*, 22 March 2022, available at https://www.foreignaffairs.com/articles/united-states/2022-03-22/toll-economic-war.

[40] Chachko E., Heath B.J., "A Watershed Moment for Sanctions? Russia, Ukraine, and the Economic Battlefield", *AJIL Unbound* (2022), 116, 135-139.

sanctions are not the leading cause behind the economic and social hardship, it cannot reasonably be argued that they improve the situation, either in Syria or Venezuela. After all, the unilateral sectoral sanctions target the countries' primary economic sectors, especially their oil and petroleum resources.[41] According to Volker Türk, UN High Commissioner for Human Rights: "While the roots of Venezuela's economic crisis predate the imposition of economic sanctions (...) it is clear that the sectorial sanctions imposed since August 2017 have exacerbated the economic crisis and hindered human rights".[42] Alena Douhan, UN Special Rapporteur on Unilateral Coercive Measures and Human Rights, noted the devastating effects of the sanctions against Syria, which are further perpetuating and aggravating the war's aftermath.[43] It has been reported that sanctions (amongst other effects) have led to inflation and food insecurity, severely diminishing households' living standards.[44]

There are doubts that sanctions can be said to violate the human rights of those living in targeted country as it is questioned whether sanctioners have extraterritorial human rights obligations.[45] Consequently, even if the

---

[41] Nephew, R., *The Art of Sanctions: A View from the Field*, Columbia University Press, 2019, 12.

For the sanctions against Syria see: Council Regulation (EU) No. 36/2012 of 18 January 2012 concerning restrictive measures in view of the situation in Syria and repealing Regulation (EU) No. 442/2011, which targets Syria's oil and petroleum sectors; in the US, Executive Order 13582 of August 17, 2011 prohibits transactions and importations relating to petrol and petroleum products. In 2019, the US adopted the Caesar Syria Civilian Protection, which as broadened the sanctions' reach.

With regard to Venezuela, US Executive Order 13808 of August 24, 2017 is directed against Petroleos de Venezuela, S.A. (PdVSA).

[42] OHCHR, *UN High Commissioner for Human Rights Volker Türk concludes official mission to Venezuela*, 2023, available at https://www.ohchr.org/en/statements/2023/01/un-high-commissioner-human-rights-volker-turk-concludes-official-mission.

[43] "Lift 'suffocating' unilateral sanctions against Syrians, urges UN human rights expert", 10 November 2022, available at https://news.un.org/en/story/2022/11/1130427.

[44] Kanfash M. "Sanctions and Food Insecurity in Syria", *World Peace Foundation* (2022), available at https://sites.tufts.edu/reinventingpeace/2022/07/06/sanctions-and-food-insecurity-in-syria/; Moret E., "A Lifeline under Threat? Syrian household remittances in light of sanctions, financial sector de-risking, Covid-19, and regional developments", *Economic and Social Commission for Western Asia* (2021), available at https://nafs.unescwa.org/sites/default/files/2023-02/A%20Lifeline-under-Threat-EN-Web.pdf; Hussain M., "Are U.S. Sanctions Against Syria Stalling Humanitarian Aid After the Earthquake?", *The Intercept*, 19 February 2023, available at https://theintercept.com/2023/02/19/syria-earthquake-us-sanctions/.

[45] Prezas I., *From Targeted Sanctions to Affected Populations: Exploring Accountability for the Negative Impact of Comprehensive Unilateral Sanctions on Human Rights* in Beaucillon C. (ed.), *Research handbook on unilateral and extraterritorial sanctions*, Edward Elgar Publishing, 2021, 385-404; Akande D., Akhavan P., Bjorge E. "Economic

sanctions have such effects this does not mean that they are unlawful.[46] The point of this section is not to engage with this debate,[47] but to argue that sanctions that cause a significant decrease in a population's well-being could be considered disproportionate.

As argued elsewhere, the proportionality principle can be considered a general principle of international law and, consequently, all sanctions, regardless of their legal nature (whether they are retorsions, countermeasures, unilateral sanctions, multilateral sanctions, etc.), should be proportionate to the goal pursued by the sender.[48] This position appears to be shared in the literature on UNSC sanctions and countermeasures.[49] In its commentaries to Article 50 on countermeasures in ARSIWA, which states *inter alia* that countermeasures should not violate fundamental human rights, the ILC seems to support the argument that countermeasures should not adversely affect the population of the targeted country.[50] There are equally indications in state practice that sanctions should be proportionate. For instance, one can read the following statement on the EU Commission website:

> *EU sanctions are carefully targeted, and designed to be proportionate to the objectives they seek to achieve. As such, they are aimed at those responsible for policies or actions the EU wants to influence, while reducing as much as possible any unintended consequences.*[51]

Sanctions, International Law, and Crimes Against Humanity: Venezuela's ICC Referral", *AJIL* (2021), 115, 3, 493-512.

[46] Afterall, for there to be a breach of international law the state needs to have violated an international obligation.

[47] But see Djourabi-Asadabadi T.'s contribution to this volume.

[48] Hofer A., "The Proportionality of Unilateral "Targeted" Sanctions: Whose Interests Should Count?", *Nordic Journal of International Law* (2020), 89, 399-421.

[49] Dawidowicz M., *Third Party Countermeasures in International Law*, Cambridge University Press, 2017, 358 ; Reisman W.M., Stevick D.L., "The Applicability of International Law Standards to United Nations Economic Sanctions Programmes", *European Journal of International Law* (1988), vol. 9, 86-141 ; Joyner D., *United Nations Counter-Proliferation Sanctions and International Law*, in van den Herik L. (ed.), *Research Handbook on United Nations Sanctions and International Law*, Edward Elgar Publishing, 2016; Jayakody N., "Refining United Nations Security Council Targeted Sanctions: "Proportionality" as a way forward for human rights protections", *Security and Human Rights* (2018), vol. 29, 90-119.

[50] "Draft articles on Responsibility of States for Internationally Wrongful Acts, with commentaries", *Yearbook of the International Law Commission* (2001), vol. II, part two, commentary to Article 50, p. 132, paras 6-7.

[51] European Commission, *Frequently Asked Questions: Restrictive Measures (sanctions),* available at https://ec.europa.eu/commission/presscorner/detail/en/qanda_22_1401.

Sanctioners also tend to include humanitarian exceptions in their sanctions' regimes.[52] This is an indication that they believe that their sanctions should not have harmful effects on civilians. This is also clear from the debate on the humanitarian consequences of the UNSC comprehensive sanctions against Iraq, Haiti and former Yugoslavia. This transition occurred following the severe humanitarian consequences of the UNSC's comprehensive sanctions regimes, after which it was decided that policymakers should ensure their sanctions are more precise. Consequently, since the early 2000s sanctions are supposed to be targeted, in the sense that they should make the distinction between those responsible for the wrongful conduct and innocent bystanders (most notably the civilian population, but it could also apply to third states and private actors).[53] Meanwhile practice demonstrates that they can still have significant repercussions.

Moret notes the "renewed humanitarian consequences of the 're-comprehensivization' of international sanctions practice".[54] Sanctioners are prone to adopting a multitude of sectoral sanctions, which are directed against important sectors of a state's economy. Iran and Syria have been sanctioned by the UNSC as well as by states unilaterally (most notably the US) and by the EU; Syria has also been sanctioned by the League of Arab States. The fact that multiple jurisdictions are involved leads to what is known as 'de-risking' or sanctions' chilling effect. Private companies fear unwittingly violating sanctions and prefer to avoid trade with a heavily sanctioned state altogether.[55] This adds barriers to accessing basic necessities, and generally impacts the most vulnerable segments of the population. In such circumstances, Moret writes, "licencing exemptions and exceptions are frequently insufficient to ensure continued supplies of essential goods to heavily sanctioned countries".[56]

Additionally, in the context of the EU restrictive measures against Russia, African states warned that the sanctions are blocking crucial exports

---

[52] On the shortcomings of the US humanitarian exceptions, see Demarais A., *op. cit.*, 58-61.

[53] Hawkins D., Lloyd J., "Questioning comprehensive sanctions: the birth of a norm", *Journal of Human Rights* (2003), 2, 3, 441-454.

[54] Moret E., *More Civilian Pain than Political Gain (Again?) The Demise of Targeted Sanctions and Associated Humanitarian Impacts,* in Charron A., Portela C. (eds.), *Multilateral Sanctions Revisited: Lessons Learned from Margaret Doxey*, McGill Queen's University Press, 2022, 179. See also Gordon J., "Revisiting Smart Sanctions", *Ethics & International Affairs* (2011), 25, 3, 315-35.

[55] Moret E., *More Civilian Pain than Political Gain,* cit., 181.

[56] *Ivi*, 180.

from Ukraine and Russia (notably fertilizer), which could lead to food insecurity in the continent.[57] Though this was staunchly rejected by the EU, member states did ask the regional organization for more guidance.[58] Part of the issue is that the EU's restrictive measures are so far-reaching that companies are uncertain about what transactions are allowed. Furthermore, Russian banks are barred from the SWIFT payment system, which is required for most international transactions. Food imports were rendered near-impossible because African companies were unable to pay.[59] Consequently, even if the sanctions do not target Russia's food sector directly, they can have unintended consequences.[60]

Ultimately, sanctions are unjust when they are imposed in a manner that punishes those who are not responsible for the policy the sanctioner wishes to change.[61] As discussed below, even if sanctions could be limited to those who are responsible, the concept of punishment is incompatible with the decentralized international order.

---

[57] "Russia sanctions hurt 'bystander' countries, South African President Ramaphosa says", *Reuters.com*, 24 May 2022, available at https://www.reuters.com/world/africa/south-africas-ramaphosa-dialogue-only-way-solve-ukraine-war-2022-05-24/.

[58] "Member states press EU to amend sanctions to unblock Russian food shipments", *Financial Times*, 7 December 2022, available at https://www.ft.com/content/1cbca193-e56f-415a-8b3b-e4208ef1def3.

[59] "African Union chief urges EU to ease food payments to Russia", *Politico.com*, 19 June 2020, available at https://www.politico.eu/article/african-union-chief-urges-eu-to-ease-food-payments-to-russia/.

[60] However, the CEOs of companies that sell fertilizer (notably EuroChem, PhosAgro, Uralchem) have been placed under an asset freeze, see Annex to Council Regulation (EU) No. 269/2014 of 17 March 2014 concerning restrictive measures in respect of actions undermining or threatening the territorial integrity, sovereignty and independence of Ukraine (OJ L 078 17 March 2014, p. 6). In order to prevent food insecurity, the EU has allowed for exceptions for the purchase, import and transport of food and agricultural goods, including fertiliser. See *ivi*, Article 6e.

On unintended consequences see: "As sanctions bite Russia, fertilizer shortage imperils world food supply", *Reuters.Com*, 23 March 2022, available at https://www.reuters.com/business/sanctions-bite-russia-fertilizer-shortage-imperils-world-food-supply-2022-03-23/.

[61] And even when they are targeted against specific individuals they can still be unjust, see Sullivan G., *The Law of the List: UN Counterterrorism Sanctions and the Politics of Global Security*, Cambridge University Press, 2021.

4.3. The counter-productiveness of punishment[62]

Political scientists tend to focus on sanctions rational objectives, yet when these tools are adopted in response to wrongdoing, they are inherently punitive. Nossal is probably most well-known for arguing that sanctions constitute international punishment. He defines punishment as the imposition "not only a concrete cost (the deprivation of something of value) but also a public expression of the community's moral disapproval of the act".[63] Even if sanctions pursue other objectives, to the extent that costs are imposed in reaction to violations their punitive characteristics cannot be denied. While punishment may be "satisfying", the imposition of costs should not be a means in and of themselves, otherwise sanctioners are just "maximizing the economic pain of ordinary [citizens] without any conception of what that will achieve".[64] For example, calls to ban ordinary Russians from travelling to Europe in summer 2022 smacked of collective punishment. The rationale was that Russian citizens should not be permitted to travel freely while their government is engaging in warfare, they should feel the costs of the war.[65] According to one analyst, such a ban would communicate to Russians that "[travelling] to Europe is a privilege, and you value it, and we're going to take it away".[66]

Inter-state punishment, imposed unilaterally by one state or collectively by a group of states against another, is at odds with the horizontal, decentralized structure of the international order. The act of punishing creates a hierarchy between the sender and the target. In broad terms, hierarchy

---

[62] This section draws from previous publications: Hofer A., *The Punitive Effect of the EU's restrictive measures against Russia: A help or a hindrance to principled pragmatism?,* in Bossuyt F., van Elsuwege P. (eds.), *Principled Pragmatism in Practice: The EU's Policy towards Russia after Crimea*, Brill, 2021; Hofer A., "Creating and contesting hierarchy: the punitive effect of sanctions in a horizontal system", *Revista CIDOB d'Afers Internacionals* (2020), 125, 15-37.

[63] Nossal R., "International sanctions as international punishment", *International Organization* (1989), vol. 43(2), 306. See also Lang A. Jr., *Punishment, Justice and International Relations: Ethics and Order in the Cold War*, Routledge, 2008, 78.

[64] Drezner D., "What is the Plan behind Sanctioning Russia?", *WashingtonPost.com*, 1 March 2022, available at https://www.washingtonpost.com/outlook/2022/03/01/what-is-plan-behind-sanctioning-russia/.

[65] "EU Under Pressure to Ban Russian Tourists from Europe", *TheGuardian.com*, 10 August 2022, available at https://www.theguardian.com/travel/2022/aug/10/eu-under-pressure-to-ban-russian-tourists-from-europe.

[66] "Europeans Debate Barring Russian Tourists Over the Invasion of Ukraine", *NYTimes.com*, 19 August 2022, available at https://www.nytimes.com/2022/08/19/world/europe/europe-russia-tourists-visas-ukraine.html.

constitutes "any system through which actors are organised into vertical relations of super- and subordination".[67] Through the imposition of sanctions, states are ranked and organized based on a system of values, between those who are assessed as 'good' (the ones imposing the measures) and those who are 'bad' (those the measures are directed against).[68] Sanctions are also illustrative of the *de facto* inequality between states. Only those that are financially and economically powerful can successfully impose costs; successful implementation of sanctions also requires substantial resources in order to gain international support and monitor coordination.

States do not respond well to being punished. It is well-documented that emotions influence decision-making and policy choices within state structures;[69] after all, behind the abstract veneer of a 'state' are the human beings (officials, bureaucrats, representatives, advisors, etc.) that represent it and make it take form domestically and internationally. Emotions influence sanctioners' decision to adopt sanctions[70] and equally influence how a targeted state responds to being sanctioned. A sanctioned state can resent the measures placed upon it, making it unwilling to give into the sender's demands and seek means to resist the costs imposed.[71] Resentment can arise in reaction to an "undeserved status".[72] Related to this discussion is identity recognition – individuals have a sense of self (their identity) and seek to be recognized by others. According to Tyler, in the context of conflict resolu-

---

[67] Bially Mattern J., Zarakol A., "Hierarchies in World Politics", *International Organization* (2016), 70, 623-656. 625.

[68] See also Simpson G., *Great Powers and Outlaw States Unequal Sovereigns in the International Legal Order*, Cambridge University Press, 2003, 5.

[69] Lerner J.S., Ye L., Valdesolo P., Kassam K.S., "Emotion and Decision Making", *Annual Review of Psychology* (2015), 66, 799-823; Franks D.D., *The Neuroscience of Emotion*, in Stets J.E., Turner J.H. (eds.), *Handbook on the Sociology of Emotions*, Springer Science, 2006; Hymans J.E.C., *The Psychology of Nuclear Proliferation: Identity, Emotions, Foreign Policy*, Cambridge University Press, 2006; McDermott R., "The Feeling of Rationality: The Meaning of Neuroscientific Advances for Political Science", *Perspectives on Politics* (2004), 2, 4, 692-706; Markwica R., *Emotion Choices: How the Logic of Affect Shapes Coercive Diplomacy*, Oxford University Press, 2018.

[70] Beauregard P., "International emotional resonance: Explaining transatlantic economic sanctions against Russia", *Cooperation and Conflict* (2022), 57, 1, 25-42.

[71] Hofer A., "Creating and contesting hierarchy: the punitive effect of sanctions in a horizontal system", cit.

[72] Wolf R., *Political Emotions as Public Processes: Analyzing Transnational Ressentiments in Discourses*, in Clément M., Sanger E. (eds.), *Research Emotions in International Relations: Methodological Perspectives on the Emotional Turn*, Palgrave Macmillan, 2018, 234. See also Wolf R., "Identifying Emotional Reactions to Status Deprivations in Discourse", *International Studies Review* (2017), 19, 491-496.

tion, individuals attach a high level of importance to being treated with respect and dignity, which includes recognition of their identity and status.[73] When identities are not recognized, this can lead to negative emotional arousal, such as guilt, anger, shame, or resentment.[74] Research has found that individuals may engage in various strategies when their sense of self is not validated.[75] They may change their behaviour or identity to increase their chances of being recognized. This is the ideal scenario from an enforcement perspective: the sanctioned will change its behaviour and comply with international law, at which point the sanctions would be lifted and they would be recognized by the sanctioners. Once again, for this to be achieved the goals pursued by the sanctions need to be clear and achievable. However, there is also the risk that they turn to other actors who will validate them.

For example, Russian leaders, which view their state as a 'Great Power', resented being punished and being placed in a 'lower' position by EU and US sanctions in 2014,[76] which undermined their identity as a 'great power'. Rather than accept this 'lesser' position, Russia has sought to project the image of an 'untouchable state', consistent with its great power identity.[77] It does not want to be seen as suffering the costs of the sanctions nor as being influenced by the senders. While the sanctions are a nuisance, they will not destroy Russia. Russian representatives and policymakers sought to demonstrate their country's strength by imposing counter-costs on the sanctioners and by framing their restrictions as illegitimate and unlawful attempts to weaken it.

Even if sanctions can impose stigma by labelling the target as a bad actor, this may backfire and cause counterproductive effects, as demonstrated by the literature on shame and stigmatization.[78] One important consequence

---

[73] Tyler T.R., *op. cit.*, 350.

[74] For an overview of the literature on identity validation and rejection, see Markwica R., *Emotional Choices: How the Logic of Affect Shapes Coercive Diplomacy*, Oxford University Press, 2018, 65-66 and accompanying sources.

[75] *Ivi*, 66.

[76] Hofer A., *The Punitive Effect of the EU's restrictive measures against Russia*, cit.

[77] Hofer A., "All the World's a Stage, and Sanctions the Merely Props: An Interactional Account of Sender-Target Dynamics in the Ukrainian Crisis", *International Peacekeeping* (2021), 28, 2, 259-284.

[78] Smetana M., Onderco M., "Bringing the outsiders in: an interactionist perspective on deviance and normative change in international politics", *Cambridge Review of International Affairs* (2018), vol. 31, issue 6, 516-536; Adler-Nissen R., "Stigma Management in International Relations: Transgressive Identities, Norms, and Order in International Society", *International Organization* (2014), 68, 1, 143-176; Zarakol A., "Ontological (In)security and State Denial of Historical Crimes: Turkey and Japan", *International Relations* (2010), 24, 1, 3-23.

(for the purpose of this chapter) is that stigmatized actors may attempt to reject or counter their stigma by becoming norm entrepreneurs and seek to transform normative orders.[79] Such strategies may undermine the system of values that the sanctioners seek to enforce. Chwieroth has written that actors engaged in counter-stigmatizing, which is when an actor accepts its stigma but takes pride in setting itself apart from those who imposed it,

> *may seek alliances with other deviants or, especially when they have sufficient material and social resources, they may pursue efforts to transform the international normative order so it is more consistent with their norms. Such alliances and resources, as well as a lack of normative agreement among the normal states, may provide a window of opportunity for the deviant states to improve their position.*[80]

We are witnessing some of this in the context of the Ukraine war. As Russia has been isolated by the West, it appears to have moved closer to China, leading to an increased rivalry between, on the one hand, the US and EU and, on the other hand, China and Russia over 'the world order'. During his visit to Moscow in March 2023, Chinese President Xi declared that his country is "ready to resolutely defend the UN-centric international system, stand guard over the world order based on international law".[81] He also remarked that: "China and Russia have natural responsibilities to make joint efforts to steer and promote global governance in a direction that meets the expectations of the international community".[82] Within this context, China put forward a proposal for peace in Ukraine. John Kirby, NSC Coordinator, commented that while Russia and China are seeking "to challenge US leadership around the world" as well as the "international rules-based order", they "do not have that same network of friends and partners" as the US.[83] Meanwhile, French President Macron is reportedly

---

[79] Chwieroth J.M., "Managing and transforming policy stigmas in international finance: Emerging markets and controlling capital inflows after the crisis", *International Political Economy* (2015), 22, 1, 44-76.

[80] *Ivi*, 49-50.

[81] "Xi Jinping says China ready to 'stand guard over world order' on Moscow visit", *TheGuardian.Com,* 20 March 2023, available at https://www.theguardian.com/world/2023/mar/20/xi-jinping-vladimir-putin-moscow-ukraine-war.

[82] The State Council, the People's Republic of China, "Xi, Putin agree to deepen comprehensive strategic partnership of coordination for new era", 22 March 2023, available at http://english.www.gov.cn/news/topnews/202303/22/content_WS641a5bd5c6d0f528699db7c2.html.

[83] Press Briefing by Press Secretary Karine Jean-Pierre, the Cast of "Ted Lasso", and NSC Coordinator for Strategic Communications John Kirby, *WhiteHouse.gov,* 20

"shocked by how much credibility we [the West] are losing in the global south",[84] which has been illustrated by their unwillingness to align on the sanctions against Russia and their preference to remain neutral. Within this context, we are also observing the expansion of BRICS, which according to some commentators is seeking to propose an alternative world order.[85]

4.4. The way forward

Even those who are critical of sanctions don't go so far as to say they should be abandoned altogether; they rather argue that sanctions should be reformed or that sanctioners should be more cautious.[86] Perhaps our unwillingness to give up on sanctions is due to the fact that we don't have an alternative.[87] This can be summed up in the following manner: "sanctions are a bad idea in principle and not very effective in practice (…) but it's worth asking what other options are available to policymakers, short of direct coercion and military might."[88] Thus, despite all their shortcomings, sanctions are the only thing we've got.

I think that the issue is that we *believe* we do not have an alternative. One exception is Chayes and Chayes, who stated in 1990 that "sanctions are a waste of time".[89] Instead, they propose a managerial approach to compliance, which views non-compliance as a problem to be solved as opposed to something that should be punished. Given the history of sanctions, and the many attempts at improving them, it seems irrational to expect sanctions will make the difference we desire. After all: "only a fool does the same thing over and over, expecting a different outcome." Yet, a

March 2023, available at https://www.whitehouse.gov/briefing-room/press-briefings/2023/03/20/press-briefing-by-press-secretary-karine-jean-pierre-the-cast-of-ted-lasso-and-nsc-coordinator-for-strategic-communications-john-kirby/.

[84] "Compare Iraq with Ukraine. It's clear the era of US global supremacy is over", *TheGuardian.com*, 20 March 2023, available at https://www.theguardian.com/commentisfree/2023/mar/20/iraq-ukraine-us-global-supremacy-washington-power-china-global-south.

[85] Giustra F., "De-dollarization: Not a matter of if, but when", *ResponsibleStatecraft.org*, 3 May 2023, available at https://responsiblestatecraft.org/2023/05/03/de-dollarization-not-a-matter-of-if-but-when/?highlight=BRICS.

[86] See, for example, Demarais A., *op. cit.*

[87] And it is precisely because the Chayeses had an alternative approach to sanctions that they were able to consider other approaches to enforcement and compliance.

[88] Beeson M., "Sanctions rarely work, but are they still the least worst option?", *The Conversation*, 28 February 2023, available at https://theconversation.com/sanctions-rarely-work-but-are-they-still-the-least-worst-option-199494.

[89] Chayes A., Handler Chayes A., *op. cit.*, 2.

Fool can go boldly where no one has gone before, have original ideas, and perhaps find (unconventional, or creative) solutions that will transcend stubborn problems.

It seems to me that the primary issue is that sanctions are based on a rational-choice approach to state behaviour: these tools are expected to influence behaviour by manipulating decision-makers' cost benefit analysis. The premise is that the imposition of costs will make the wrongful behaviour less attractive, and therefore the sanctioned actor will change its behaviour and comply with the sender's demands. Applying pressure, or coercion, can thus yield results. There are multiple issues with this perspective, and the shortcomings to this approach are reflected in the discussion above. Most importantly, perhaps, this approach to state behaviour depends on the sanctioner's ability to break the target's resolve.[90] Yet, as discussed above, the target may resent this and seek to resist. At the end of the day, decision-making is far more complicated than the ideal presented by rational-choice models. Human beings are influenced by biases,[91] in-group dynamics and identities,[92] and, as mentioned above, emotions. As also mentioned above, behaviour is also very dependent on our interactions and how we perceive them.

Emily and Laurence Alison's (who are a counsellor and psychologist respectively) research has focused on how to persuade individual's being interrogated by the police to share information.[93] They have demonstrated that coercion rarely works in inter-personal communication. Instead, building a rapport that is based on empathy and a balance of power leads to more successful results. To foster co-operation, it is necessary to be seen as a friend and not as an enemy. This would most likely resonate with the reader. We have no doubt all experienced that improved communication skills leads to better results in our personal relationships, be that in exchanges with close personal connections or colleagues.[94] I would argue that it can equally be applied between states – especially if a state is aiming to persuade another to change its behaviour. The challenge can be to build the rapport during confrontational exchanges, and especially if we are deal-

---

[90] Nephew R., *op cit.*

[91] Kunda Z., "The case for motivated reasoning", *Psychological Bulletin* (1990), 108, 3, 480-498.

[92] Tajfel H., *Social Identity and Intergroup Relations*, Cambridge University Press, 1982; Stets J., Burke P.J., "Identity Theory and Social Identity Theory", *Social Psychology Quarterly* (2000), 63, 3, 224-237.

[93] Alison E., Alison L., *Rapport: The Four Ways to Read People*, Vermilion, 2020.

[94] As stated by Alison E., Alison L., *op. cit.*, 17-21.

ing with attitudes that trigger emotional responses such as anger that give the incentive to be punitive. However, it is in such circumstances that de-escalating becomes crucial.

American psychologist Carl Rogers applied his person-centred approach[95] to facilitate communication and mediate disputes between different groups. In his view:

> *One of our greatest difficulties in any dispute is to recognize or, even more difficult, to accept that the certitude we feel about our own rightness and goodness. If tension can be reduced, is it this pattern that must somehow be resolved.*[96]

His approach also emphasizes the importance of humility (acknowledging our own shortcomings), communication and understanding the other's perspective.[97] In this way, people and groups come to realize that they share a lot more than they had previously thought and can start to build a more humane world.

Important in this discussion is identity recognition. Robin Markwica's analysis of Khrushchev's decision-making process during the 1962 Cuban Missile Crisis draws attention to the importance the Russian president attached to being respected and validated by his US counterpart.[98] A defining moment was when Khrushchev had "the impression that Kennedy was at long last recognizing him as a co-equal power",[99] leading him to agree to remove the Soviet rockets from Cuba. Trita Parsi's study of the US-Iran secret negotiations, which led to the Joint Comprehensive Plan of Action, also emphasises the importance of mutual respect and recognition. According to his analysis, one of the determining factors of the negotiations' success was then-US President Obama's and then-US Secretary of State John Kerry's "unusual ability to see the world through the eyes of their counter-

---

[95] Rogers describes this method as one where a psychologist assists an individual in tapping into their vast resources for self-understanding and for adjusting their concepts, beliefs and behaviour. In order for the psychologist to facilitate this, they have to adopt a position of genuineness, acceptance and empathy. Their exchange must also be based on trust. See generally: Rogers C., *A Client-centred/Person-centred Approach in Theory (1986)*, in Kirschenbaum H., Land Henderson V. (eds.), *The Carl Rogers Reader*, Houghton Miflin Company, 1989.

[96] Rogers C., *Resolving Intercutural Tensions (1977)*, in Kirschenbaum H., Land Henderson V. (eds.), *op. cit.*, 438.

[97] Rogers C., *A Psychologist Looks at Nuclear War (1982)*, in Kirschenbaum H., Land Henderson V. (eds.), *op. cit.*, 455.

[98] Markwica R., *op. cit.*, 172-175.

[99] *Ivi*, 178.

parts", which was critical to building trust.[100] Mutual respect, where the US recognized Iran as a nation and accepted its collective identity, was essential to reaching an agreement. These examples are consistent with Tyler's studies on procedural justice, which find that identity is central to perceptions of justice and fair treatment.[101] After all, human beings are fundamentally social animals who are concerned about their relations with others.[102]

If we adopt such an approach to state behaviour, then sanctions, which are punitive and stigmatizing, appear as highly counterproductive and even harmful. Policies grounded on empathy, which entail a willingness to see the other as an equal and an openness to dialogue, making room for diplomacy and negotiations, could create an environment that would be more conducive to international norms being upheld. Such policies require letting go of sanctions.

---

[100] Parsi T., *Losing an Enemy: Obama, Iran and the Triumph of Diplomacy*, Yale University Press, 2017, 371.

[101] Tyler T.R., *op. cit.*, 356-358. See also: Tyler T.R., *Why People Cooperate: The Role of Social Motivations*, Princeton University Press, 2010.

[102] Tyler T.R., *op. cit.*, 359.

Chapter 5
THE JURISDICTIONAL INTRICACIES OF SECONDARY SANCTIONS CONSISTING OF ACCESS RESTRICTIONS

Felipe Rodríguez Silvestre

ABSTRACT: *Secondary access restrictions, defined as measures adopted to deny admission to third states' companies or individuals into the internal market, financial institutions, or territory of the sanctioning state, are the most prevalent type of secondary sanction employed by powerful economies. Despite their straightforward implementation and comparative advantages over other forms of secondary sanctions, their conformity with the customary rules governing the exercise of jurisdiction by states remains a highly contested matter. This chapter aims to elucidate the jurisdictional scope of secondary access restrictions, in order to ascertain the rules applicable to these measures and provide an answer regarding their overall legality.*

5.1. The taxonomy of unilateral sanctions in the international legal order

The threat and adoption of sanctions by states and international organizations have become part and parcel of foreign relations. However, for such a prevalent practice, few concepts are as shrouded under a veil of ambiguity concerning their applicable legal framework as sanctions are.

Traditionally, sanctions were regarded as measures adopted by centralized organs within a collective structure to counter unlawful behavior and reinstate legality. However, over the last few decades, some states and regional organizations, such as the EU, have employed non-forcible coercive measures against third states autonomously. These unilateral measures are increasingly being adopted to exert pressure on the target state to alter its policies or conduct, with the ultimate aim of achieving a particular geopolitical goal.[1] Currently, sanctions of an economic nature, are the preferred foreign policy instrument of powerful states to achieve their diverse objectives.[2]

In the absence of an institutional framework coordinating their collective implementation, the effectiveness or strength of a given unilateral sanction is conditioned by the voluntary alignment of third states, and how widespread this endorsement is within the international community. As Beaucillon points out, 'the more States that implement a specific threat of economic sanctions, the smaller the potential for the State target to circumvent the measures by turning to other partners and markets.'[3] Nevertheless, reality paints a different picture, as other nations are frequently willing to seize the opportunity and fill the outstanding trade gap left by the adoption of unilateral economic sanctions.[4] This practice is known as backfilling.

5.2. The distinction between primary and secondary sanctions

As a response to the circumvention of unilateral sanctions, secondary sanctions emerged with the objective of economically isolating and amplifying the pressure on the target state. While primary sanctions restrict economic interactions between individuals and companies under the territorial or national jurisdiction of the sanctioning state and the target state, including economic actors operating within its territory,[5] secondary sanctions aim to deter, restrict or prohibit, the economic or financial interactions between a third state, including the companies or individuals either residing or legally

---

[1] Krisch N., "International Law in Times of Hegemony: Unequal Power and the Shaping of the International Legal Order", *European Journal of International Law* (2005), 16, 369, 403; Lowenfeld A.F., *International Economic Law*, 2nd ed., Oxford University Press, 2008, 698.

[2] Joyner D., *International Legal Limits on the Ability of States to Lawfully Impose International Economic/Financial Sanctions*, in Ronzitti N. (ed.), *Coercive Diplomacy, Sanctions and International Law*, Brill-Nijhoff, 2016, 193.

[3] Beaucillon C., *Practice Makes Perfect, Eventually? Unilateral State Sanctions and the Extraterritorial Effects of National Legislation*, in Ronzitti N. (ed.), *Coercive Diplomacy*, cit., 103, at 109.

[4] Meyer J.A., "Second Thoughts on Secondary Sanctions", *University of Pennsylvania Journal of International Law* (2009), 30, 905, 924; Terry P.C.R., "Enforcing U.S. Foreign Policy by Imposing Unilateral Secondary Sanctions: Is Might Right in Public International Law?", *Washington International Law Journal* (2020), 30, 1, 3.

[5] Ruys T., Ryngaert C., "Secondary Sanctions: A Weapon out of Control? The International Legality of, and European Responses to, US Secondary Sanctions", British *Yearbook of International Law* (2020), 7.

incorporated in its territory, and the primary sanctions' target state, including the economic agents operating within its territory. [6] Hence, secondary sanctions aim to govern transactions carried out by foreign entities outside the territory of the sanctioning state, ergo they are often referred to as extraterritorial sanctions.

In practice, secondary and extraterritorial sanctions share conceptual similarities but are not identical. Primary sanctions can also be extraterritorial when founded on a jurisdictional nexus based on nationality, in cases where a given regulation governs the conduct of nationals abroad. While secondary sanctions have indeed an intrinsic extraterritorial character, [7] their distinctive feature is that they regulate and punish conduct that cannot be linked to the sanctioning state by a territorial or personal jurisdictional nexus.

Primary sanctions are generally less problematic from a jurisdictional perspective compared to secondary sanctions. [8] However certain primary sanctions are grounded on controversial wide-ranging interpretations of territory or nationality. For instance, the United States (US) has adopted primary sanctions on the basis of the utilization of US dollars in transactions performed overseas between two foreign subjects, [9] the re-export of US technology already located abroad, [10] or the control of a US parent company over foreign branches or subsidiaries registered in another country. [11] While these measures could be catalogued as primary sanctions, the overstretched jurisdictional connection invoked in each case described is remarkably faint and could hardly qualify as genuine, so that they could also be viewed as having a secondary character.

Secondary sanctions may adopt several formats, ranging from hefty monetary fines on foreign companies [12] to trade embargoes, freezing of as-

---

[6] Sossai M., *Legality of Extraterritorial Sanctions*, in Masahiko Asada (ed.), *Economic sanctions in international law and practice*, Routledge, 2020, 63.

[7] Beaucillon C., *An Introduction to Unilateral and Extraterritorial Sanctions: Definitions, State of Practice and Contemporary Challenges,* in Ead., *Research Handbook on Unilateral and Extraterritorial Sanctions*, Edward Elgar Publishing. 2021, 6.

[8] Lowenfeld A.F., "Congress and Cuba: The Helms-Burton Act", *American Journal of International Law* (1996), 90, 419, 429; Mills A., "Rethinking Jurisdiction in International Law", *British Yearbook of International Law* (2014), 84, 187, 196.

[9] Ruys T., Ryngaert C., *op. cit.*, 22.

[10] *Ivi*, 7.

[11] Bechky P., "Sanctions and the Blurred Boundaries of International Economic Law", *Mo. L. Rev.* (2018), 83, 1, 11.

[12] An illustrative example is the 8.9 billion USD fine imposed against BNP Paribas by the United States in 2014. See "BNP Paribas Agrees to Plead Guilty and to Pay $8.9

sets, withdrawal of financial aid, criminal prosecution and the measures that inform the present study, access restrictions. Regardless of their typology, secondary sanctions operate as a supplement to primary sanctions.[13] To this end, secondary sanctions exert pressure upon foreign companies to choose between continue trading with the primary sanctions target and face one of the consequences listed above,[14] or cease their transactions with the latter, at the same time compelling the third states where these companies operate to change their foreign and economic policies,[15] thus aligning with the interests of the sanctioning state.

5.3. Identifying secondary sanctions consisting of access restrictions and their *modus operandi*

Access restrictions, in the context of unilateral sanctions, may refer to any measure adopted to deny the admission of third state's companies or individuals into the territory of the sanctioning state, but most importantly into its domestic market and financial institutions. It should be mentioned that the legality of market access restrictions has been discussed in other contexts, most notably within the framework of environmental protection through process and production methods restrictions (PPMs), whereby states set standards that foreign companies must comply with to maintain their trading privileges or access to its market.[16]

The classic modus operandi of secondary sanctions involving access restrictions is straightforward. The sanctioning state enacts a rule, decree, or regulation, which establishes that companies or individuals located abroad will be prohibited from trading or accessing the market and financial insti-

---

Billion for Illegally Processing Financial Transactions for Countries Subject to U.S. Economic Sanctions", 29 August 2014, available at https://www.justice.gov/opa/pr/bnp-paribas-agrees-plead-guilty-and-pay-89-billion-illegally-processing-financial accessed on 20 April 2023.

[13] Sossai, M., *op. cit.*, 63.

[14] Beaucillon C., *An Introduction to Unilateral and Extraterritorial Sanctions*, cit., 6.

[15] Ruys T., Ryngaert C., *op. cit.*, 4.

[16] See Cooreman B., *Global Environmental Protection through Trade: A Systematic Approach to Extraterritoriality*, Edward Elgar Publishing Limited, 2017; Charnovitz S., "Rethinking WTO Trade Sanctions", *American Journal of International Law* (2001), 95, 792; Howse R., Regan D., "The Product/Process Distinction - an Illusory Basis for Disciplining "unilateralism" in Trade Policy", *European Journal of International Law* (2000), 11, 249; Vranes E., *Trade and the Environment: Fundamental Issues in International Law, WTO Law, and Legal Theory*, Oxford University Press, 2009.

tutions of the sanctioning state if they continue to invest in a country subject to a primary sanction regime or trade with their economic counterparts in such a state.

While secondary boycotts are the most typical example of these types of measures, access restrictions are diverse in kind.[17] For example, the consolidated sanctions regime enacted by the US against Iran contains arguably the most far-ranging menu-based list of access restrictions to be applied against third states' companies or individuals.[18] These include the denial of Export-Import Bank loans, credits, or credit guarantees for US exports to the sanctioned entity; denial of US bank loans exceeding $10 million in one year to the sanctioned entity; prohibition of the sanctioned entity from acquiring, holding, using, or trading any US-based property which the sanctioned entity has a financial interest in; prohibition on transactions in foreign exchange by the entity; prohibition on any credit or payments between the entity and any US financial institution; exclusion from the US of corporate officers or controlling shareholders of a sanctioned firm, among others. Access restrictions may also encompass measures denying visas or revoking existing ones, as well as the denial of admission into the territory of the sanctioning state.

Access restrictions are particularly appealing as a secondary sanction. Firstly, they can be implemented almost immediately by the sanctioning state, unlike fines that usually require lengthy judicial or administrative proceedings.[19] Secondly, the effectiveness of access restrictions relies entirely on the economic leverage of the state whose market is being restricted, whereas the enforcement of fines requires the sanctioned entity to have assets in the territory of the sanctioning state. Thus, as the recent practice of the US illustrates, access restrictions can have a greater detrimental impact on foreign companies than economic fines.[20]

Secondary sanctions, as opposed to primary unilateral sanctions employed by a wider group of states, have been historically developed almost exclusively by the US. However, in recent times there have been signs that the European Union (EU) and China are considering the use of these far-

---

[17] See further, Ryngaert C., "Extraterritorial Export Controls (Secondary Boycotts)", *Chinese Journal of International Law* (2008), 7, 625.

[18] See further https://home.treasury.gov/policy-issues/financial-sanctions/sanctions-programs-and-country-information/iran-sanctions.

[19] Ruys T., Ryngaert C., *op. cit.*, 12.

[20] Viterbo A., *Extraterritorial Sanctions and International Economic Law*, in European Central Bank (ed.), *Building bridges: central banking law in an interconnected world: ECB Legal Conference 2019*, European Central Bank, 2019, 162.

ranging measures.[21] Be that as it may, it is important to note that this remains a relatively new development, and it is unclear how extensively these countries will employ secondary sanctions. The US has been able to successfully incorporate secondary sanctions, and especially access restrictions, into its economic statecraft repertoire. This is largely due to a combination of factors, including the size and strength of its market, the power of its currency, and its central position in the global financial architecture. To date, the US market enjoys a hegemonic position in global trade, and the US dollar remains the standard currency employed in the majority of significant international transactions between large and medium-sized companies.[22]

5.4. Prolegomena: the contested legality of secondary access restrictions under the rules governing the exercise of jurisdiction by states

Now that access restrictions have been identified and situated within the framework of secondary sanctions, the central point of this contribution can be addressed, i.e. their conformity with the customary rules on jurisdiction. Secondary access restrictions pose challenges that cut across the very foundations of the way in which international law delimits the allocation of regulatory competences of states.

As follows, before addressing the conformity of access restrictions with international law, it is important to examine the concept of jurisdiction in more detail. The legal framework governing the exercise of jurisdiction by states is considered as one of the cornerstones of the international legal or-

[21] As will be discussed below, the EU sanctions imposed against Russia have expanded the traditionally conservative operational scope of the EU in the context of sanctions. At the same time, there are a few past and recent examples of other nations imposing these kinds of measures, such as the Arab boycott on Israel, or the recent sanctions imposed against Qatar in 2017. Similarly, the silent boycott imposed by China against Lithuania in September 2021, as a result of the latter allowing Taiwan to open a representation office in Vilnius under that name, instead of "Chinese Taipei", had secondary features.

[22] Meagher D., "Caught in the Economic Crosshairs: Secondary Sanctions and the American Sanctions Regime", *Fordham Law Review* (2020), 89, 999, 1006; Emmenegger S., "Extraterritorial Economic Sanctions and Their Foundation in International Law", *Arizona Journal of International and Comparative Law* (2016), 33, 631, 655; Stoll T., et al., "Extraterritorial Sanctions on Trade and Investments and European Responses", Study requested by the Committee on International Trade (INTA) of the European Parliament and published as doc. PE 653.618 by the Policy Department for External Relations 76.

der and it corresponds to the power that a state is entitled to, under international law, to regulate the conduct, and its consequences, of natural and legal persons.[23] This power or authority is exercised over persons, their property or a given conduct, and has traditionally been divided into three, albeit generally only two, separate categories. The first is prescriptive or legislative jurisdiction, which concerns the competence of a state to enact rules, in whichever form they may assume and adopted by any state organ authorized under its domestic legislation, attaching legal consequences to a given act. Secondly, adjudicative jurisdiction has generally been understood to share features from both prescription and enforcement,[24] and refers to the authority of states to subject individuals to judicial or administrative procedures, as well as establishing such procedures aimed at applying the existing legal rules and identifying potential breaches and the consequences arising from them in each case. Enforcement jurisdiction, lastly, pertains to the power of a state to pursue and compel compliance with its laws and regulations. For the purposes of this chapter, we will focus on the limitations that apply to prescriptive and enforcement jurisdiction in the context of secondary sanctions.

5.5. The legal character of secondary access restrictions: disentangling prescriptive and enforcement jurisdiction

At the outset, the first issue to be examined concerns the classification of secondary access restrictions, particularly whether these measures fall un-

[23] Mann F.A., *The Doctrine of Jurisdiction in International Law*, vol. 111, Collected Courses of the Hague Academy of International Law, 1964; Besson S., *Why and What (State) Jurisdiction: Legal Plurality, Individual Equality and Territorial Legitimacy*, in Klabbers J., Palombella G. (eds.), *The Challenge of Inter-Legality*, 1st ed., Cambridge University Press, 2019, 100; Crawford J., *Brownlie's Principles of Public International Law*, 9th ed., Oxford University Press, 2019, 440; Oppenheim L., et al., *Oppenheim's International Law*, vol. 1, *Peace*, 9th ed., Longman, 1996, 45; Akehurst M., "Jurisdiction in International Law", *British Year Book of International Law* (1972), 46, 145; Maier H.G., "Extraterritorial Jurisdiction at a Crossroads: An Intersection Between Public and Private International Law", *American Journal of International Law* (1982), 76, 280; Olmstead C.J. (ed.), *Extra-Territorial Application of Laws and Responses Thereto*, International Law Association in association with ESC Pub, 1984. Report of the International Law Commission on the Work of its 58th Session (1 May-9 June and 3 July-11 August 2006) UN Doc A/61/10, Annex E (ILC Report on Extraterritorial Jurisdiction), 236-237.

[24] Mills A., *Private Interests and Private Law Regulation in Public International Law Jurisdiction*, in Allen S., Mills A., et al. (eds.), *The Oxford Handbook of Jurisdiction in International Law*, Oxford University Press, 2019, 331. However, some authors do not include adjudicative jurisdiction as a separate category.

der the category of prescriptive jurisdiction or correspond to measures amounting to enforcement jurisdiction. This distinction is critical, as each category is subject to different constraints under international law. Nonetheless, there appears to be a conceptual entanglement between the two categories that permeates the secondary access restrictions debate and blurs the discussion regarding their legality.

In an international system composed of equal sovereign states, territoriality is the most uncontested basis of jurisdictional authority,[25] according to which the conduct taking place within the legal and geographical boundaries of a state falls under its regulatory authority. Thus, the question over the legality of a jurisdictional assertion only arises when it goes beyond the geographical boundaries of one state and enters another sovereign's regulatory space.[26]

Within this framework, some authors claim that secondary access restrictions do not raise concerns under the legal framework on jurisdiction as their implementation creates obligations exclusively binding upon entities located in the territory of the sanctioning state.[27] At the same time, as Ruys and Ryngaert have argued, access restrictions rest on the foundation that states 'enjoy discretionary power to control their borders',[28] as well as their internal market and domestic financial institutions. Following this argument, from a jurisdictional perspective a state would not be subject to any real limitation to impose access restrictions, as these measures are always linked to the sanctioning country either by a territorial or personal nexus.[29]

However, the preceding approach overlooks an entire category of jurisdiction, that is prescriptive or legislative jurisdiction, which is triggered in the process of enacting a secondary access restriction, and whose legality needs to be examined before deciding on whether these measures contravene in-

---

[25] Mann F.A., *The Doctrine of Jurisdiction in International Law*, cit., at 20; Oppenheim L., et al., *Oppenheim's International Law*, cit., at 458.

[26] Ryngaert C., *Jurisdiction in International Law*, 2nd ed., Oxford University Press, 2015, 6.

[27] Rathbone M., Jeydel P., Lentz A., "Sanctions, Sanctions Everywhere: Forging a Path through Complex Transnational Sanctions Laws", *Georgetown Journal of International Law* (2012), 44, 1055, 1071; Bismuth R., "Pour une appréhension nuancée de l'extraterritorialité du droit américain – Quelques réflexions autour des procédures et sanctions visant Alstom et BNP Paribas", *Annuaire Français de Droit International* (2015), 61, 785, 789; Dunning T., "D'Amato in a China Shop: Problems of Extraterritoriality with the Iran and Libya Sanctions Act of 1996", *University of Pennsylvania Journal of International Law* (1998), 19, 169, 184; Ruys T., Ryngaert C., *op. cit.*, 12.

[28] Ruys T., Ryngaert C., *op. cit.*, 12.

[29] Meyer J.A., "Second Thoughts on Secondary Sanctions", cit., 908-909.

ternational law. In the context of secondary sanctions, access restrictions indeed qualify as enforcement measures, however these do not emerge out of thin air, on the contrary, they are the deliberate consequence of sanctions' legislation which attaches specific consequences to the breach of its provisions. In other words, the underlying regulation that stipulates the imposition of access restrictions as a form of punishment for, in general terms, refusing to comply with a prohibition or restriction to trade with the primary sanctions target state,[30] represents an exercise of prescriptive powers.

For instance, the US sanctions regime against Iran is composed of a complex web of legislative sources, including public statutes passed by Congress, executive orders issued by the President and Codes of Federal Regulation prepared by OFAC.[31] Some of these regulations, such as the Trading with the Enemy Act of 1917,[32] have been laying the groundwork for the adoption of unilateral sanctions long before their actual implementation. Hence, secondary sanctions, including access restrictions, cannot be deemed as measures that solely constitute an exercise of enforcement jurisdiction, as they are a direct consequence of a previously prescribed rule. Some additional examples of US sanctions regulations, where access restrictions are prescribed as an enforcement mechanism for the breach of a given normative command, include the Iran Sanctions Act of 1996,[33] the Comprehensive Iran Sanctions, Accountability, and Divestment Act of 2010,[34] or the 2017 Countering America's Adversaries Through Sanctions Act.[35]

As follows, the traditional approach to access restrictions or any other secondary sanctions involves a two-step process of prescription and subsequent enforcement.[36] However, while secondary sanctions laws or regulations may attach legal consequences to foreign conduct, their enforcement

[30] Vazquez C.M., "Trade Sanctions and Human Rights - Past, Present, and Future", *Journal of International Economic Law* (2003), 6, 797, 813.

[31] See further, "Iran Sanctions | Office of Foreign Assets Control", 19 April 2023, available at https://ofac.treasury.gov/sanctions-programs-and-country-information/iran-sanctions, accessed on 21 April 2023.

[32] Trading With the Enemy Act of 1917, 50 App. U.S.C.A. §10; Fed. Reg. 2503-04 (1942).

[33] Iran Sanctions Act of 1996 (as amended by Iran Sanctions Extension Act, Pub L No. 114- 277 (2016).

[34] Comprehensive Iran Sanctions, Accountability, and Divestment Act, Pub L No. 111-195 (2010).

[35] Countering America's Adversaries Through Sanctions Act, Pub L No. 115-44 (2017).

[36] Stern B., "Can the United States Set Rules for the World? – A French View", *Journal of World Trade* (1997), 31, 5, 13-14.

must be confined to the territorial limits of the sanctioning state. This is consistent with the uncontested jurisdictional rule under international law according to which enforcement is strictly territorial, except when explicit consent is granted by another state.

Thus, the legality of a given secondary access restriction should not be presumed *prima facie* by merely assessing the location of its implementation or the nationality of those tasked with its enforcement.[37] If a sanction qualifies as extraterritorial due to its prescriptive reach, a contentious issue in the context of secondary access restrictions that will be discussed in depth in the following section, the territorial character of its enforcement does not 'conceal or erase the fact that the prescription is extraterritorial'.[38] In the same tone, O'Keefe argues that 'regardless of how it is enforced, an assertion of prescriptive jurisdiction over conduct taking place outside the territory of the prescribing state is an assertion of extraterritorial jurisdiction, for which an alternative legal justification must be found.'[39] Accordingly, the relevant point to determine the extraterritoriality of a secondary access restriction is 'the location outside the territory of the act (sale, export, granting of financing, etc.) that falls under the sanctions.[40] Any assessment of the legality of an access restriction must therefore begin by a determination of the reach of the underlying regulation that substantiates the implementation of access restrictions as an enforcement mechanism.

The Third Restatement of Foreign Relations Law of the US published in 1987 shared this position, at a time when secondary sanctions were shaping up to become a major transatlantic rift between the EU and the US, after the latter adopted the soviet pipeline embargo in 1982. The Restatement affirmed that the denial of export privileges solely grounded on the basis that a third state maintains its trade relationships with the primary sanctions target, would constitute a breach of jurisdictional rules, due to the US

---

[37] Stoll T., et al., *Extraterritorial Sanctions on Trade and Investments and European responses*, Study requested by the Committee on International Trade (INTA) of the European Parliament, 2020, 52.

[38] Stern B., "Can the United States Set Rules for the World? – A French View", cit., 14; von Lutterotti L., *The US Extraterritorial Sanctions of 1996 and the EU Reaction*, in Griller S., Weidel B. (eds.), *External Economic Relations and Foreign Policy in the European Union*, vol. 20, Springer, 2002, 245-246.

[39] O'Keefe R., "Universal Jurisdiction: Clarifying the Basic Concept", *Journal of International Criminal Justice* (2004), 2, 735, 742.

[40] Kerbrat Y., *Unilateral/Extraterritorial Sanctions as a Challenge to the Theory of Jurisdiction*, in Beaucillon C., *Research Handbook on Unilateral and Extraterritorial Sanctions*, Edward Elgar Publishing, 2021,167; Meyer J.A., "Second Thoughts on Secondary Sanctions", cit., 954.

lacking jurisdictional power to prescribe rules that aimed to regulate the economic interactions occurring between third states.[41]

Upon closer scrutiny, the position arguing that access restrictions as an entirely territorial endeavour based on the location of their enforcement or nationality of its enforcers, appears to be rooted in an understatement of the relevance of the rules governing prescriptive jurisdiction, arguably a consequence of the 1927 Lotus dictum. This landmark judgment has often, yet mistakenly, been interpreted to support the claim that hardly any limits exist for the extraterritorial exercise of prescriptive jurisdiction by states.[42] Nevertheless, if secondary sanctions consisting of access restrictions were to be automatically labelled as territorial due to their being enforced within the borders of the sanctioning state, the distinction between prescriptive and enforcement jurisdiction would dilute to the point any state could disguise their exorbitant assertions of jurisdiction by recharacterizing them as mere access restriction to its territory.[43]

From a practical perspective, the distinction between prescriptive and enforcement jurisdiction is pivotal in the context of secondary sanctions, given that these measures do not even require, in most cases, to reach the phase of enforcement in order to be highly effective.[44] The practice of the US in this field suggests that the mere prescription of secondary sanctions by a dominant economy is often sufficient to compel foreign entities, and the third states where these operate, to modify their conduct, as the risk of being fined or locked out of their domestic market often outweighs the benefits from continuing to trade with a state being targeted by primary sanctions.[45] This is clearly portrayed by the secondary sanctions imposed

[41] Restatement of the Law (Third): The Foreign Relations Law of the United States, § 431.

[42] *Lotus', Judgment No. 9, 1927, PCIJ, Ser A, No. 10*, 18-19: "Far from laying down a general prohibition to the effect that States may not extend the application of their laws and the jurisdiction of their courts to persons, property and acts outside their territory, it leaves them in this respect a wide measure of discretion which is only limited in certain cases by prohibitive rules".

[43] Vazquez C.M., "Trade Sanctions and Human Rights - Past, Present, and Future", cit., 814 ("If the argument were accepted, however, no law would violate limits on prescriptive jurisdiction; every law could simply be recharacterize as a regulation of access to the regulating state's territory."); Staker C., *Jurisdiction*, in Evans M.D., *International Law*, Oxford University Press, 2018, 308.

[44] von Lutterotti L., *The US Extraterritorial Sanctions of 1996 and the EU Reaction*, cit., 247; Schmidt J., "The Legality of Unilateral Extra-Territorial Sanctions under International Law", *Journal of Conflict and Security Law* (2022), 27, 53, 65.

[45] Rathbone M., Jeydel P., Lentz A., "Sanctions, Sanctions Everywhere: Forging a Path through Complex Transnational Sanctions Laws", cit., at 1119; Ruys T., Ryngaert C., *op. cit.*, at 16.

by the US against Iran, where the cost-benefit analysis led EU companies to abandon ongoing and potential trade interactions with Iran, before risking losing access to the US market.[46]

With regard to the rules applicable to prescriptive jurisdiction, there is widespread consensus that states may only exercise such regulatory authority if a permissive principle is present.[47] These principles, also referred to as jurisdictional bases, are all justified by the existence of a genuine or sufficiently close connection between the state asserting jurisdiction and the conduct or persons subject to regulation.[48] Therefore, since enforcement is a logical consequence of prescription, to lawfully enforce a given rule this must have been enacted through a valid exercise of prescriptive jurisdiction in the first place.[49] No enforcement, as territorial as it may be, will be lawful if the exercise of prescriptive jurisdiction that preceded it was not justified under international law.[50]

As explained earlier, secondary sanctions are measures enacted where a state holds no territorial or personal nexus with the conduct regulated, although this is disputed in the case of secondary access restrictions, as will be explored below. Nonetheless, the fact that the prescription of secondary access restrictions may not be justified on a territorial or nationality nexus, does not necessarily mean that these measures contravene international law, as they could be justified on different jurisdictional grounds.[51] The recog-

---

[46] *See* Geranmayeh Rapnouil E., Lafont M., "Meeting the Challenge of Secondary Sanctions – European Council on Foreign Relations", *ECFR*, 25 June 2019, available at https://ecfr.eu/publication/meeting_the_challenge_of_secondary_sanctions/, accessed on 21 April 2023.

[47] Ryngaert, C., *Jurisdiction in International Law*, cit., 35.

[48] Mann F.A., *The Doctrine of International Jurisdiction Revisited after Twenty Years*, vol. 186, Collected Courses of the Hague Academy of International Law, 1984, 9, 29; Ryngaert, C., *Jurisdiction in International Law*, cit., 43; Reinisch A., "Widening the US Embargo Against Cuba Extraterritorially: A Few Public International Law Comments on the 'Cuban Liberty and Democratic Solidarity (LIBERTAD) Act of 1996'", *European Journal of International Law* (1996), 7, 545, 552; Stern B., *How to Regulate Globalization?*, in Byers M. (ed.), *The Role of Law in International Politics*, Oxford University Press, 2001, 256; Bianchi A., *Reply to Professor Maier*, in Meessen K.M. (ed.), *Extraterritorial jurisdiction in theory and practice*, Kluwer Law International, 1996, 90.

[49] Bowett D.W., "Jurisdiction: Changing Patterns of Authority over Activities and Resources", *British Yearbook of International Law* (1983), 53, 1, 1; Brownlie I., *Principles of Public International Law*, 4th ed., Clarendon Press-Oxford University Press, 1990, 309; ILC Report on Extraterritorial Jurisdiction, cit., at 236.

[50] Mann F.A., *The Doctrine of Jurisdiction in International Law*, cit., 47.

[51] Meyer J.A., "Second Thoughts on Secondary Sanctions", cit., 908.

nized bases of jurisdiction, considered as an exception to the territoriality primacy,[52] are the nationality, protective, and universality principles.

Under universal jurisdiction states are entitled to exercise jurisdiction with regard to the gravest international crimes recognized by international law, in cases when these have been committed abroad and no other connection exists between the criminal offence and the state asserting jurisdiction.[53] Hence, it can be easily concluded that secondary access restrictions normally fall outside the scope of universal jurisdiction, unless these have been adopted as a response to such heinous crimes.

The protective principle, on the other hand, grants states jurisdiction over matters taking place abroad that threaten or endanger the vital interests or security of a state.[54] This jurisdictional basis, however, is not unfettered, as it relates to conducts which specifically imperil the sovereignty or political independence of a country. Bowett, for instance, suggested the following examples: 'espionage, sedition, counterfeiting of currency, perjury in relation to official documents such as visas, or attacks against embassies and consulates abroad'.[55] The protective principle is arguably the sole feasible jurisdictional nexus that states could invoke to lawfully prescribe secondary sanctions,[56] notably, when these measures are adopted with the intention to curtail policies such as the proliferation of nuclear weapons and in an attempt to prohibit transactions facilitating this endeavour. Nevertheless, it should be noted that in most cases secondary sanctions are prescribed without the existence of a valid jurisdictional nexus.

Whereas in the case of secondary sanctions that impose fines or other types of criminal or civil penalties, it can be held with certainty that the sanctioning state attaches legal consequences to foreign conduct, thus entailing an exercise of extraterritorial jurisdiction,[57] access restrictions present an additional challenge, since the determination of their scope is not as straightforward as it appears at first sight.

---

[52] Ryngaert, C., *Jurisdiction in International Law*, cit., 34.

[53] O'Keefe R., "Universal Jurisdiction: Clarifying the Basic Concept", cit., 745; Stern, B., *How to Regulate Globalization?*, cit., 258.

[54] Emmenegger S., "Extraterritorial Economic Sanctions and Their Foundation in International Law", cit., 655.

[55] Bowett D.W., "Jurisdiction: Changing Patterns of Authority over Activities and Resources", cit., 11.

[56] Ryngaert, C., *Jurisdiction in International Law*, cit., 117.

[57] Kerbrat Y., *Unilateral/Extraterritorial Sanctions*, cit., 182.

5.6. The elusive jurisdictional scope of secondary access restrictions

In the first section of this chapter, I attempted to disentangle prescription and enforcement to clarify their separate role in the process of implementing a secondary access restriction. The second part explores perhaps the most challenging aspect of the debate surrounding the jurisdictional validity of these measures. As explained earlier, the legality of the exercise of prescriptive jurisdiction will depend on the existence of a nexus between the sanctioning state and the conduct or actors under regulation. Accordingly, the question that arises is whether there is a way to unequivocally identify the scope and addressee of a given sanction law.[58] In simple terms, since prescriptive jurisdiction equates to making law applicable to persons, property, or conduct,[59] the pressing inquiry becomes whose and what conduct is regulated when states decide to adopt secondary access restrictions.

At first glance, the question may not appear exceedingly complex. After all secondary sanctions have explicit extraterritorial objectives, as they generally aim to modify the conduct of companies or individuals located beyond the territorial limits of the sanctioning state with regards to their economic or financial interactions with the primary sanctions target.[60] However, whether the efforts to alter foreign behaviour necessarily translate into exercising extraterritorial jurisdiction is contested. Specifically, secondary access restrictions appear to sit right in the middle between domestic regulation and extraterritorial jurisdiction. This liminal space of regulatory authority has been referred to as territorial extension[61] or indirect extraterritoriality,[62] and its relevance in the context of the present chapter will be explored in depth below.

As follows, the determination of the scope or content of a rule, and whose conduct is subjected to its regulation, is not as straightforward as it may prima facie appear. As a first criterion, the wording of a regulation needs to be scrutinized. In the context of secondary sanctions, it is not un-

---

[58] Meyer J.A., "Second Thoughts on Secondary Sanctions", cit., 954; Bismuth R., "Pour une appréhension nuancée", cit., 789.

[59] Restatement of the Law (Fourth): The Foreign Relations Law of the United States (2018), § 402 Prescription.

[60] Kerbrat Y., *Unilateral/Extraterritorial Sanctions*, cit., 167.

[61] Scott J., "Extraterritoriality and Territorial Extension in EU Law", *American Journal of Comparative Law* (2014), 62, 87, 90.

[62] Bianchi A., "Extraterritoriality and Export Controls: Some Remarks on the Alleged Antimony between European and U.S. Approaches", *German Yearbook of International Law* (1992), 35, 366, 373.

common to find statutes, decrees, or executive orders, that expressly define the normative command arising from the regulation, and its respective addressee(s). From a cursory review of some of the US most stringent sanctions regimes, it is not difficult to find provisions that directly impose obligations upon foreign entities. For instance, Section 6 of the Iran Sanctions Act of 1996 allows for the implementation of different types of market or territory access restrictions for breaching the provisions included in Section 5, some of which apply to foreign entities, such as those restricting investments relating to the energy sector of Iran.[63] Another example is Section 232 of the Countering America's Adversaries Through Sanctions Act of 2017, which authorizes the implementation of five or more of the sanctions described in Section 235 of the same act, including several types of access restrictions, against a person that 'makes an investment described in subsection (b) or sells, leases, or provides to the Russian Federation, for the construction of Russian energy export pipelines, goods, services, technology, information, or support described in subsection (c)'.[64]

As illustrated by the examples, these regulations roughly target various forms of economic or financial interactions between third-state entities and the primary sanctions target. The sanctioning state seeks to limit or prohibit these exchanges by threatening to implement market or territory access restrictions in case of non-compliance. As a result, the latter must demonstrate the existence of a jurisdictional basis allowing it to govern the extraterritorial acts described.

The jurisdictional scope of a provision is, however, often not explicitly stated, or easy to discern from the text of the regulation itself. While the extraterritorial character of the examples presented above is relatively clear, this is not always the case. Quite on the contrary, legislation enacting secondary sanctions is often highly sophisticated and intentionally ambiguous, a characteristic which has led to over-compliance by foreign economic operators.[65] This ambiguity also encompasses the *ratione personae* scope of jurisdiction, as it not unusual for countries to enact sanctions with an open-ended target, avoiding circumscribing the regulation to national or foreign conduct.

This is largely due to the fact that extraterritorial jurisdiction is one of the thorniest topics of international law, and is generally viewed in a negative light by states.[66] As a result, countries may rather pursue the same ob-

---

[63] Iran Sanctions Act of 1996, cit.

[64] Countering America's Adversaries Through Sanctions Act, cit.

[65] See Viterbo A., *Extraterritorial Sanctions and International Economic Law*, cit., 162.

[66] Ryngaert, C., *Jurisdiction in International Law*, cit., 8.

jective behind explicitly extraterritorial secondary access restrictions, that of altering the behaviour of third states' companies or individuals with the intention to economically isolate and maximize the pressure applied against the primary sanctions target, by prescribing sanctions in terms that impose obligations strictly upon domestic entities.

Joanne Scott coined this regulatory practice as territorial extension, consisting of a regulation whose 'application depends upon the existence of a relevant territorial connection, but where the relevant regulatory determination will be shaped as a matter of law, by conduct or circumstances abroad'.[67] Similarly, Bianchi suggested a classification between direct extraterritoriality, corresponding to regulations that impose obligations directly against foreign companies or individuals, along the lines of US sanctions legislation explored above, and indirect extraterritoriality, when a provision only imposes direct obligations upon domestic entities,[68] even though the underlying motive of shaping conduct abroad remains unfettered.

For illustrative purposes, in the case of secondary access restrictions, a provision may be drafted in the following terms: "No individual or company subject to the jurisdiction of state A will engage in economic dealings with any actor involved in transactions with entities operating in state C". An alternative provision could read as follows: "Banks operating in the jurisdiction of state A are forbidden to provide any financial service to companies or individuals that remain engaged in economic interactions with the primary sanctions target, including the re-export of goods originating in the latter". These sample provisions are drafted in a way that implies the existence of exclusively domestic obligations arising from them. The relevant territorial nexus is present in both provisions, as domestic entities are the ones directly ordered to block non-complying third-state entities from the territory or market of the sanctioning state. However, at the same time, compliance with the regulation entirely depends on extraterritorial conduct, specifically such domestic entities are required to monitor whether foreign entities comply with the implicit normative command imposed against them by the provision.

Therefore, the potential negative consequences against foreign subjects arising in case of non-compliance are still implicitly present, albeit surreptitiously disguised in the regulation, even if from a strictly textual standpoint, the obligations imposed solely target domestic entities.[69]

---

[67] Scott J., "Extraterritoriality and Territorial Extension in EU Law", cit., 90.

[68] Bianchi A., *op. cit.*, 373.

[69] Schmidt J., "The Legality of Unilateral Extra-Territorial Sanctions", cit., 67.

As things stand, territorial extension switches the immediate target of a regulation from a foreign to a domestic one. However, is this modification enough to completely alter the scope of a jurisdictional assertion from extraterritorial to territorial, even though the underlying objective of the regulation remains the same? Put differently, do secondary access restrictions enacted via territorial extension regulate the conduct of foreign entities, or do they merely influence and generate ancillary extraterritorial effects? The question is topical since, as Vranes correctly points out, 'mere extraterritorial *effects* of domestic regulations do not transform such prescriptions into extraterritorial regulations.'[70] Accordingly, the question begs, where is the threshold? When do extraterritorial effects reach the level of regulation?

In light of this question, some authors have shown an excessive reliance on textual or exceedingly formal approaches to establish the scope of a jurisdictional assertion, claiming that an access restriction 'does not pose a significant risk of being extraterritorial, if it is channelled through the regulation of the conduct of domestically incorporated companies',[71] provided these measures only create obligations binding upon subjects connected to the sanctioning state by a territorial nexus.[72] Hence, following a strictly textual interpretation, any underlying extraterritorial intention or effect suffered by third-state entities is merely ancillary or incidental, falling short of qualifying as an exercise of extraterritorial jurisdiction.[73]

In the course of his influential studies on jurisdiction, Mann briefly addressed the subject from a broad perspective, affirming that there is no international rule precluding states from exercising indirect extraterritorial jurisdiction.[74] In the same light and in the context of secondary sanctions, Meyer has suggested that 'the fact that the United States may lack a proper prescriptive jurisdictional basis to regulate business deals between China

---

[70] Vranes E., *Trade and the Environment*, cit., 168.

[71] Bogdanova I., *Unilateral Sanctions in International Law and the Enforcement of Human Rights*, Brill-Nijhoff, 2022, 98; on the same note, Meyer J.A., "Dual Illegality and Geoambiguous Law: A New Rule for Extraterritorial Application of U.S. Law" *Minnesota Law Review* (2010), 95, 110, 124. ("If, for example, a U.S. law prohibits consumers in the United States from purchasing African elephant tusks, this is a territorial regulation of consumer conduct within the United States, despite its apparent purpose or effect in part to discourage killing of endangered elephants in Africa.").

[72] Ruys T., Ryngaert C., *op. cit.*, 12; Schmidt J., "The Legality of Unilateral Extra-Territorial Sanctions", cit., 67; Bismuth R., "Pour une appréhension nuancée", cit., 795.

[73] Blattner C.E., *Protecting Animals within and across Borders: Extraterritorial Jurisdiction and the Challenges of Globalization*, Oxford University Press, 2019, 90.

[74] Mann F.A., *The Doctrine of International Jurisdiction Revisited after Twenty Years*, vol. 186, Collected Courses of the Hague Academy of International Law, 1984, 78.

and Sudan does not dispel US authority to regulate the conduct of US companies in US territory to prohibit them from doing business with Sudan's Chinese business partner.'[75] At a state level, this regulatory technique appears to have been endorsed by the former US Under Secretary for Terrorism and Financial Intelligence who, in an effort to deny the extraterritorial reach of certain sections of the CISADA Act of 2010, affirmed that the regulation merely 'provides authority to the Secretary of the Treasury to regulate US financial institutions, limiting our banks' ability to transact with certain foreign banks'.[76]

Territorial extension also appears to be the backbone of wider-reaching EU sanctions.[77] To date, the EU has adopted 10 sanctions packages against Russia, as a response to the latter's invasion against Ukraine.[78] While traditionally opposed to extraterritorial sanctions,[79] Europe has tightened its grip on Russia with each new package, implementing increasingly far-reaching restrictions. A significant number of these measures employ territorial extension as a regulatory technique. For instance, import restrictions on iron and steel products apply not only to direct imports from Russia but also to products incorporating materials of Russian origin processed in a third country.[80] Although these restrictions solely impose obligations on subjects under the jurisdiction of the EU, their intention is, at least partially, to influence the behaviour of third-state companies or individuals trading with Russia.

Indeed, the wording behind a regulation has a strong bearing on whether a measure is to be regarded as territorial or extraterritorial. However, a provision's scope should not be determined solely by a verbatim reading of its text. Examining the underlying intention can serve as a second criterion to decipher its true scope. A given statute's underlying claim to jurisdiction

---

[75] Meyer J.A., "Second Thoughts on Secondary Sanctions", cit., 955.

[76] "Remarks of Under Secretary for Terrorism and Financial Intelligence David Cohen before the New York University School of Law on 'The Law and Policy of Iran Sanctions'", U.S. Department of the Treasury, 12 September 2012, available at https://home.treasury.gov/news/press-releases/tg1706 accessed 20 April 2023.

[77] Scott J., "Extraterritoriality and Territorial Extension in EU Law", cit., 119-122.

[78] See "EU Sanctions against Russia Explained", 14 April 2023, available at https://www.consilium.europa.eu/en/policies/sanctions/restrictive-measures-against-russia-over-ukraine/sanctions-against-russia-explained/ accessed 21 April 2023.

[79] Council of the European Union, Guidelines on implementation and evaluation of restrictive measures (sanctions) in the framework of the EU Common Foreign and Security Policy, DOC. 5664/18, 4 May 2018, at 19.

[80] Council Regulation (EU) 2022/1904 of 6 October 2022 amending Regulation (EU) No. 833/2014 concerning restrictive measures in view of Russia's actions destabilising the situation in Ukraine 2022 (OJ L).

may differ from what appears on the face of the statute, hence a statute that appears to be limited to "intraterritorial" conduct may actually regulate extraterritorial behaviour. [81]

Despite the relevance of regulatory intention as a criterion to distinguish between extraterritorial and territorial jurisdiction, there are fair concerns about its reliability, [82] given the difficulties derived from the determination of a subjective element (intention) arising from an abstract entity (states). In the same vein, Blattner has suggested a *sine qua non* test to uncover the *raison d'être* or primary purpose behind a regulation. In essence, the author claims that '[if] the purpose of a norm is to alter conduct abroad, then failure to attain this purpose renders the norm redundant'. [83] Conversely, if the regulation still has a regulatory purpose regardless of whether extraterritorial conduct is modified or not, it is to be regarded as primarily territorial.

As mentioned earlier, secondary sanctions legislation imposing different types of market or territory access restrictions share the ultimate purpose of modifying foreign conduct. [84] If these access restrictions fail to alter their behaviour, the regulation loses all purpose. Given the supplementary nature of secondary sanctions, it must be assumed that primary sanctions with the purpose of restricting the conduct of domestic entities towards the target state already exist independently.

Accordingly, just because a given measure is framed in terms that directly impose obligations exclusively upon nationals or subjects operating within the territorial jurisdiction of the sanctioning state, this does not remove the fact that the regulation could be governing the behaviour of foreign entities. As Bartels notes, 'a measure *defined* by something located or occurring abroad should be considered just as extraterritorial as a measure specifically mandating or forbidding conduct abroad'. [85]

However, this affirmation is not uncontested in legal doctrine. The jurisdictional compatibility of market access restrictions was debated at large

---

[81] Lowe A.V., "The Problems of Extraterritorial Jurisdiction: Economic Sovereignty and the Search for a Solution", *International and Comparative Law Quarterly* (1985), 34, 724, 736.

[82] Vranes E., *Trade and the Environment*, cit., 163.

[83] Blattner C.E., *Protecting Animals within and across Borders*, cit., 90.

[84] Vazquez C.M., "Trade Sanctions and Human Rights - Past, Present, and Future", cit., 813. In the context of import bans derived from PPMs adopted by the United States, Vazquez affirmed that "Given that the whole point of the import ban is to induce a change in the production process, it makes considerable sense to view the US law as an attempt to regulate conduct taking place in another country".

[85] Bartels L., "Article XX of GATT and the Problem of Extraterritorial Jurisdiction The Case of Trade Measures for the Protection of Human Rights", *Journal of World Trade* (2002), 36, 353, 381.

long before in a different context than sanctions. Trade restrictions based on PPMs imposed to address environmental concerns were the object of much scholarly attention and led to three World Trade Organization (WTO) Panel Reports addressing the subject (two of them unadopted), and one Appellate Body Report.[86] While the WTO jurisprudence has favoured the view that market access restrictions can be extraterritorial, there are several dissenting voices in this debate, with a number of authors claiming that measures that limit access to a state's market do not constitute an exercise of extraterritorial jurisdiction in the proper sense of the term,[87] regardless of their underlying intention to shape conduct abroad.

Aside from the text and intention of the drafters, authors generally agree that a line must be drawn between provisions that mandate or compel a certain behaviour, and those that merely influence foreign conduct, as only the former would constitute extraterritorial jurisdiction.[88] The capacity to command or compel foreign entities is closely linked to the coercive strength of the state behind the regulation, meaning the degree of pressure that a state can exert through the prescription of a rule. Put differently, the coercive force behind a regulation relates to the capacity of states of swaying foreign entities towards a certain course of action, which certainly depends on a country's factual power within the international community. Thus, a third and final criterion that could help elucidating the reach of a jurisdictional assertion is the coercive force or strength of a given regulation. In other words, jurisdiction is rooted in the relative power of a state and its capacity co coerce. As Ryngaert puts it, '[p]owerful States will be able to impose their legislation on weaker

---

[86] WTO, *United States - Restrictions on Imports* of *Tuna,* unadopted, 3 September 1991, DS21/R; WTO, *United States-Restrictions on Imports of Tuna,* unadopted, 16 June 1994, DS29/R; WTO, *United States-Import Prohibition of Certain Shrimp and Shrimp Products,* WT /DS58/R, 15 May 1998; WTO, *United States-Import Prohibition of Certain Shrimp and Shrimp Products,* 12 October 1997 WT /DS58/ AB/R.

[87] Zleptnig S., *Non-Economic Objectives in WTO Law*, Martinus Nijhoff Publishers, 2010, 308; Cleveland S.H., "Human Rights Sanctions and International Trade: A Theory of Compatibility", *Journal of International Economic Law* (2002), 5, 133, 160; Nollkaemper A., *Rethinking States' Rights to Promote Extra-Territorial Values,* in Weiss F., Denters E., de Waart P.J.I.M. (eds.), *International Economic Law with a Human Face,* Kluwer Law International, 1998, 189; Cooreman B., *Global Environmental Protection,* cit., 54; Howse R., Regan D., "The Product/Process Distinction", cit., 274. ("Nothing in customary international law bars a state from conditioning access to its own markets in this manner").

[88] Meng W., *Extraterritoriale Jurisdiktion im öffentlichen Wirtschaftsrecht =: Extraterritorial jurisdiction in public economic law,* Springer, 1994, 74; Anderson B., "Unilateral Trade Measures and Environmental Protection Policy", *Temple Law Review* (1993) 66, 751, 755.

States, while weaker States will almost never be able to impose their legislation on more powerful States.'[89]

As Mann identified over 50 years ago, there are instances where the exercise of prescriptive jurisdiction 'plainly implies the likelihood of enforcement'.[90] Moreover, certain states have such a significant geopolitical or economic pull that third state's entities targeted by their regulations 'cannot reasonably afford to disregard the order without suffering considerable hardship.'[91]

Along these lines, Meng proposed an approach that combines both intent and coercion, suggesting that behind every extraterritorial exercise of jurisdiction there is a clear intention to produce coercive effects abroad, in the sense of persuading or dissuading foreign subjects to adopt a certain conduct or to abstain from it.[92] In the same vein, the definition of extraterritorial jurisdiction provided by Bianchi incorporates the two criteria. The author suggests that extraterritorial regulations are those 'aimed at controlling the conduct of entities abroad, thus *overriding the power of the foreign territorial sovereign to regulate the same course of conduct.*'[93]

The fact that relative power or coercive force of a state has some bearing in the determination of the jurisdictional scope of a regulation is foreseeable. The capacity of states to exercise prescriptive jurisdiction through territorial extension operates under the same power dynamics of secondary sanctions. Specifically, to be effective they require to be adopted by hegemonic states at the helm of dominant economies. The asymmetric economic interdependence[94] characteristic of the current global trade provides fertile ground for both practices, as most states cannot afford to lose access to certain markets such as the US, EU, or China, given that their economic stability frequently depends on that.[95]

---

[89] Ryngaert C., *Jurisdiction in International Law*, cit., 41.

[90] Mann F.A., *The Doctrine of Jurisdiction in International Law*, vol. 111, Collected Courses of the Hague Academy of International Law, 1964, 14.

[91] Meng W., *Extraterritoriale Jurisdiktion*, cit., 156.

[92] *Ivi*, 86; See further the translations and respective analyses of Meng's approach by Vranes E., *Trade and the Environment*, cit., 162; Bartels L., "Article XX of GATT", cit., 379.

[93] Bianchi A., *op. cit.*, 373.

[94] See Farrell H., Newman A.L., "Weaponized Interdependence: How Global Economic Networks Shape State Coercion", *International Security* (2019), 44, 42.

[95] von Lutterotti L., *The US Extraterritorial Sanctions of 1996 and the EU Reaction*, cit., 246.

5.7. Concluding remarks: the inescapable dual nature of secondary access restrictions

Secondary sanctions are widely regarded as a controversial practice whose legality under international law is highly suspect. Still, access restrictions have managed to pass muster to a certain extent, as their incursion into extraterritorial behaviour is debated between commentators and states.

As things stand, and considering the different criteria to determine the scope of a regulation, wording, intention, and coerciveness, there can be few doubts that the enactment of secondary access restrictions constitutes an exercise of extraterritorial prescriptive jurisdiction, going far beyond a mere denial of privileges.[96] Admittedly, access restrictions are not *prima facie* unlawful, as they could potentially be justified under the protective principle of jurisdiction. Yet, it appears that in most cases secondary access restrictions are imposed without a valid jurisdictional nexus between the sanctioning state and the entities (the primary sanctions target and the third state economic operators) or the conduct (the economic transactions between the cited parties) subject to regulation.

In practical terms, however, despite constituting a clear attempt to regulate extraterritorial behaviour,[97] secondary market or territory access restrictions have a residual 'terrinational' rooting that is difficult to dispel.[98] Certainly, the entry of goods or persons into their own territory is inexorably linked to the domestic sovereignty of a state.[99] Moreover, as explored in the present contribution, states can easily mischaracterize their assertions of jurisdiction via territorial extension, directly imposing obligations upon domestic entities to regulate foreign behaviour. Accordingly, Meyer has argued that it is irrelevant whether the sanctioning state has a valid jurisdictional nexus to prescribe conduct extraterritorially or not, since it will always be entitled to regulate the conduct taking place in its territory or that of its nationals.[100]

Nevertheless, it is submitted that the preceding view must respectfully

---

[96] See however, arguing the opposite view, Ruys T., Ryngaert C., *op. cit.*, 12; Rathbone M., Jeydel P., Lentz A., "Sanctions, Sanctions Everywhere: Forging a Path through Complex Transnational Sanctions Laws", cit., 1071.

[97] von Lutterotti L., *The US Extraterritorial Sanctions of 1996 and the EU Reaction*, cit., 248.

[98] Meyer J.A., "Second Thoughts on Secondary Sanctions", cit., 908.

[99] Stern, B., "Can the United States Set Rules for the World? – A French View", cit., 14; Lowe V., "Us Extraterritorial Jurisdiction: The Helms-Burton and D'Amato Acts", *International and Comparative Law Quarterly* (1997), 46, 378, 385.

[100] Meyer J.A., "Second Thoughts on Secondary Sanctions", cit., at 957.

be set aside. With regard to the territorial link, it has been argued that while it is certainly present in the enforcement phase of access restrictions, it is doubtful whether it can be found in the prescriptive part. As Mills notes, 'the distinction between the categories of jurisdiction remains important, even if it is not always clearly recognised in practice.'[101] Although states are certainly free to regulate access to their territory or market as they see fit, if these measures are prescribed with the intention to regulate extraterritorial behaviour, they amount to an exercise of extraterritorial jurisdiction which requires a valid justification under international law. In the case of a nationality nexus, the technique of exercising jurisdiction via territorial extension admittedly constitutes an efficient method to disguise the real intention and target of a given sanctioning state. However, as discussed earlier, the jurisdictional scope of a sanction provision is not solely determined by its wording, therefore such drafting technique should not enable states to circumvent the limitations that international law places in relation to their exercise of jurisdiction.

In spite of the above, it remains challenging to escape the fact that albeit primarily extraterritorial, secondary access restrictions appear to have a dual nature, amounting to territorial and extraterritorial regulation at the same time.[102] This is largely due to the primitive nature of the jurisdictional regime under international law, whereby any requirements concerning the strength of a link or nexus are yet to be outlined. Thus, any residual territorial or national connection that a sanctioning state may be able to invoke to justify the prescription of secondary access restrictions, as faint or farfetched as it may be, can be exploited to claim jurisdiction over conduct taking place virtually anywhere in the world. Furthermore, contrary to international law provides no clearly defined rules or principles to determine which state has a stronger or more genuine claim of authority over a certain conduct or subject. Hence, the current framework fosters concurrent assertions of jurisdiction, as international law fails to establish a hierarchy between different links that could aid untangling conflicts of regulatory authority.[103]

This is ultimately the greatest issue that secondary access restrictions present for the jurisdictional regime, as their residual territorial anchor enables sanctioning states to supplant 'regulation enacted by regulators who may in fact have a stronger nexus to the situation'.[104] As Krisch puts it, for

---

[101] Mills A., "Rethinking Jurisdiction in International Law", cit., 196.

[102] Li K., *Reconceiving Extraterritorial Jurisdiction: From Formality to Function*, Nomos Verlagsgesellschaft mbH & Co KG, 2022, 249.

[103] Besson S., *Why and What (State) Jurisdiction*, cit., 105.

[104] Ryngaert C., *Jurisdiction in International Law*, cit., 96.

third-state companies on the receiving end of secondary access restrictions, '[t]he price to be paid for access – to a territory or market – is submission to jurisdiction of a much wider scope', many times to the detriment of the sovereign authority of the territorial state where they are situated.[105] The consequences of the foregoing are dire for sovereign equality, as weak territorial links can give rise to far-reaching jurisdictional claims enabling dominant powers to extend their regulatory claws far beyond territorial constraints,[106] confirming that the degree of success of exercise of extraterritorial jurisdiction is a function of relative power.[107]

At the core of the issue examined across the present contribution lies the following question: should states be allowed to freely adopt secondary sanctions involving market or territory access restrictions, that aim to regulate the behaviour of individuals or companies located beyond their territorial or national jurisdiction? Put differently, does international law allow hegemonic states to 'set rules for the world'[108] and impose their foreign policy views upon their peers through the adoption of secondary access restrictions? From a strictly jurisdictional standpoint, the answer remains unsettled. Nevertheless, it should not be omitted that other principles of international law, such as sovereign equality, the prohibition of intervention,[109] and abuse of rights, inform every exercise of jurisdiction and their observance could potentially provide a solution to arbitrary or exorbitant assertions of jurisdiction in the shape of secondary access restrictions, or alternatively could serve to solve conflicting assertions of jurisdiction.

[105] Krisch N., "Jurisdiction Unbound: (Extra)Territorial Regulation as Global Governance", *European Journal of International Law* (2022), 33, 481, 497.

[106] *Ivi*, 497.

[107] Ryngaert C., *Jurisdiction in International Law*, cit., 41.

[108] Stern, B., "Can the United States Set Rules for the World? – A French View", cit.

[109] Jamnejad M., Wood M., "The Principle of Non-Intervention", *Leiden Journal of International Law* (2009), 22, 345, 372. ("The limits on a state's prescriptive jurisdiction can be viewed as a question of nonintervention.").

Chapter 6

UNILATERAL SANCTIONS AND EXTRATERRITORIAL OBLIGATIONS IN THE AREA OF ECONOMIC, SOCIAL AND CULTURAL RIGHTS

Tabasom Djourabi-Asadabadi

ABSTRACT: *The International Covenant on Economic, Social and Cultural Rights provides an extraterritorial scope of application. Thus, it is conceivable that a sanction sender state that is a state party to the Covenant may owe human rights obligations vis-à-vis people located within the targeted country. It needs to be explored whether a jurisdictional link between state und individual is required in order to establish so-called "extraterritorial" human rights obligations. Such a high threshold would however cause difficulties in the context of sanctions as it will be pointed out in this chapter.*

6.1. Introduction

Due to the effects of multiple economic, trade and financial sanctions, targeted states such as Iran, Syria and Venezuela were severely affected in reacting to the challenges of the COVID-19-pandemic[1]. As they had to struggle to obtain and purchase medical equipment and health care supplies the virus spread rapidly, causing high rates of infection and death. This had severe impact on the enjoyment of human rights, such as the right to health, of individuals trapped within the targeted countries. Hence several actors, including the United Nations Special Rapporteur on the negative impact of unilateral coercive measures on the enjoyment of human rights, called for sanctions to be lifted.

---

[1] The World Health Organization declared on March 11, 2020 the coronavirus (COVID-19), an infectious disease caused by the severe acute respiratory syndrome coronavirus 2 (SARS-CoV-2), a global pandemic. The pandemic had devastating health and economic consequences, particularly between 2020 and 2021, with unprecedented disruption to people's lives, the global economy, and world trade.

Considering that the impact on the enjoyment of human rights gave rise to the call to lift sanctions, one may raise the question whether *international human rights law* requires states to act accordingly. However, such an assumption would presuppose *human rights obligations* of sanction sender states in regard to individuals located in targeted countries. Traditionally, a state would only owe human rights duties vis-à-vis its own nationals who would normally be located on its territory. Obligations vis-à-vis foreign nationals are nevertheless well established in the case of state conduct on foreign territory affecting foreign nationals – although this is considered exceptional. Whether extraterritorial obligations can also be established in the context of unilateral sanctions, i.e., *intra-territorial acts* with extraterritorial effects, is unclear.

Since unilateral sanctions seem to affect the enjoyment of *economic, social and cultural* (ESC) *rights* primarily, the quest for extraterritorial human rights obligations will be embedded in the analysis of the extraterritorial scope of application of the main treaty in the area of ESC rights, namely The International Covenant on Economic, Social and Cultural Rights (ICESCR). The first section of this chapter demonstrates that the ICESCR provides a scope for extraterritorial application. Section 2 examines whether establishing extraterritorial obligations under the framework of the ICESCR depends on a jurisdictional threshold to be met. Section 3 applies the findings of Section 2 to the context of unilateral sanctions and examines whether sanction sender states owe human rights obligations towards affected individuals located within the targeted country.

6.2. Extraterritorial scope of application of the ICESCR

Several human rights treaties contain provisions defining their scope of application. In that regard Article 2(1) of The International Covenant on Civil and Political Rights (ICCPR) limits a state party's obligations to respect and to ensure Covenant rights to "individuals within its *territory* and subject to its *jurisdiction* [emphasis by the author]". The text of the ICESCR lacks a pendant to Article 2(1) ICCPR. Instead, Article 2(1) ICESCR speaks of state parties undertaking steps "individually and through international assistance and co-operation" to achieve "the full realization of the rights recognized in the present Covenant".[2] Compared

[2] The text of the Covenant also refers to the relevance of international cooperation for the implementation of the obligations under the Covenant in other provisions (Art. 11(1), 22, 23).

to the ICCPR, the ICESCR has a much more global and international outlook.[3]

Accordingly, the absence of a provision limiting the scope of application and the emphasis on the realisation of ESC rights through international assistance and cooperation has predominantly been interpreted in favour of an extraterritorial scope of application of the ICESCR.[4]

This seems to be in line with the *travaux preparatoires* of the Covenant.[5] *Gondek's* analysis concludes that "the drafters of the Covenant did not explicitly restrict its scope of application to the territory or jurisdiction of a state party."[6] He further notes that "the work of the CESCR, the International Court of Justice and other mechanisms has to some extent resolved the debate in favour of a certain extraterritorial scope of the ICESCR."[7]

The Committee on Economic, Social and Cultural Rights (CESCR) has pointed out on several occasions that the scope of the Covenant is not limited.[8] It has mainly dealt with the issue in General Comments (GC) on

---

[3] Coomans F., *Some Remarks on the Extraterritorial Application of the International Covenant on Economic, Social and Cultural Rights*, in Coomans F., Kaminga M. (eds.), *Extraterritorial Application of Human Rights Treaties*, Intersentia, 2004, 183, 185.

[4] See e.g., Coomans F., "The Extraterritorial Scope of the International Covenant on Economic, Social and Cultural Rights in the Work of the United Nations Committee on Economic, Social and Cultural Rights", *Human Rights Law Review* (2011), 11, 1; Künnemann R., *Extraterritorial Application of the International Covenant on Economic, Social and Cultural Rights*, in Coomans F., Kaminga M. (eds.), *Extraterritorial Application of Human Rights Treaties*, cit., 201; Papp A., *Extraterritoriale Schutzpflichten*, Duncker & Humblot, 2013.

[5] Gondek M., *The Reach of Human Rights in a Globalising World: Extraterritorial Application of Human Rights Treaties*, Intersentia, 2009, 299-302; see for a contrary view Dennis M., "Application of Human Rights Treaties Extraterritorially in Times of Armed Conflict and Military Occupation", *The American Journal of International Law* (2005), 99, 119, 127.

[6] *Ivi*, 302.

[7] *Ibidem*.

[8] There has been some uncertainty regarding the legal status of the Committee's pronouncements for the purpose of the interpretation of the Covenant. The International Law Commission has addressed this issue noting that pronouncements of treaty bodies can be used as supplementary means of interpretation in the sense of Article 32 VCLT and that they also contribute to the determination of the ordinary meaning of the terms in their context and in light of the object and purpose of the treaty (ILC, Text of the draft conclusions on subsequent agreements and subsequent practice in relation to the interpretation of treaties with commentaries, UN Doc. A/73/10, 2018, available at http://legal.un.org/docs/?path=../ilc/reports/2018/english/a_73_10_advance.pdf&lang =E). This position is shared by States, domestic courts and most authors, see e.g. General Assembly, A/C.6/70/SR.22, 8 f.; Federal Court of Australia, Minister for Immigration and Citizenship v Anochie (18 December 2012), cited by Kanetake M., *Giving due*

state parties' obligations resulting from Article 2(1) (GC No. 3), concerning specific rights (e.g., GC No.12 on the right to food) or specific issues (e.g., GC No. 8 on the issue of economic sanctions). In its general comment No. 19 (2007) on the right to social security, the CESCR underscores that "States parties should *extraterritorially* protect the right to social security by preventing their own citizens and national entities from violating this right in other countries [emphasis by the author]". [9] Another reference has been made in GC No. 15, where the CESCR expressed that "to comply with their international obligations in relation to the right to water, states parties have to respect the enjoyment of the right *in other countries* [emphasis by the author]." [10] Further, GC No. 15 points out how the term "cooperation" has to be interpreted in regard to the realisation of the right to water: "International cooperation requires states parties to refrain from actions that interfere, directly or indirectly, with the enjoyment of the right to water *in other countries* [emphasis added by author]." Another very well-known example of the Committee's position regarding the ICESCR's scope of application can be found in its concluding observations on Israel's first state report to the Committee. Israel only provided information on the enjoyment of ESC rights by Israeli settlers in the Occupied Palestinian Territories. The CESCR reacted by noting that "the Palestinian population within the same jurisdictional areas were excluded from both the report and the protection of the Covenant" and further, that "the State's obligations under the Covenant apply to all territories and populations under its effective control.". [11]

The CESCR's position regarding Israel's scope of obligations was even endorsed by the International Court of Justice (ICJ). The ICJ rejected Israel's view that the ICESCR would not apply extraterritorially in its advisory opinion on *Legal Consequences of the Construction of a Wall in the Occupied Palestinian Territory* [12] clarifying that it applies to "both the territories

---

consideration, in Krisch N. (ed), *Entangled Legalities Beyond the State*, Cambridge University Press, 2021, 131, 147; Schlütter B., *Aspects of human rights interpretation by the UN treaty bodies*, in Keller H., Ulfstein G. (eds.), *UN Human Rights Treaty Bodies*, Cambridge University Press, 2012, 261, 289 f.; Mechlem K., "Treaty Bodies and the Interpretation of Human Rights", *Vanderbilt Journal of Transnational Law* (2005), 42, 905, 920 f.; Wheatley S., *The idea of International Human Rights Law*, Oxford University Press, 2019, 124.

[9] GC No. 19: The right to social security (Art. 9), 4 February 2008, E/C.12/GC/19 at para 54.

[10] GC No. 15: The right to water (Arts. 11 and 12), 20 January 2003, E/C.12/2002/11 at para 31.

[11] Concluding Observations on Israel, 4 December 1998 E/C.12/1/Add.27 at para 8.

[12] Legal Consequences of the Construction of a Wall in the Occupied Palestinian Territory, Advisory Opinion, ICJ Reports 2004, 136.

over which a state party has sovereignty *and* to those over which that State exercises territorial jurisdiction [emphasis by the author]." [13] The Court recalled these findings in the judgement in *Armed Activities on the Territory of the Congo.* [14] It underlined that "international human rights instruments are applicable 'in respect of acts done by a State in the exercise of its jurisdiction *outside* its own territory', particularly in occupied territories [*emphasis by the author*].". [15]

6.3. Jurisdiction as a 'threshold criterion'

In summary, *Gondek's* aforementioned conclusion seems convincing: The interpretative work of the CESCR as well as the case law of the ICJ speak in favour of an extraterritorial scope of application of the ICESCR. However, the ICJ and the CESCR (at least in its conclusions regarding Israel's obligations) assumed that the treaty only applies in an extraterritorial context given a *jurisdictional link* between state party and individual.

The term "jurisdiction" has a wide range of meanings in different contexts of international law. [16] (State) jurisdiction in general international law relates to sovereignty [17] and therefore to the authority of a state to regulate its public order by its domestic law. Thus, the concept of jurisdiction serves to determine the extent of a state's sovereignty [18] as well as to delimit state competences [19] and is, hence, understood as primarily territorial.

In human rights law, the term jurisdiction appears as mentioned above in human rights treaties in order to determine whom state parties are obliged to. [20] The European Convention on Human Rights (ECHR), for

---

[13] *Ivi*, para. 112.

[14] Armed Activities on the Territory of the Congo (Democratic Republic of the Congo v Uganda), Judgment, ICJ Reports 2005, 168.

[15] *Ivi*, para. 216.

[16] See Milanovic M., *Extraterritorial Application of Human Rights Treaties*, Oxford University Press, 2011, 21-44.

[17] Ryngaert C., *Jurisdiction in International Law*, 2nd ed., Oxford University Press, 2015, 5.

[18] Ryngaert C., *The Concept of Jurisdiction in International Law*, in Orakhelashvili A. (ed.), *Research Handbook on Jurisdiction and Immunities in International Law*, Edward Elgar Publishing, 2015, 50, 51.

[19] Ryngaert C., *Jurisdiction, Towards a Reasonableness Test*, in Langford M., Vandenhole W., Scheinin M., van Genugten W. (eds.), *Global Justice, State Duties*, Cambridge University Press, 2012, 192, 194.

[20] Ryngaert C., *Jurisdiction in International Law*, cit., 22.

example, contains a jurisdictional clause in its Article 1, where it says that state parties shall secure the rights under the treaty to "everyone within their jurisdiction". The European Court of Human Rights (ECtHR) seems to define jurisdiction largely along the lines of how the term is used in general international law, i.e., primarily territorial. Therefore, it considers the extraterritorial application of the ECHR *exceptional.* Accordingly, an extraterritorial application is only justified in the case of a state party's exercise of *effective (overall) control* over a territory (spatial model) or persons (personal model).[21]

The Human Rights Council (HRC), the treaty body of the ICCPR, defines jurisdiction less narrowly. Although it also uses the term *effective control*, it considers the exercise of *de facto* control as sufficient.[22] This is mainly based on the assumption that the notion of jurisdiction in the context of human rights law has – to say it with *Milanovic's* words – "precisely *nothing*" to do with the notion in general international law.[23]

It remains unclear which concept of jurisdiction the ICJ and the CESCR referred to and whether they considered the exercise of jurisdiction as a threshold criterion for the extraterritorial application of the ICESCR. Such a conclusion seems to be contrary to the wording and purpose of the treaty. As already pointed out, the ICESCR does not contain a jurisdiction clause. Besides, it would contradict the CESCR's position towards the extraterritorial application of the treaty.[24] However, it seems that the ICJ was referring to the notion of jurisdiction in general international law as it declared that the rights under the ICESCR are "essentially territorial".[25]

Nonetheless, some scholars demand a jurisdictional link to establish extraterritorial human rights obligations at least with respect to *positive obligations.* This has been argued in order to distinguish between *positive* and *negative* human rights obligations regarding the extraterritorial scope of the ICESCR.[26] While the negative obligation to *respect* human rights, i.e., to

---

[21] See Milanovic M., *Extraterritorial Application of Human Rights Treaties*, cit., 127-173, 173-208.

[22] GC No. 31, The nature of the general legal obligation imposed on States Parties to the Covenant, 26 May 2004, CCPR/C/21/Rev.1/Add. 13, para. 10 by stating that the rights also apply to those within the power or effective control of a state party, "*regardless of the circumstances in which such power or effective control was obtained*".

[23] Milanovic M., *op. cit.*, 26.

[24] See Section 1.

[25] ICJ Advisory Opinion, *supra*, para. 112.

[26] See, e.g., Künnemann R., *Extraterritorial Application*, cit., 212; Craven M., *Human Rights in the Realm of Order: Sanctions and Extraterritoriality,* in Coomans F., Kaminga M. (eds.), *Extraterritorial Application of Human Rights Treaties*, cit., 233, 247; den Hei-

refrain from interfering with or curtailing the enjoyment of rights, would apply without any restrictions, obligations to *protect* and *fulfil* rights would only be triggered if a person falls under the jurisdiction of the foreign state. Such a distinction has also been made for obligations deriving from the ICCPR.[27] Just like the state is obliged to refrain from conduct that violates the rights of individuals on its territory, it should be obliged in the same way to those outside its territory.[28] However, given the lack of jurisprudence or other sources endorsing the latter view, it remains (to some extent) unclear whether the ICESCR applies extraterritorially in a limited or unlimited manner.

6.4. Extraterritorial effects of unilateral sanctions and the concept of jurisdiction

Considering extraterritorial negative obligations to apply in all circumstances, state parties to the ICESCR imposing unilateral sanctions would have obligations to *respect* ESC rights of persons located in targeted countries.[29] The more restrictive interpretation of the ICESCR's extraterritorial application would instead require a jurisdictional link between the state party and the individual claiming deprivation of its rights. Individuals located in targeted countries would therefore need to fall under the jurisdiction of the sanction sender state in order to be entitled to protection. As has been pointed out above, at least in the context of extraterritorial acts and the deprivation of civil and political rights, jurisdiction results from a state's control over a territory or a person. But can a person within the targeted state fall under the jurisdiction and therefore under the control of a sanction sender state due to the effects of the sanction?

Unilateral sanctions constitute domestic policy measures addressing

---

jer M., Lawson R., *Extraterritorial Human Rights and the Concept of 'Jurisidction'*, in Langford M., Vandenhole W., Scheinin M., van Genugten W. (eds.), *Global Justice, State Duties*, cit., 153, 182 as they only examine *positive obligations* and jurisdiction.

[27] Künnemann R., *Extraterritorial Application*, cit., 228; Milanovic M., *op. cit.*, 215.

[28] The CESCR seems to follow a similar approach. In GC 12 on the right to food, it emphasised that states parties "should refrain *at all times* from food embargoes or similar measures", thereby pointing out that the negative obligations of state parties should apply *under all circumstances*.

[29] It is important to distinguish at this point between the question of the extraterritorial obligation to respect ESC rights and the question whether sanctions cause human rights violations. A sanction does not violate human rights *per se*. In order to provide a comprehensive answer in this regard, an intensive study on the *causation* of sanctions for the deprivation of ESC rights would be needed.

natural and legal persons within the targeting state's own territory.[30] Hence, unilateral sanctions are considered as *intra-territorial acts*, although their effects arise *extraterritorially* as sanctions aim to induce the target to change its behaviour. As pointed out, the effects of sanctions lead to circumstances that inevitably affect the enjoyment of ESC-rights in targeted states. But these extraterritorial effects do *not* depend on the exercise of effective control over a territory or a person. The doctrine of effective control, thus, is too restrictive with regard to domestic acts causing extraterritorial effects.[31] Accordingly, extraterritorial effects of sanctions do not trigger extraterritorial obligations under the jurisdictional threshold of effective control.

Considering the indirect effect of sanctions, however, the question arises as to whether "jurisdiction" cannot be defined differently in order to establish extraterritorial obligations of sanction sender states, or whether a jurisdictional threshold is required at all.

The "Maastricht Principles on Extraterritorial Obligations of States in the Area of Economic, Social and Cultural Rights"[32] might offer two fruitful approaches. Principle 9 defines three kinds of situation where a state has extraterritorial obligations to respect, protect and fulfil ESC rights: while Principle 9 a) takes into account situations where a state exercises effective control, Principle 9 b) identifies situations where a state's "acts or omissions bring about *foreseeable effects* on the enjoyment of economic, social and cultural rights [emphasis added by author]". "Jurisdiction" based on Principle 9 b) is the result of what one would consider as careless or negligent state behaviour. The imposition of unilateral sanctions might therefore be a case that Principle 9 b) seeks to cover (the required degree of "negligence" would then have to be defined and determined in the specific individual case). Although, the inclusion of humanitarian exemptions in unilateral sanction regimes could be used to justify why the damage was not expected and therefore not foreseeable. Principle 9 c) refers to the obligation under Article 2(1) ICESCR

[30] In some circumstances sanctions can also bind foreign natural and legal persons. This is the case for so called *secondary sanctions*. They are intended to prevent third parties from interacting with individuals, entities or states that are subject to sanctions.

[31] This presumption does, however, not apply in cases of occupation or similar situations where the state is acting on foreign territory, e.g., the Israeli occupation of Palestinian territory which the ICJ Advisory Opinion on Legal Consequences of the Construction of a Wall in the Occupied Palestinian Territory was based on.

[32] Maastricht Principles on Extraterritorial Obligations of States in the Area of Economic, Social and Cultural Rights available at https://www.fidh.org/IMG/pdf/maastricht-eto-principles-uk_web.pdf; The Maastricht Principles constitute an international expert opinion on extraterritorial obligations issued on 28 September 2011.

to take measures individually and jointly through international cooperation in order to fulfil ESC rights while taking into account the capacity and resources to act accordingly. Thus, in applying Principle 9(c) in the sanction situation, it would be required to determine whether a sanction sender state possesses the capacity and means necessary to realize the ESC rights of individuals affected by the impact of its sanctions.

Narula proposes a different approach to determine whether an individual falls under the jurisdiction of a state by suggesting the threshold criterion of "effective *economic* control [emphasis added by author]":[33] Practising control over economic policies or markets outside a state's territory is sufficient to assume that the state exercises "jurisdiction". *Narula* argues that "social and economic rights are more easily violated under globalization's deterioration of economic sovereignty"[34] and furthermore, that it is reasonable to "argue that the jurisdictional scope of the ICESCR should be adapted to reflect erosions and expansions of economic jurisdiction." Unfortunately, *Narula* does not elaborate on this approach further. However, there is much to be gained from this proposal as it deals with the *de facto* influence of a state on the interdependence of the economy of another state which might be the situation in a sanction context.[35]

Another suggestion extends the standard test of effective control to "control *over situations* (with extraterritorial *effects on the enjoyment of human rights*) [emphasis added by author]."[36] *Altwicker* restricts this concept to effects on "identifiable individuals" to prevent unlimited jurisdiction in human rights cases.[37] Besides, *Altwicker* considers that the concept only applies when a specific degree of "dangerousness of the effects, impact duration, choice of means and the vulnerability of the targeted or affected individuals, as well as the overall security context in the state where the affected individuals reside [...]" has been reached.[38] *Altwicker's* proposal seems to be partly applicable to the case of extraterritorial effects of sanctions as he distinguishes between *direct* and *indirect* effects and refers the

[33] Narula S., "The Right to Food: Holding Global Actors Accountable Under International Law", *Columbia Journal of Transnational Law* (2006), 44, 691, 734.

[34] *Ibidem.*

[35] Especially with regard to very broad sanction regimes, such as the "maximum pressure campaign" by the Trump administration against Iran after the United States exited the Joint Comprehensive Plan of Action (JCPOA) in 2018.

[36] Altwicker T., "Transnationalizing Rights: International Human Rights Law in Cross-Border Contexts", *The European Journal of International Law* (2018), 29, 581, 590.

[37] *Ibidem.*

[38] *Ibidem.*

concept of control over situations only to the former. That means, in the case where the subject of a targeted sanction is a clearly definable individual which would be the case with a travel ban, that this person would fall under the jurisdiction of the sanction sender state (assuming that the impact intensity is high enough). It is difficult to determine whether broader unilateral sanction regimes targeting state sectors would also be regarded as having *direct* effects on individuals.

The outlined approaches have in common that they take particular aspects into account that arise due to the peculiarity of domestic acts triggering effects abroad. However, regarding the broad concept of the Maastricht Principles and *Narula's* proposal, it is rather difficult to assume that they reflect international law *de lege lata.* Nevertheless, the concepts and proposals intend to close gaps where the standard threshold of effective control is *unsuitable*. With respect to a more globalised world, "a 'shift of perspective' in international human rights law, away from a state-centred 'territorial' approach towards a more 'functional' approach"[39] should be considered when assessing the concept of jurisdiction. This view, that international law does not intend to disregard cases where an act within a state's territory has harmful effects abroad, is well established in international environmental law as well as human rights law when it comes to human rights violations rooted in transboundary environmental harm.

In a precedential dispute between Canada and the USA (the so-called Trail Smelter case[40]) the smelter plant in Trail close to the US borders processed lead and zinc. The fumes emitted by the smelter caused damages to land located in the State of Washington which was mainly used for farming. The arbitral tribunal found that Canada was "responsible" for the damage caused by the company and that the latter should refrain from causing any further damage. It stated that

> *Under the principles of international law [...] no state has the right to use or permit the use of its territory in such a manner as to cause injury by fumes or in the* territory of another or the properties or persons therein *[...].*[41]

---

[39] Askin E., MPEPIL, Economic and Social Rights, Extraterritorial Application, para. 22, available at https://opil.ouplaw.com/display/10.1093/law-epil/9780199231690/law-9780199231690-e2213.

[40] Ad Hoc International Arbitral Tribunal, *Trail Smelter Arbitration* (United States v. Canada), III United Nations Reports of International Arbitral Awards 1911, 138, (1941), 1905-1982.

[41] *Ivi*, 1965.

Human Rights Courts took up this position and argued that individuals are subject to the jurisdiction of the State of origin of the environmental harm.[42] International legal literature shares this view.[43]

From this it follows that an act and its effects may very well fall apart and that the effects may trigger responsibility, even occurring on foreign territory.

Against the background of the paradigm change of individuals becoming the primary international legal subjects, the international community must consider the effective protection of the individual regardless of where the person is physically present. In addition, the increase of global transactions entails particularly risks for the protection of ESC rights. Therefore, the CESCR expressed grave concerns as it commented on the process of globalisation as a risk "downgrading the *central place* accorded to human rights by the Charter of the United Nations in general and the International Bill of Human Rights in particular [*emphasis added by the author*].".[44]

Unilateral sanctions, thus, need to be seen as what they are, coercive measures that by their very nature and due to the increase of global transactions endanger the protection of ESC rights.[45] Therefore, a tendency to play down the extent of such measures fails to recognise the *central place* of human rights and in particular *human dignity*.[46] Indeed the CESCR, after experiencing the devastative humanitarian outcome of the Iraqi sanctions in the 1990s, devoted a GC on the compatibility of economic sanctions and ESC rights.[47] It highlighted that "sanctions should always take full account of the provisions of the International Covenant on Economic, Social and Cultural Rights.".[48] Further, the Committee indicated that economic sanctions' impact on the enjoyment of human rights should not be underesti-

---

[42] See e.g., Inter-American Court of Human Rights. Advisory Opinion OC 23/17 of November 15th, 2017, 35-43, in particular para. 102.

[43] See e.g., Boyle A., "Human Rights and the Environment: Where next?", *European Journal of International Law* (2012), 23, 613; see also, among others Viñuales J., *A Human Rights Approach to Extraterritorial Environmental Protection – An Assessment*, in Bhuta N. (ed.), *The Frontiers of Human Rights*, Oxford University Press, 2016, 177.

[44] Statement by the CESCR "Globalization and its impact on the enjoyment of economic, social and cultural rights", E/1999/22, para. 515.

[45] See Craven M., *Human Rights in the Realm of Order*, cit., 243.

[46] See Le Moli G., Viñuales J., "Today as Yesterday? Unilateral Coercive Measures and Human Dignity", *Chinese Journal of International Law* (2019), 18, 437.

[47] GC No. 8, The relationship between economic sanctions and respect for economic, social and cultural rights 12 December 1997 E/C.12/1997/8.

[48] *Ivi*, para. 1.

mated as it stated that "lawlessness of one kind should not be met by lawlessness of another kind [...].".[49]

Against this background, it is not apparent why states should not be held accountable for acts undermining the enjoyment of human rights in other parts of the globe even beyond the realm of their *effective control.*[50] Otherwise, the responsibility for the protection of human rights would lie solely with the territorial state. As the pandemic proves, it is not always possible for the latter to live up to its positive human rights obligations in that regard. How should targeted states such as Iran, Syria or Venezuela comply with the protection of the *right to health* in the absence of medical goods due to the burden of sanctions?

6.5. Conclusion

This paper set out to determine whether effects of unilateral sanctions on ESC rights can trigger extraterritorial human rights obligations of sanction sender states. It was outlined that the ICESCR as the main treaty on ESC rights does provide an extraterritorial scope of application. Yet, it could not be clearly determined whether extraterritorial obligations under the ICESCR can only arise towards individuals that fall under the jurisdiction of a state party. According to a broad approach, state parties owe obligations to *respect* human rights vis-à-vis any individual. Thus, sanction sender states have to refrain from any conduct or omission that affect rights of individuals located in targeted countries. A more restrictive approach considers a jurisdictional link between state party and individual as an indispensable requirement. Yet, it proved difficult to identify such a link in the context of sanctions under the well-known *effective control* test as sanctions constitute domestic acts with extraterritorial effects. Therefore, this paper presented other possible approaches aimed at defining *jurisdiction* beyond the traditional *effective control* criterion. What has clearly emerged in the course of this study is that there is an urgent need to review and adapt the traditional jurisdiction criteria with a view to more effectively protect individual rights in the context of the far-reaching effects of sanction measures.

---

[49] *Ivi*, para 16.

[50] Craven M., *Human Rights in the Realm of Order*, cit., 249.

Chapter 7

THE POLITICAL-ECONOMIC IMPACT OF SANCTIONS: A COMPARATIVE ANALYSIS OF THE CASES OF RUSSIA AND IRAN*

Peter A.G. van Bergeijk, Sajjad F. Dizaji

ABSTRACT: *This chapter analyses the interaction between economic and political variables paying special attention to how this interaction develops over time. We use an innovative approach to sanctions that provides a dynamic, forward-looking, perspective and deals with the economic and political outcome of sanctions simultaneously. We use Impulse Response Functions to report the main results of a comprehensive set of unrestricted Vector Auto Regression models that we use to analyse how negative oil and gas shocks impact on the economy and politics in Russia and Iran in order to find out differences and agreements between those cases. In both cases we find that the limitation of energy rents can improve political conditions in the short to medium term, but also that the beneficial impact of sanctions is limited as both economic and political behaviour adjust when time passes by.*

7.1. Introduction

Sanction research has often been characterized as a black box.[1] Typically, the empirical literature reports quasi reduced form equations based on a review of the relevant literature rather than a well specified structural model. There are basically two approaches that can be distinguished by the assumed direction of causality: (a) the argument that takes the target's political behavior as the dependent variable and (b) the strand of the literature that investigates how sanctions exert an impact on the economy.

---

* Useful comments by the Editors are gratefully acknowledged.

[1] Bergeijk P.A.G. van (ed.), *Research Handbook on Economic Sanctions*, Edward Elgar, 2021.

– *The determinants of the sanction target's political behavior.* The first strand of the literature would seem to be the domain of political science, but actually has been produced by political scientists and economists a like. The lefthand side variable of the black box equation is often some measure of success or failure, that is: the extent to which a sanction changes the target's political behavior. For economists, this was initially a focal point, because of their interest in the effectiveness of the sanction instrument rather than the actual damage of sanctions.[2] This strand of the literature has been significantly broadened as other variables have been used to investigate the socio-political impact of economic sanctions (e.g., human rights or changes in the political system).

The righthand side of the black box equation consists of a set of explanatory variables that relate to

- economic vulnerability and resilience,
- economic impact including observed evasion,
- characteristics of the type of sanction and its goals and/or
- political indicators that reflect the relationship between sanction sender and sanction target as well as alliances with one of the parties.

Typically, and for obvious reasons, these explanatory variables are measured in the year before sanction threat and or imposition. Occasionally timing issues are considered, for example, to allow for adjustment and learning.[3]

– *The impact of sanctions on the target economy.* In this strand of literature, the lefthand side variable is some measure of economic impact. A great many dimensions have been investigated: trade flows (exports, imports, goods, services), capital flows (foreign investment, lending, development aid, remittances) firm level (e.q. productivity) or a macroeconomic impact measure for the target economy (production, unemployment, etc.). The righthand side variables typically use

- a dummy variable for the application of a sanction (threat),
- indicators for the kind of sanction and
- indicators for vulnerability and resilience (some of which are economic, and some are political).

[2] Bergeijk P.A.G. van, "The Effectivity of Economic Sanctions: Illusion or Reality", *Peace Science, Peace Economics and Public Policy* (1994), 2, 1, 24-35.

[3] Bergeijk P.A.G. van, van Marrewijk C., "Why Do Sanctions Need Time to Work? Adjustment, Learning and Anticipation", *Economc Modelling* (1995), 12, 2, 75-86.

The second strand typically would seem to be the domain of economists proper. Indeed, it consists of many recent contributions that thanks to the availability of new data sets focus on the impact of sanctions on international trade and investment flows, Gross Domestic Product and its distribution, (un)employment and inflation. It is, however, not the realm of the economic tribe alone; it is noteworthy that the seminal paper in this strand appeared in a peace science journal.[4] Typically, the approach in this strand of the literature is time series analysis and the research mainly covers the target economy but it sometimes also studies the countries that are imposing or threatening economic sanctions. Due to the sanctions on Russia, there has been a recent surge in the use of Applied General Equilibrium that model the impact on sanction targets and sanctions simultaneously.

The main point that this chapter addresses is the fact that the causality in these strands of the literature predominantly is mono-directional by assumption. This mono-directionality is not a consequence of a lack of disciplinary dialogue and/or interplay in sanctions research, but rather reflects how scientists structure their research questions and it is a common characteristic of the available sanctions research. There is a clear cost: as the hypotheses on the direction of causality differ, it is not really a surprise that the sanctions literature is not converging.[5] This all strongly suggests that theory and application explicitly need to consider that politics and economics mutually influence each other in the case of sanctions. It is this third way that this c proposes (Figure 7.1).

---

[4] See, for example, Caruso R., "The Impact of International Economic Sanctions on Trade An Empirical Analysis", *Peace Economics, Peace Science and Public Policy* (2003), 9 (2), Article 2.

[5] Clifton M.T., et al., "Economic sanctions: Evolution, consequences, and challenges", *Journal of Economic Perspectives* (2023), 37, 1, 3-29 and Demena B.A., et al., *Publication bias of economic sanction research: a meta-analysis of the impact of trade linkage, duration and prior relations on sanctions success*, in Bergeijk P.A.G. van (ed.), *Research Handbook on Economic Sanctions*, Edward Elgar, 2021, 126-50. Relatedly, a problem is that the different vintages of data sets play havoc, see Irina M., *FDI and Sanctions*, in Bergeijk P.A.G. van (ed.), *Research Handbook on Economic Sanctions*, Edward Elgar, 2021, 369-87 and Bergeijk P.A.G. van, M. Siddiquee S.H., "Biased Sanctions? Methodological Change in Economic Sanctions Reconsidered and Its Implications", *International Interactions* (2017), 43, 879-93.

Figure 7.1. Different approaches to sanction modelling

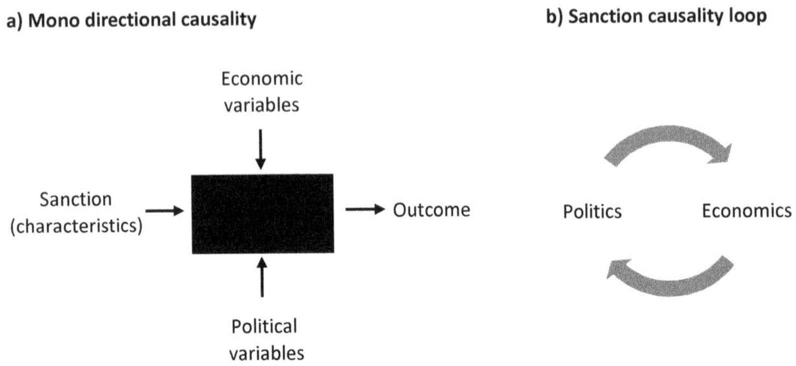

Source: the authors.

This chapter sketches an approach that takes the mutual dependence of economics and politics as the point of departure, introducing a loop between political and economic variables (Figure 7.1).[6] Our approach neither pre-imposes an economic structure nor a lag structure. The reason to use a dynamic statistical approach (Vector Auto Regression) is that we do not want to rely on specific theoretical assumptions, for example (neo) Keynesian, monetarist or (neo) classical. Theoretical *priors*, although sometimes suggested by conditions of time and place in actual cases, would moreover reduce the more general applicability that we strive for.

We will discuss two cases from a comparative perspective: the sanctions against Iran in 2012 and against Russia in 2022, respectively.[7] It should on the one hand, be clear from the start that the sanctions are to a large extent quite different both in terms of sanction goals (non-proliferation/military), sanction instruments (largely macroeconomic/initially mainly targeted) and external economic environment (the aftermath of the Great Recession/Covid-19 pandemic).[8] On the other hand, similarities exist, including a history

---

[6] See for a mono-directional VAR analysis of sanction damage: Pestovanna M., et al., "The price of war: Macroeconomic effects of the 2022 sanctions on Russia", *VoxEU*, 15 April 2022.

[7] We use these two cases because our analyses have been peer-reviewed and published: Dizaji, S.F., Bergeijk P.A.G. van, "Potential early phase success and ultimate failure of economic sanctions: A VAR approach with an application to Iran", *Journal of Peace Research* (2013), 50 (6), 721-36 and Dizaji S.F., Bergeijk P.A.G. van, *Sanctions and Russian autocracy*, in Bali M. (ed.), *Sanctions and the Impact of the Russia-Ukraine Conflict*, Nova Publishers, 2023, in print.

[8] See: Bergeijk P.A.G. van, *Sanctions against Iran-A preliminary economic assessment*,

of earlier imposed sanctions by the US and EU, an autocratic governing structure and the fact that both countries are energy exporters and may therefore suffer from the Resource Curse. While the differences may convince the reader that our approach is applicable in different cases, the similarities may warrant caution regarding applicability: the bottom line is that this chapter only demonstrates two cases and that we hope that our findings stimulate the development of such models for other sanction cases in order to find out whether our approach is generally applicable.

The remainder of this chapter is organized as follows. section 7.2 provides our motivation for VAR-modelling of sanctions and offers a succinct introduction to this method. Section 7.3 deals with econometric and simulation issues. Section 7.4 compares the findings of the two cases, illustrating the use of impulse response functions and variance decomposition. Section 7.5 analyses the benefits and costs of VAR modelling of economic sanctions, from the perspective of policy makers, policy analysts and academic researchers. Section 7.6 draws some conclusions and section 7.7 offers suggestions avenues for future research.

7.2. Vector auto regressive sanction modelling

Sanction research builds on a long history of qualitative case studies and descriptive statistics. Quantitative country case studies did exist, but formed a minority of studies, possibly due to data requirements, computational constraints, and complexity of macro-economic modelling.[9] As of 1985 the dominant approach in sanction research became the analysis of so-called large-*N* data sets, that are: collections of sanction case characteristics of which Hufbauer and Schott's *Economic Sanctions Reconsidered*[10] is

---

in Dreyer I., Luengo-Cabrera J. (eds.), *On target? EU sanctions as security policy tools*, EIUSS, 2015, 49-58 and Bergeijk P.A.G. van, "Sanctions against the Russian war on Ukraine: Lessons from history and current prospects", *Journal of World Trade* (2022), 56, 4, 571-586.

[9] Examples are: Bayard T.O., et al., *An Economic Model of United States and Western Controls on Exports to the Soviet Union and Eastern Europe*, in Joint Economic Committee, *Soviet Economy in the 1980s: Problems and Prospects,* Congress of the United States, 1983, 507-55; Hughes Hallett A.J., Brandsma A.S., "How Effective Could Sanctions Against the Soviet Union Be?", *Weltwirtschaftliches Archiv* (1983), 119, 498-522.; Khan H.A., "Impact of Trade Sanctions on South Africa: A Social Accounting Matrix Approach", *Contemporary Policy Issues* (1988), 6, 130-40., and Porter R.C., "International Trade and Investment Sanctions: Potential Impact on the South African Economy", *Journal of Conflict Resolution* (1979), 23, 4, 579-612.

[10] Hufbauer G.C., Schott J.J., *Economic Sanctions Reconsidered: History and Current Policy*, Peterson Institute for International Economics, 1985.

the seminal start and the Global Sanctions Data Base is the most recent best practice example.[11] While important improvements have been made in coverage both in terms of cases and in period covered by the large-*N* data sets,[12] the approach appears to have reached its limits.[13] The empirical literature is by and large based on a limited number of data collections that essentially use the approach pioneered by Hufbauer and Schott.[14] In the core these data sets do not consider the channels by which politics and economics interact in the case of sanction threats and applications. How can we shift the literature's focus from essentially static observations (outcome of sanction cases and pre-sanction values of 'determinants') towards an approach that recognizes the dynamic interplay of macroeconomic and political variables and also investigates how these factors *codetermine* the political impact of sanctions? Our aim is to discuss such an approach.

We recognize that such an ambition implies that we need to acknowledge practical constraints. To be useful the method needs to be applicable to a large domain of

- *economic conditions*, ranging from underconsumption to excess demand,
- *economic structures*, ranging from countries with a large public sector to economies dominated by private firms,
- *levels of development,* and
- *political systems*, ranging from autocracies to democracies.

The implication is that structural models (such as large econometric models or computational general equilibrium models) with a significant number of fixed parameters to be established by means of econometric research are less fit for our goal. It is after all difficult to imagine a structural model that would be useful on this large domain. Therefore, rather than imposing an *a priori* theoretical structure, we decided to let the data speak by means of a Vector Autoregressive (VAR) model, that enables us to consider all variables to be (potentially) conjointly endogenous. A VAR more-

---

[11] Kirilakha A., et al., *The Global Sanctions Data Base (GSDB): an update to include the years of the Trump presidency*, in Bergeijk P.A.G. van (ed.), *Research Handbook on Economic Sanctions*, Edward Elgar, 2021, 62-107.

[12] See Portela C., Charron A., "The Evolution of Databases in the Age of Targeted Sanctions", *International Studies Review* (2023), 25, 1, doi.org/10.1093/isr/viac061.

[13] Bergeijk P.A.G. van, "Can the sanction debate be resolved?", *CESifo Forum* (2019), 20 (4), 3-8.

[14] Peksen D., "When Do Imposed Economic Sanctions Work? A Critical Review of the Sanctions Effectiveness Literature", *Defence and Peace Economics* (2019), 30, 6, 635-47.

over does not impose the kind of a priori restrictions on structural relationships that we want to avoid. Our methodology has its roots in economics [15] but is also acknowledged as a useful approach in political science [16] especially when the short-run and long-run impact of interventions is important. [17]

Essentially, a VAR provides a multivariate framework relating changes in a particular variable to changes in its own lags and to changes in (the lags of) other variables:

$$y_t = A_1 y_{t-1} + \cdots + A_p y_{t-p} + Bx_t + \varepsilon_t \tag{7.1}$$

where y_t is a vector of k endogenous variables, x_t is a vector of d exogenous variables, $A_1, \ldots, A_p$ and B are matrices of coefficients to be estimated, and ε_t is a vector of unexpected shocks that may be contemporaneously correlated but are uncorrelated both with their own lagged values and with all of the right-hand side variables. Since only lagged values of the endogenous variables appear on the righthand side of the equation, simultaneity is not an issue and OLS yields consistent estimates. The VAR treats all variables as jointly endogenous and does not impose *a priori* restrictions on structural relationships. Since the VAR expresses the dependent variables in terms of predetermined lagged variables, it is a reduced-form model.

Estimation of a VAR model with a political-economic sanction loop in the real world encounters a number of challenges related to data availability. Typically, many of the variables are available on an annual basis only. This is in our experience especially true for the political variables, although public opinion polls and Big Data (e.g. based on analysis of social media) may offer an alternative way out in specific cases. Many economic data are already available with high frequency. [18] The exchange rate, the interest rate and stock market data are available on a daily basis. Inflation, unemployment and trade flows are reported monthly. Many countries report Gross Domestic Product, investment and consumption on a quarterly or biannual

---

[15] Sims C.A., "Macroeconomics and reality", *Econometrica* (1980), 48, 1, 1-48.

[16] See, for example, Freeman J.R., et al., "Vector autoregression and the study of politics", *American Journal of Political Science* (1989), 33, 4, 842-877.

[17] See Enders W. and Sandler T., "The effectiveness of anti-terrorism polices: A vector-autoregression-intervention analysis", *American Political Science Review* (1993), 87 (4), 829-44., and Dizaji S.F., "The impact of negative oil shocks on military spending and democracy in the oil states of the greater Middle East: Implications for the oil sanctions", *Journal of Peace Research* (2022) available at https://doi.org/10.1177/0022343 3221116654.

[18] Typically, at lower levels of development the frequency for these data is lower.

basis. However, also for economic observations annual observations are still the dominant or determining frequency.[19] By implication the data available for estimation may typically be of an annual frequency putting a clear restriction on the number of observations. Estimating large VARs would therefore be hindered by too limited a degree of freedom. This is why we propose to estimate a large family of small models. In these specifications one can distinguish between different sanction shocks, consider the impacts of sanctions on different sets of economic variables and analyse several indicators for movements along the autocracy-democracy spectrum. Running different specifications of the VAR model has the side benefit that it allows the researcher to test for robustness of the findings[20] which is also relevant since indicators for the political system although coded by academic experts are prone to bias due to subjectivity and methodology.

The main tools in the VAR approach are:

1. *impulse response functions (IRFs)* IRFs are reported as graphs and allow us to examine the dynamic effects of sanction shocks on the other variables. The dynamic response of macroeconomic and political variables to unexpected shocks in a particular variable can be traced out by using the simulated responses of the estimated VAR system. Through the IRF graphs, we can observe the magnitude and statistical significance of such responses to a sanction shock;
2. *variance decomposition*. The variance decomposition can be used to analyze the proportion of the changes in the time series of a specific variable that are due to innovations in other variables. In particular this is useful to investigate the comparative importance of variables in the sanction loop.

Given the intellectual, computational and data collection requirements it is fair that we demonstrate the viability of this approach in concrete sanction cases. Therefore, we will discuss two sanctions cases where we have applied the VAR methodology in the next section.

7.3. Econometric and simulation issues

As already stated, the cases of the sanctions against Iran and Russia share

---

[19] For example, the level of development is mainly determined on an annual basis, firm level data are produced on an annual basis while census data that report on one specific year may be collected only at long intervals.

[20] Dizaji S.F., "Trade openness, political institutions, and military spending (Evidence from lifting Iran's sanctions)", *Empirical Economics* (2019), 57 (6), 2013-2041.

similarities but also have important differences. We start this section with a discussion of the differences and similarities that occur in our modelling of both cases. Table 7.1 provides a summary of econometric aspects.[21] Both cases are built on a family of VAR models and use a 10-year horizon for the IRFs and variance decomposition. We start with a similar set of explanatory variables. According to the Phillips-Perron and Augmented Dickey Fuller unit root tests our variables are integrated of order one I(1). Generally speaking, if all the variables in the system are non-stationary, it is better to use a VAR in levels. On the other hand, estimating a VAR in levels in the case of cointegration may lead to the neglect of important constraints. Following the approach of Johansen and Juselius (1990)[22], we reject the hypothesis of no cointegration among the variables for both Iran and Russia. We have applied several statistical criteria to find the optimal lag length of our VAR models. These information criteria are LR, FPE (final prediction error), AIC (Akaike information criterion), SC (Schwarz information criterion), and HQ (Hannan-Quinn information criterion).

Ordering of variables in VAR models is also important and can change the dynamics of a VAR system. The first variable in the Cholesky ordering is usually the most exogenous variable among the variables of the VAR system. We suppose that oil and gas revenues have been restricted by the international sanctions, and therefore they are determined by them. Then, we expect that significant shocks in oil and gas rents affect contemporaneously the other key variables in the system. Additionally, we have also applied a group of generalized impulse responses, as suggested by Pesaran and Shin,[23] which are independent of the VAR ordering. The general results do not change. The VAR stability condition test (roots of characteristic polynomial) indicates that the VAR satisfies the stability condition and the results are reliable.

---

[21] The table compares Dizaji, S.F., Bergeijk P.A.G. van, "Potential early phase success and ultimate failure of economic sanctions: A VAR approach with an application to Iran", op cit. and Bergeijk P.A.G. van, Dizaji S.F., "Energy sanctions and Russia's democracy – autocracy: a dynamic VAR analysis", *IISS working paper 703*, Erasmus University, 2022.

[22] Johansen S., Juselius K., "Maximum likelihood estimation and inference on cointegration – with applications to the demand for money", *Oxford Bulletin of Economics and statistics* (1990), 52, 2, 169-210.

[23] Pesaran M.H., Shin Y., "Generalised impulse response analysis in linear multivariate models", *Economics Letters* (1998), 58, 1, 17-29.

Table 7.1. Comparative econometric similarities and differences

	Iran	Russia
Model	VAR	VAR
Estimation period	48 years	31 years
Time horizon	10 years	10years
Sanction shock variable(s)	Total oil and gas rents p.c.	Oil rents p.c. Gas rents p.c.(*)
Family of models	20	14
Economic variables	Government consumption p.c. Imports p.c. Gross capital formation p.c. GDP p.c. Exchange rate CPI	Government consumption p.c., Imports p.c. Gross capital formation p.c. GDP p.c. (#) Exchange rate CPI (#) Defense spending p.c. (*)
Political variables	Polity Vanhanen	Polity V-Dem indicators for electoral, liberal, deliberative, egalitarian and participatory democracy

Notes: (*) robustness analysis; (#) not included in VAR because of failed tests

Source: the authors.

For economic variables we used defense expenditure per capita as a robustness analysis for the case of Russia.[24] For political variables both cases investigate *Polity.*[25] *Polity* is a net indicator based on an assessment of autocratic and democratic aspects of the target country and has a very good country coverage. An estimation issue is that the data does not show a lot of variation and for this reason we used alternative indicators also to test for robustness. The Iran case uses *Vanhanen* indicator[26] as an alternative; in the case of Russia five *V-Dem* indicators for democracy[27] have been used.

[24] Economic data have been derived from World Bank's World Development Indicators (WDI) online database (World Bank, 2022).

[25] These data on democracy/autocracy dimension are derived from the Polity5 project of the Center for Systemic. See Marshall M.G., et al., *POLITY™ IV project*, Center for Systemic Peace, 2017.

[26] Vanhanen T., "Measures of Democracy 1810-2010", FSD1289, version 5.0, Finnish Social Science Data Archive 2011, available at https://www.prio.org/Data/Governance/Vanhanens-index-of-democracy/.

[27] Coppedge M., et al., "Measuring high level democratic principles using the V-Dem data", *International Political Science Review* (2015), 37, 5, 580-593.

Practical reasons and judgement play a role in the differences in the actual applications. Since the VAR modelling strategy is new to the field of sanctions research and because we wanted to keep the exposition transparent and focused on the methodological innovation, we have limited ourselves in the choice of political variables, but future research could certainly consider alternative indicators. When comparing the analyses for Iran and Russia, three issues are especially relevant:

1. *The estimation period* differs considerably from 48 years for Iran to 31 years for Russia. The shorter estimation period is due to the economic and political break of the collapse of the Union of Soviet Socialist Republics (USSR) – thus, for practical reasons the economic data series on modern days Russia start in 1990.[28] The time series is shorter than one would like, but the econometric results are still sufficiently reliable to do the analysis. However, this may be considered as a minimum requirement limiting the number of cases potentially available for our research strategy. For example, the 2014 EU sanctions against the Russian invasion of the Crimea could not have been analyzed with our approach since at that time we would only have had 23 annual economic observations (the start of the series for Russia rather that the USSR in 1990 until the most recent available numbers, that is the year 2013).
2. *The family of reported models*. The number of alternative models that are presented differs basically due to the lower degrees of freedom for Russia that makes it more difficult to establish reliable VARs. Indeed, we do not have "preferred equations" but rather equations that pass the required tests or not. Note that in the Russian models both the choice of the five political (*V-Dem*) variables as well as the use of two sanction shocks (gas versus oil) increases the size of the family of models.
3. *The sanction shock variables*. The differences relate to the actual sanctions discussed at the time of the modelling exercises. For Iran the total gas and oil rent was at stake.[29] For Russia, sanctions were phased in

[28] Bergeijk P.A.G. van, Oldersma H., "Détente, Market-oriented Reform and German Unification: Potential Consequences for the World Trade System", *Kyklos* (1990), 43, 4, 599-609. Not? that is not only the geography and structural change of the sanction target economy that plays havoc. We also limit ourselves to the post 1989 period since Eastern European data during the Cold War period were to a large extent manipulated; see Bergeijk P.A.G. van, "The accuracy of international economic observations", *Bulletin of Economic Research* (1995), 47, 1, 1-20.

[29] Note, however, that Dizaji S.F., Bergeijk P.AG. van, "Early phase success and long run failure of economic sanctions: With an application to Iran", *IISS working paper*

with initially no role for gas sanctions due to the high European dependence on Russian gas.

It should be clear from this discussion that the results should be interpreted with caution in the comparative case study. With this caveat in mind, we proceed to take a look at the findings for the sanctions against Iran and Russia.

7.4. Comparative case study findings for Iran and Russia

We focus our discussion on results for the political economic sanction loop. The comparison is limited to two variables that appear in all models and form the nucleus from an economic and political perspective:

- *gross capital formation per capita* (that is: gross investment) because this component of effective demand also translates into production capacity (and thus future production) and thus has both short-term (demand) and long-term (supply) effects;
- *polity* (a numerical indicator on where a country is located in the autocracy-democracy spectrum). An increase in Polity indicates that a country becomes more democratic.[30]

First, we will look at the impulse response functions and then we consider the variance decomposition.

Impulse response functions are reported in Figure 7.2. Horizontally the IRFs shows the time period after the initial sanction shock in years. Vertically the IRFs shows the magnitude of response to shocks. The middle line in the IRFs displays the response of the variables of interest to a one standard deviation shock in oil (gas) rents per capita.[31] On the vertical axis we measure the impact on the variables of interest in terms of their standard deviation. As an indication of significance, we have estimated 68% confidence intervals for the IRFs (dashed lines represent confidence bands).[32] When the horizontal line (x-axis; representing zero impact) in the IRFs falls between confidence bands, the impulse responses are not statistically sig-

No. 544, Erasmus University, 2012, provides additional testing for real oil revenues 1965-2008 (for which 44 observations are available.).

[30] Cross country comparisons are also possible, so to indicate that a country is more (less) democratic.

[31] The numerical size of the shocks differs of course but since we use one standard deviation shocks a comparison is possible.

[32] Sims C.A., Zha T., "Error bands for impulse responses", *Econometrica* (1999), 67, 5, 1113-55.

nificant. In other words, the null hypothesis of "no effects of changes in oil (gas) rents per capita" on the specific variable cannot be rejected.[33]

From Figure 7.2 we learn that the adjustment patterns for Iran and Russia to sanctions are quite different. While the direct magnitude of the sanction impact on gross capital formation is significant and of the same order of magnitude in terms of standard deviations in both cases, the impact pattern for Iran is more or less stable over time while the IRF for Russia shows fluctuations and actually gross capital formation per capita becomes significantly positive in the 8th year (panel 2a). Also, in the political domain (panel 2b) the response patterns are quite different. The initial (first year) reaction of *Polity* to a sanction shock in Iran is significant and positive; in Russia the impact is initially significantly negative before turning significantly positive in the 2nd to 5th year, inclusive.

It is important to note that the interpretation and translation of these findings into a concrete assessment always needs consideration. For example, the impact of the EU and US sanctions against Russia that we assess with the VARs definitely did not start with the announcement of the first sanction packages. Moreover, while the US imposed a full ban on Russian oil, gas and derivative products, the EU did only impose a ban on Russian crude oil shipping on December 5, 2022, and a ban on petroleum on February 5, 2023. (Also, exemptions were granted to several EU members.) The EU at the time of writing did not impose sanctions on gas but only strived for significant independence from Russia. Moreover, price movements of oil and gas initially significantly increased compensation for quantity reductions. By implication the start of the oil sanction shock in the case of Russia should probably be located early 2023 so that gross capital formation per capita and *Polity* could be expected to deteriorate in 2023 and 2024, while the positive political impact of sanctions according to the VAR could only emerge starting 2024.

---

[33] Berument M.H., et al., "The impact of oil price shocks on the economic growth of selected MENA countries", *Energy Journal* (2010), 31, 1, 149-76.

Figure 7.2. Impulse response functions

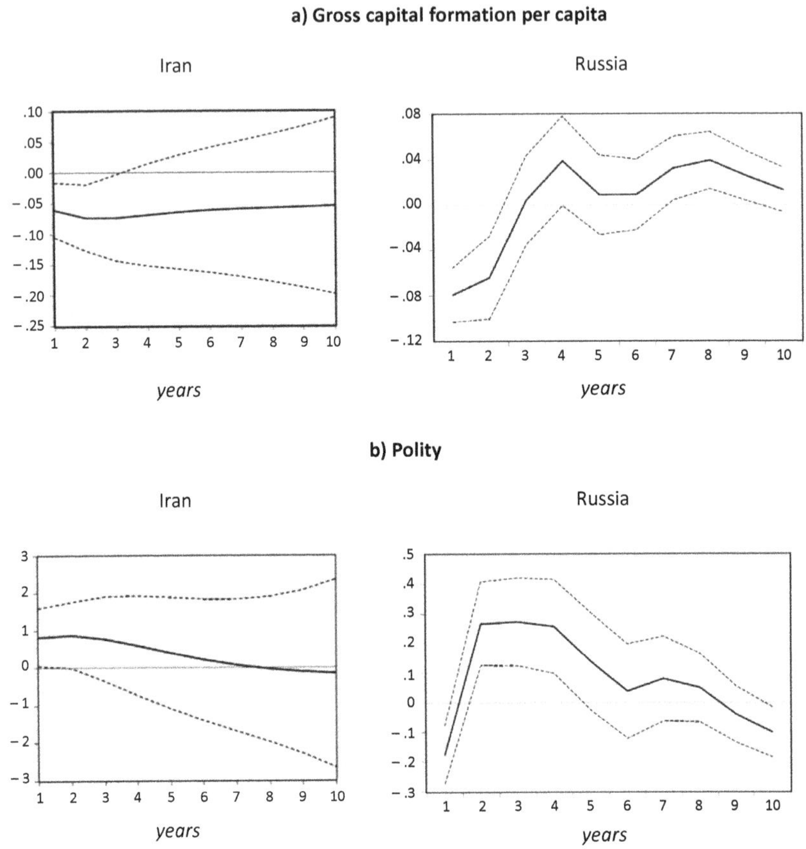

Source: the authors.

The second lens that we use to compare the two cases is based on the variance decomposition of forecasting error so that we can analyze the proportion of the changes in the time series that are due to innovations in a variable's own time series as opposed to innovations in other variables. Again, we focus on gross capital formation per capita and *Polity* (Figure 7.3) in order to assess the political economic sanction loop. Again, we find meaningful quantitative and qualitative differences between the two sanction cases.

Figure 7.3. Variance decomposition

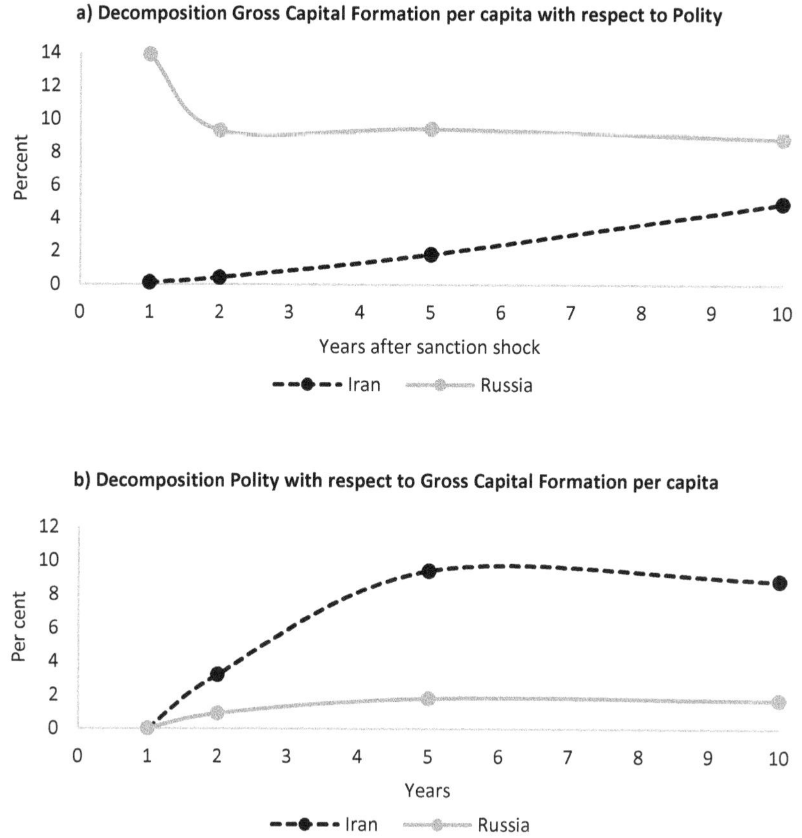

Source: the authors.

The variance decomposition shows for the considered sanction cases that politics (*Polity*) has a persistently stronger impact on economics (Gross capital formation per capita) in Russia than in Iran even as Iran over the ten-year period that we consider in the VAR has been on an upward trend. For the impact of the economy on politics we find the opposite. Again, the VAR methodology brings differences in political and economic dynamics to the fore. We cannot at this stage attempt to answer the question of what drives this intriguing difference.[34] This is an issue that can only be addressed once VAR models for more cases are available and we must therefore leave this as an issue for future research.

---

[34] We owe this point to an anonymous referee.

From a methodological point of view several observations could be made:

- a consistent finding is that the political and economic impact of sanctions changes over time. For one thing this means that political and economic interaction need to be considered simultaneously. For another thing, the time dimension of a sanction evaluation both with respect to sanction outcome (a measure for political change) and sanction contribution is a relevant dimension that should be considered more explicitly in sanction research.[35] A key issue to consider is therefore how much time has passed since the case was initiated at the moment of evaluation;
- it is important that the modelling approach that we propose in this Chapter is able to describe such different patterns and thereby can provide fresh perspectives on the dynamic adjustment of the target's political-economic system. An important caveat is that we have only analyzed two cases yet and that it is difficult to generalize on the basis of these two cases (and also as noted earlier to explain why exactly we find differences between Iran and Russia). Application of VAR models on dissimilar cases, i.e. for democracies and/or non-oil exporting countries would be an important first step to investigate the further potential of our research strategy;
- VAR modelling is not a one size fits all project. Although we start the modelling exercise with a comparable set of variables and were able to have at least a core of identical explanatory variable technical case characteristics related to the availability of data, the possible estimation period and time series characteristics need to be assessed in a comprehensive case by case basis.

7.5. Benefits and costs of VAR modelling of economic sanctions

This section investigates the benefits and costs of our modelling strategy from three perspectives: academic knowledge production, policy advise and communication. It should be recognized beforehand that the reader may want to disagree on what we label costs and benefits. Indeed, what may appear to be a cost in one area may be a benefit in another area and sometimes what we identify as a cost may actually be a characteristic that is

[35] By implication new vintages of data sets will have different observations and often different measures as well, compare Bergeijk P.A.G. van, M. Siddiquee S.H., "Biased Sanctions?", cit.

warranted under certain conditions of time and place. Analytical clarity may, for example, not be in the interest of parties involved in a conflict.

From an *academic point of view* the major benefit is that this method is much more transparent than the traditional coding of sanctions that are graded on a spectrum from total failure to total success by experts and this is true for both the element related to the sanction contribution as well as the component that assesses its impact on the target's behavior. Replication and changes due to data revisions enable a much stronger evidence base. An important side benefit is that the simultaneous analysis of politics and economics may work as a bridge between the fields of economics and political science. The academic costs, however, also need to be considered. Meaningful VAR modelling is impossible without sufficiently long time series for both the sanction shock variable and the political and economic variables. Data needs may create a biased sample of cases (for example it will in general not pe possible to assess cases of the 1960s and 1970s) – in this sense one should not rely on assessment of sanction cases by VARs alone.

For *policy makers* the major benefit of our research strategy consists probably of the option to provide a quick evidence-based assessment of the dynamic effects and impacts of considered sanctions, in particular their timing. In the strategic context of threats and applications of economic sanctions timing (that is: the moment that an impact can be expected to be strongest) is key, but also it is important to know what such measures can and cannot achieve and also to understand which channels are important for achieving results. There are two costs that are particularly relevant to consider. First, rather than point estimates our research strategy provides confidence intervals and as we use families of VARs a great many outcomes need to be evaluated.[36] Second, the organizational costs of inhouse VAR estimation may be considered too high – this could be especially the case if potential sanction assessment is in the domain of the Ministry of Foreign Affairs where econometric capacity probably is scarce.

Communication is key both for academic researchers and for policy makers. VAR estimation helps to underpin many key insights, such as the extent to which policy changes can be expected to result from economic sanctions and the finding (at least in the two cases that we discussed) that the major

[36] Most policy makers would consider this lack of an unambiguous outcome a cost; we believe it is an opportunity to communicate uncertainty in the findings. Typically, model uncertainty is also relevant for structural models. For example, the estimates of nine independent modelling exercise of the negative economic impact of sanctions on Russian GDP ranged from -1% to -29% (medium -11%) with both intra and inter study variation (Dizaji, S.F., Bergeijk P.A.G. van, "Potential early phase success and ultimate failure of economic sanctions", cit., Table 1).

economic damage and political impact occur on the short to medium term but fade away due to economic and political adjustments. The IRFs are useful to communicate such findings, avoid the pretense of accuracy and have an intuitive interpretation. It is also quite possible to show the impacts on all the variables in the model although a focus on a few graphs is preferable from a communication point of view. A danger exists in relying too much on the econometric toolbox. Often important aspects cannot be modelled and therefore sanction assessment is often an art rather than a science.

7.6. Conclusions

With a sample of only two cases, it is of course difficult to generalize, but with this caveat in mind this chapter has still brought several issues to the fore. Our comparative case study has demonstrated the do-ability and versatility of the use of VAR modelling of the economic and political processes of the sanction target simultaneously. Concrete cases can be analyzed on relatively short notice in a transparent framework open for replication. The two cases illustrate that these processes can, to differing degrees, play a role in concrete sanction cases. An important finding of both cases is that the impact of sanctions wanes over time. Sanctions open a window of opportunity to find political solutions, but that window closes after some time. In the case of Iran, the recent history seems to vindicate that *ex ante* research finding (published as a working paper in June 2012);[37] for the case of Russia the jury is still out.

VAR modelling is not a panacea: the requirement data may simply not be available (North Korea is a case in point), the time series may be too short (we can analyze the sanctions against the Russian invasion of the Ukraine in 2021 but cannot build a VAR model for the sanctions against the Russian occupation of the Crimea in 2014). Also, structural breaks may change an economy in such a way that the stability of a modelling exercise is compromised.

7.7. Suggestions for future research

We hope that this chapter stimulates VAR applications to economic sanction cases. At some future point in time when more and more VAR studies of sanction cases become available, research synthesis will move beyond narra-

---

[37] Dizaji S.F., van Bergeijk P.A.G., "Early Phase Success and Long Run Failure of Economic Sanctions: With an Application to Iran", *Institute of Social Studies Working Paper No. 544*, Erasmus University, 2012.

tive reviews of literature (such as the present one) and meta-analysis will become possible so that researchers will be able to assess (a) genuine effects, (b) the impact of heterogeneous methodological characteristics of primary VAR studies and (c) the extent to which political and economic country characteristics contribute to differences in the speed and intensity of the established relationships. Given the data requirements for meta-analysis it should be standard practice to report transparently on data and methodological issues as well as to provide confidence intervals in IRFs.[38] A further avenue for research would be to combine the standard VAR model with panel data techniques making it possible to develop a family of Panel-VAR models to find more general economic and political impact of sanctions on target countries.[39]

A second avenue of research that could be pursued with the use of VARs is the analysis of the impact of sanctions on indicators of human development.[40] This would offer the possibility to analyze in a consistent empirical framework some of the unintended sanction impacts on livelihoods of a population that often has little or nothing to do with the activities of the elite that sanctions try to influence. Indeed, sanctions often violate basic rights. Sanctions tend to increase income inequality[41] and thus, a negative trade-off exists with SDG 10 (reduction of inequality). A potentially negative trade-off also exists for such diverse areas as SDG 2 ('End hunger.'),[42] SDG 4 (education),[43] SDG 5 (gender equality),[44] SDG 3 (health)[45] and SDG 13-15 (envi-

---

[38] See Nguyen M, et al., "Publication Bias in the Price Effects of Monetary Policy: A Meta-Regression Analysis for Emerging and Developing Economies", *International review of economics and finance* (2020), for an example of a metaregression analysis based on IRFs.

[39] Dizaji S.F., Murshed S.M., "External Arms Embargoes and their Implications for Government Expenditure, Democracy and Internal Conflict", *World Development* (2023) (in print).

[40] By their very design, sanctions carry a negative impact on economic growth and employment (SDG 8).20.

[41] Afesorgbor S.K., Mahadevan R., "The impact of economic sanctions on income inequality of target states", *World Development* (2016), 83, 1, 1-11.

[42] Afesorgbor S.K., *Sanctioned to starve? The impact of economic sanctions on food security in targeted states*, in Bergeijk P.A.G. van (ed.), *Research Handbook on Economic Sanctions*, Edward Elgar, 2021, Chapter 23.

[43] Hwami M., "A comparative scoping review of the impact of international economic sanctions on education", *Compare: A Journal of Comparative and International Education* (2021), doi: 10.1080/03057925.2020.1846120.

[44] Drury A.C., Peksen D., "Women and economic statecraft: The negative impact international economic sanctions visit on women", *European Journal of International Relations* (2014), 20, 2, 463-490.

[45] Gutmann J., et al., "Sanctioned to death? The impact of economic sanctions on life expectancy and its gender gap", *Journal of Development Studies* (2021), 57, 1, 139-162.

ronment).[46] The debate about the sign and significance is still ongoing[47] and our modelling strategy could very well help to strengthen the empirical analysis of unintended effects. Indeed, Nowadays, it is widely accepted that the design and implementation of sanctions need to be improved, and their humanitarian costs to ordinary citizens minimized as far as possible. Further empirical research is needed to directly compare smart against traditional sanctions with respect to their impact on human rights. It is also useful to take into account the intensity of sanctions when we are investigating their impact on the government and citizens of target countries as multilateral and unilateral sanctions may have different consequences.

---

[46] Fu Q., et al., "The impact of international sanctions on environmental performance", *Science of The Total Environment* (2020), 745, doi: 10.1016/j.scitotenv.2020.141007.

[47] Gutmann J., et al., "Precision-guided or blunt? The effects of US economic sanctions on human rights", *Public Choice* (2020), 185, 1, 161-182.

Chapter 8
"A FAREWELL TO ARMS": ARMS EMBARGO BUSTING AND THE CHALLENGES OF ARMS EXPORT HARMONIZATION

Keith A. Preble

ABSTRACT: *The EU's Common Position on arms exports (2008/944/CFSP of 8 December 2008) has generated a "race away from Brussels" whereby member states resist efforts to consolidate policy with Brussels and move closer to national policies and interests. This "race away from Brussel" is an effort to reduce EU interference in member states' arms industries, interference that could potentially harm the competitiveness of member states' in this arena while removing a potent foreign policy tool. I theorize that the increased transparency and reporting of arms transfers by member states in response to efforts at harmonizing EU arms export policy have stimulated intra-EU competition. This competitive process – driven by greater information sharing and transparency – has had an impact on the effectiveness of arms embargoes by rendering them less effective at inhibiting arms transfers to states and groups targeted by multilateral arms embargoes. I discuss how arms embargoes are made less effective by EU harmonization policies. The EU's Common Position, which seeks to regulate and rein in arms exports, reflects how calls for greater transparency and centralization of policy may generate negative externalities and undermine the very problem such policies were meant to counter. Member states and their respective arms industries face not only economic competition and pressure due to increasing competition in the arms market but also barriers to carrying out arms trade due to the perception (real or otherwise) of burdensome supranational regulations.*

8.1. Introduction

EU member states are trusted to devise national rules to ensure that arms sales do not find their way into embargoed states, but these weapons still find their way to places barred by the spirit of the Common Position. In total, France, Germany, Italy, Spain, Sweden, and the United Kingdom (before it left the EU) granted permits to countries routinely violating UN sanctions and arms embargo totalling more than 1 billion euro.[1] Arms sales, especially of modern conventional weapons (MCWs), are highly regulated by national governments (as is most military equipment), and export licenses must be granted before transfers can occur.[2] Within the EU (and in most arms producing countries), arms export policies are implemented and enforced at the national level, which allows member states to ignore the EU's Common Position and exploit loopholes with few political or economic consequences.[3]

The Common Position and the former EU Code of Conduct were designed to reduce the flow of arms transfers and harmonize arms exports across a single EU policy, especially when the sale of such weapons undermined international legal commitments and human rights, destabilized "internal situations" of countries where arms were destined, and preserving regional peace, security and stability.[4] Rettman has noted that arms exports from European member states routinely find their way into arms embargoed Libya owing to the lack of oversight within the EU Council in Brussels.[5] Stefano Trevisan has also observed how the European Union (EU) contributes to the arms problem in Libya, noting that "defense companies are untouchable by law… The role of arms-control laws in this organized irresponsibility is neither incidental nor sustainable. Member states' laws and licensing systems structurally enable them to break the arms embargoes that the EU is seeking to enforce."[6] While Trevisan's description of

[1] Rettman A., "Why Do EU Arms End up in Libya despite UN Ban?", *EUobserver*, 24 January 2020, available at https://euobserver.com/foreign/147256.

[2] Stohl R.J., Grillot S., *The International Arms Trade, War and Conflict in the Modern World*, Cambridge-Polity, 2009, 63-69.

[3] Besch S., Oppenheim B., "Up in Arms: Warring over Europe's Arms Export Regime", *Centre for European Reform* (2019), available at https://www.cer.eu/publications/archive/policy-brief/2019/arms-warring-over-europes-arms-export-regime; Hansen S.T., Marsh N., "Normative Power and Organized Hypocrisy: European Union Member States' Arms Export to Libya", *European Security*, 3 April 2015, 24, No. 2: 264-86, available at https://doi.org/10.1080/09662839.2014.967763; Ministerie van Buitenlandse Zaken, "When Do I Need an Export Licence for Military Goods? – Government.Nl", onderwerp (Ministerie van Algemene Zaken, 2021), available at https://www.government.nl/topics/export-controls-of-strategic-goods/question-and-answer/topics/-controls-of-strategic-goods/question-and-answer/when-do-i-need-an-export-licence-for-military-goods; Oppenheim B., "Europe Is at War Over Arms Exports", *Foreign Policy blog* (2019), available at https://foreignpolicy.com/2019/09/18/europe-is-at-war-over-arms-exports/.

[4] European Council, "European Union Code of Conduct on Arms Exports", 1998, available at https://www.europarl.europa.eu/meetdocs/2004_2009/documents/dv/031006codeofconduct1998_/031006codeofconduct1998_en.pdf.

[5] Rettman A., "Why Do EU Arms End up in Libya despite UN Ban?", cit.

[6] Trevisan S.,"Revealed: Loopholes Letting EU Firms "break' Arms Embargoes", *EUobserver*, 25 May 2021, available at https://euobserver.com/investigations/151880.

the problem addresses deficiencies in the system, the EU's Common Position has provided an avenue for some accountability as nongovernmental organizations (NGOs) and civil society groups have filed legal cases in several member states and achieved notable success for selling arms that fuel regional instability and violate international humanitarian law.[7]

While the EU's Common Position is overridden once arms embargoes are imposed, the language of arms embargoes may limit not only *who* might receive arms transfers but also the types of arms that could be transferred. Arms embargoes may not prohibit all military equipment, and equipment not explicitly barred may still be transferred despite the presence of the embargo and still covered by the EU's Common Position. Arms embargoes often do not apply to existing orders or contracts, as well. EU member states may exploit these loopholes and avenues for commerce, which are not explicit violations in the letter of the embargo but still violate the spirit of the embargo. Reports and studies have consistently demonstrated how member states routinely seek exemptions at their respective national levels to the Common Position even when such licenses contravene the principles and spirit of the EU's Common Position.[8] The language of the Common Position itself is at times paradoxical. While urging member states to use caution when exporting to recipient countries, the Common Position simultaneously privileges member states' sovereignty and signals the importance of arms and defense industries to member states in the preamble of the Common Position. Further complicating matters is that these *Common Positions* often "occupy something of a gray zone between legislation and political cooperation" within EU governance.[9] The lack of a formal enforcement mechanism also means that states are relied upon to support the EU's security policies.[10] Thus, EU member states export arms even to embargoed states with few if any consequences, which at their core undermine the effectiveness (if not the spirit) of arms embargoes. Recent reports by the Stockholm International Peace Research Institute (SIPRI) indicate that, since 2011, the European Union accounts for 26% of global exports of modern conventional weapons. During the 2016-2020 period profiled in a

---

[7] Wisotzki S., Mutschler M., "No Common Position! European Arms Export Control in Crisis", *Zeitschrift Für Friedens- Und Konfliktforschung*, 1 October 2021, 10, 2, 282-83, available at https://doi.org/10.1007/s42597-022-00071-x.

[8] Hansen S.T., Marsh N., "Normative Power and Organized Hypocrisy", cit.; Oppenheim B., "Europe Is at War Over Arms Exports", cit.

[9] Dix D.E., "The European Union: Foreign and Security Policy", *CRS Report*, R41959, Congressional Research Service, 2013, 7, available at https://fas.org/sgp/crs/row/R41959.pdf.

[10] *Ibidem*.

recent SIPRI report, France, Germany, the UK (still part of the EU before Brexit), Spain, and Italy account for 22% of global arms exports, a slight uptick from the 2011-2015 period examined in previous reports.[11] European defense industries exist in almost all EU member states with "the bulk of SMEs [small and medium enterprises]" engaged in arms manufacturing located mainly in Austria, Czechia, France, Germany, Italy, Poland, Spain, Sweden, and the United Kingdom."[12] As of 2014, these industries employed over 500,000 individuals and created – directly or indirectly – more than 1.2 million jobs.[13] This level of exports demonstrates the importance that national governments place on arms exports and supporting these industries.

Kranz has argued that the issues related to compliance and arms embargo effectiveness are due to the way that arms embargoes and other restrictive measures (EU sanctions) are designed that privilege national sovereignty where national imperatives take precedence over joint foreign and security policy goals at the EU level.[14] Conversely, Erickson has shown arms embargoes *are effective* at restricting arms to partial and fully embargoed states.[15] I argue that the answer lies somewhere in the middle: arms embargoes are conditionally effective, but the EU's Common Position on arms exports has had an opposite and unintended effect of undermining the effectiveness of arms embargoes. I argue that EU efforts at harmonizing arms export policy through an increase in transparency has undermined the effectiveness of arms embargoes due to increased transfers to embargoed states since the implementation of the EU Common Position in 2008.

I take the position that the Common Position has generated a "race away from Brussels" whereby member states resist efforts to consolidate policy with Brussels and instead move closer to their respective national policies and interests. This "race away from Brussel" is an effort to reduce EU inter-

---

[11] Wezeman P.D., Kuimova A., Wezeman S., "Trends in International Arms Transfers, 2020", *SIPRI Fact Sheet*, Stockholm International Peace Research Institute, 2021, available at https://sipri.org/sites/default/files/2021-03/fs_2103_at_2020.pdf.

[12] Roth A., "The Size and Location of Europe's Defence Industry", *Breugel* (blog) (2017), available at https://www.bruegel.org/2017/06/the-size-and-location-of-europes-defence-industry/; Stockholm International Peace Research Institute (SIPRI), "SIPRI Arms Transfers Database", 2021, available at https://www.sipri.org/databases/armstransfers.

[13] Roth A., "The Size and Location of Europe's Defence Industry", cit.

[14] Kranz K., "European Union Arms Embargoes: The Relationship between Institutional Design and Norms", *Cambridge Review of International Affairs*, 2 July 2016, 29, 3, 970-96, available at https://doi.org/10.1080/09557571.2016.1233938.

[15] Erickson J.L., "Stopping the Legal Flow of Weapons: Compliance with Arms Embargoes, 1981-2004", *Journal of Peace Research*, 1 March 2013, 50, 2, 159-74, available at https://doi.org/10.1177/0022343312470472.

ference in member states' arms industries, interference that could potentially harm the competitiveness of member states' in this arena while removing a potent foreign policy tool. I define harm as the disproportionate gains, real or perceived, that EU member states and their constituents gain or potentially gain over other EU member states and their firms. I theorize that the increased transparency and reporting of arms transfers by member states in response to efforts at harmonizing EU arms export policy have stimulated intra-EU competition. As more information on the activities of competing arms manufacturers and licenses granted (and denied) has become publicly available, increased competition arose, pushing EU member states and their respective arms manufacturers to preserve control over their respective arms export policies of their national governments by "racing away from Brussels" and eschewing greater EU-wide cooperation and control by the EU.

This competitive process – driven by greater information sharing and transparency – has had an impact on the effectiveness of arms embargoes by rendering them less effective at inhibiting arms transfers to states and groups targeted by multilateral arms embargoes. I do not argue here that arms embargoes are ineffective[16] as evidence exists to the contrary.[17] Instead, they are *made less effective* by EU harmonization policies, which undermines arms embargo effectiveness due to greater transparency of arms transfers by member states.

As this "race away from Brussels" begins to accelerate, it reflects efforts by member states to slow or ignore harmonized arms export control policies by taking advantage of and exploiting loopholes in an effort to mitigate potential harms created by the Common Position. The "race away from Brussels," stands in sharp contrast with Holzinger and Sommerer's "race to Brussels," whereby both industry and government benefit through harmonization of standards and increasing delegation.[18] Because increased harmonization of arms exports potentially *harms* both industry (profit margins) and government (loss of access to a critical foreign policy tool) in the

---

[16] Bromley M., Brzoska M., "Towards a Common Restrictive EU Arms Export Policy; The Impact of the EU Code of Conduct on Major Conventional Arms Exports", *European Foreign Affairs Review*, 1 August 2008, 13, 3 available at https://Kluwerlawonline.com/journalarticle/European+Foreign+Affairs+Review/13.3/EERR2008026; Fruchart et al., "United Nations Arms Embargoes: Their Impact on Arms Flows and Target Behaviour", Stockholm International Peace Research Institute and Uppsala Universitet, 2007, 1-56.

[17] Erickson J.L., "Stopping the Legal Flow of Weapons", cit.

[18] Holzinger K., Sommerer T., "'Race to the Bottom' or 'Race to Brussels'? Environmental Competition in Europe: Environmental Competition in Europe", *JCMS: Journal of Common Market Studies* (2011), 49, 2, 315-39, available at https://doi.org/10.1111/j.1468-5965.2010.02135.x.

EU, member states, often at the behest of their national arms industries, resist efforts to harmonize arms exports in an effort to preserve their control and sovereignty over this key aspect of the EU's Common Foreign and Security Policy (CFSP).

This "race away from Brussels" is the result of both greater transparency of arms exports and intra-EU competition among arms manufacturers. This information that member states capture, report, and subsequently make public on their arms export activity exacerbates already present intra-EU competition among arms exporters. If the Common Position has driven an increase in arms exports, there should be a notable change in the average transfer of military equipment from EU member states to embargoed states. I employ SIPRI arms transfer data from 1993-2018 of EU member states and Norway[19] to study arms transfers from EU member states and Norway during three periods: 1993-1997 (Pre-EU Code of Conduct), 1998-2007 (EU Code of Conduct), and 2008-2018 (EU Common Position). I commence the analysis in 1993 since consolidation and internationalization of the European defense industry, a shift in focus to ethically motivated foreign policies and conflict prevention, and Europe's role in the first Persian Gulf War served a three motivating factors for EU-wide policy change.[20] I find that arms exports to embargoed targets increases 74% after the EU's Common Position is implemented. Because there is an increase in the average arms transfers across all three levels, the effects witnessed are unlikely to be solely the result of the commercial opportunities created by network effects generated by arms embargoes.[21]

The EU's Common Position, which seeks to regulate and rein in arms exports, reflects how calls for greater transparency and centralization of policy may generate negative externalities and undermine the very problem

[19] Stockholm International Peace Research Institute (SIPRI), "SIPRI Arms Transfers Database", cit.; Since 1998, Norway has cooperated with the EU on export control, so it is included in the sample. See Norwegian Ministry of Foreign Affairs, "Norwegian exports of defence-related products in 2021, export control and international non-proliferation cooperation", Recommendation of 3 June 2022 from the Ministry of Foreign Affairs, approved in the Counsil of State the same day, available at https://www.regjeringen.no/en/aktuelt/exports_2021/id2917453/.

[20] Bromley M., *The EU Common Position on Arms Exports and National Export Control Policies*, in Bailes A.J.K., Depauw S. (eds.), *The EU Defense Market: Balancing Effectiveness with Responsibility*, Flemish Peace Institute, 2011, 39, available at https://www.sipri.org/sites/default/files/2016-03/Conference-report-EU-defence-market.pdf.

[21] Caruso R., "The Impact of International Economic Sanctions on Trade: An Empirical Analysis", *Peace Economics, Peace Science and Public Policy* (2003), 9, No. 2, 1-37; Bergeijk P.A.G. van, *Economic Diplomacy, Trade, and Commercial Policy: Positive and Negative Sanctions in a New World Order*, Edward Elgar, 1994.

such policies were meant to counter. Member states and their respective arms industries face not only economic competition and pressure due to increasing competition in the arms market but also barriers to carrying out arms trade due to the perception (real or otherwise) of burdensome supranational regulations. The "race away from Brussels" may exist in other policy areas, as well, such as the rise of vaccine nationalism in the EU during the Covid-19 pandemic as well as the hesitancy of member states to accept additional refugees and migrants during the Syrian civil war, warranting further investigation.

8.2. Between the ethics and economics of arms embargoes

Much of the literature on the arms trade addresses the ethical and human rights concerns involved in such transfers. Such approaches focus on the consequences of both unregulated and, in some cases, regulated legal arms trade without properly considering the impetus driving such trade. Some studies have noted that many arms supplying states – such as France, Germany, the UK, and the United States – fail to exercise sufficient export controls, noting that most transfers seek to advance the domestic interests of the arms supplying state to further security and economic interests. [22]

The arms market, however, is not constant and has changed with developments in the international system. Lerna K. Yanik's work has sought to show how the decline of the Cold War has created a buyer's market and largely attributes human rights abuses to how national laws and international norms are structured to allow for arms transfers to embargoed states to occur. [23] Arms exporting states create export controls designed so that such regulations do not inhibit their ability to market and sell products as well as use those products as forms of positive sanctions. Yanik's logic assumes, however, that the "buyer's [export] market" drives sales in sufficient quantities. Such an explanation might imply that arms manufacturers are *desperate* to sell their modern conventional weaponry to whoever has ready cash to purchase. While many arms manufacturers may indeed need the funds that sales generate, such an explanation is insufficient to explain

[22] Perkins R., Neumayer E., "The Organized Hypocrisy of Ethical Foreign Policy: Human Rights, Democracy and Western Arms Sales", *Geoforum*, 1 March 2010, Themed Issue: Mobilizing Policy, 41, 2, 247-56, available at https://doi.org/10.1016/j.geoforum.2009.09.011.

[23] "Guns and Human Rights: Major Powers, Global Arms Transfers, and Human Rights Violations", *Human Rights Quarterly* (2006), 28, 2, 357-88.

the proliferation of MCWs to embargoed states. Given that many buyers often purchase from multiple suppliers,[24] the availability of potential buyers and the need for buyers to diversify their supplies may play an important role in the proliferation of arms.

What is missing from many explanations is how arms manufacturers compete for business and how this competition impacts arms transfers, especially to embargoed states. Europe and the European Union represent an important case for understanding the dynamics of arms export competition, especially when supranationally driven Common Positions with little enforcement power seek to regulate national governments' ability to issue arms export licenses to embargoed and non-embargoed customers. These regulations that promote arms exports reflect shrinking military budgets and defense spending as arms manufacturers rely less on domestic markets for sales and profit. This "dangerous trade" has caused untold human rights abuses, and scholars have sought to highlight the dangers of arms transfers and their effects on human rights in several conflicts.[25]

While arms may represent "big business" for many states,[26] other industries and sectors for many countries are much more profitable. In 2006, conventional arms transfers amounted to nearly $60 billion in 2006, which accounts for only the legal trade in modern conventional weapons. While $60 billion represents significant trade, other forms of legitimate trade generate significantly greater revenue. Oil and gas and agricultural products, for example, generated $1.7 trillion and $852 million, respectively, during the same period.[27] Given the oligopolistic nature of the arms market since the end of the Cold War,[28] the ability of new countries to break into a

[24] Thurner P.W., et al., "Network Interdependencies and the Evolution of the International Arms Trade", *Journal of Conflict Resolution* (2019), 63, 7, 1736-64, available at https://doi.org/10.1177/0022002718801965.

[25] Erickson J.L., *Dangerous Trade: Arms Exports, Human Rights, and International Reputation*, Columbia University Press, 2015.

[26] Amnesty International, Oxfam, and International Action Network on Small Arms, *Arms without Borders: Why a Globalised Trade Needs Global Controls*, Control Arms, 2006, available at https://www.amnesty.org/en/documents/POL34/006/2006/en/; Stockholm International Peace Research Institute (SIPRI), "Global Military Spending Remains High at $1.7 Trillion", 2018, available at https://www.sipri.org/media/press-release/2018/global-military-spending-remains-high-17-trillion.

[27] Stohl R.J., Grillot S., *The International Arms Trade*, cit.

[28] Speers K., Rear Admiral Baker S.H. (ret.), *Economic Arguments for Arms Export Reform*, in Gabelnick T., Stohl R. (eds.), *Challenging Conventional Wisdom: Debunking the Myths and Exposing the Risks of Arms Export Reform*, Center for Defense Information and Federation of American Scientsits, 2003, 53-64.

market and achieve true competition may be exceedingly difficult;[29] this dynamic may explain the importance and support governments provide as both governments and arms manufacturers may be unwilling to lose access to these markets. Yet, it is not unusual for multiple suppliers to sell to a single buyer, a common occurrence throughout the network of the legitimate arms trade. While breaking into a state's market may be difficult, once such a market is broken into, the competition to retain that market may stimulate competition among suppliers of various companies, especially if those suppliers come from different countries.

Are arms embargoes effective under such complex market dynamics?[30] Arms embargoes, a 'smart' or targeted form of economic sanctions are routinely violated.[31] However, they are a frequent international policy that multilateral organizations like the United Nations (UN) and EU utilize to bring an end to inter- and intra-state conflicts, protect human rights, promote democracy, and seek to improve international security.[32] Studying the effects of arms trade and the issues that come with such trade is key for understanding the interaction between foreign policy and economic issues, which may reflect a delicate balance of competing interests.[33] These competing interests may potentially have an impact on the effectiveness of arms embargoes. The literature on the effectiveness of arms embargoes is mixed and intersects with the effectiveness of economic sanctions generally. Economic sanctions are argued by some to be ineffective and unsuccessful[34] while others find that success is conditional on the policy's stated aims and the behaviors seeking the target to cease.[35] Previous studies have employed case studies to explore the effectiveness of arms embargoes, which have in-

---

[29] Stohl R.J., Grillot S., *The International Arms Trade*, cit., 44.

[30] Brzoska M., "Measuring the Effectiveness of Arms Embargoes", *Peace Economics, Peace Science and Public Policy*, 23 January 2008, 14, 2-2, available at https://doi.org/10.2202/1554-8597.1118; Control Arms, *UN Arms Embargoes: An Overview of the Last Ten Years*, Arms, 2006; Erickson J.L., "Stopping the Legal Flow of Weapons", cit.

[31] Moore M., "Arming the Embargoed: A Supply-Side Understanding of Arms Embargo Violations", *Journal of Conflict Resolution* (August 2010), 54, 4, 593-615, available at https://doi.org/10.1177/0022002710369085.

[32] Brzoska M., "Measuring the Effectiveness of Arms Embargoes", cit.

[33] Smith R.P., Tasiran A., "The Demand for Arms Imports", *Journal of Peace Research*, 1 March 2005, 42, 2, 167-81, available at https://doi.org/10.1177/0022343305050689.

[34] Pape R.A., "Why Economic Sanctions Do Not Work", *International Security* (1997), 22, No. 2, 90-136; Pape R.A., "Why Economic Sanctions Still Do Not Work", *International Security* (1998), 23, 1, 66-77, available at https://doi.org/10.2307/2539263.

[35] Elliott K.A., "The Sanctions Glass: Half Full or Completely Empty?", *International Security* (1998), 23, No. 1, 50-65, available at https://doi.org/10.2307/2539262.

dicated that they are frequently violated.[36] However, such violations may not be illegal depending on the nature of the language of the embargo itself. In the UN, members of the UN Security Council often take such steps, as well, to undermine the effectiveness of arms embargoes prior to their implementation by limiting what goods are prohibited.[37] Erickson, however, revisits the efficacy of arms embargoes given their frequency and perceived ineffectiveness. She argues that arms embargoes do have an impact on the sender states' arms exports on average[38] despite the paucity of mechanisms to punish violators and the incentives for arms exporting states to violate embargoes.

Understanding the role of arms embargoes in arms transfer networks (mainly of MCWs) is key to understanding when and if arms embargoes work as their implementers intend. Thurner et al. use temporal exponential random graph models (TERGMs) to describe, explain, and predict the structure and dynamics of international arms trade from 1950 to 2013, although they do not consider how the presence of arms embargoes or other institutional arrangements may alter these networks.[39] Their model, though, demonstrates that political and economic factors play a key role in where arms are directed globally, but that other effects, such as path dependencies resulting from previous exchanges, trade hierarchies, and importer and exporter effects also play a role in shaping these networks. Their work departs from the common approach of dyadic independence, which has largely ignored dependence structures in data. By modeling international trade as a dynamic network, these assumptions are relaxed, which allows for greater explanatory and predictive power across time.[40] Such approaches have the potential to help policymakers understand why arms embargoes fail to inhibit arms transfers, especially from Europe where the concentration of arms manufacturers is significant[41] despite the consolidation that has occurred in the European defense and arms industries.

---

[36] Control Arms, *UN Arms Embargoes: An Overview of the Last Ten Years*, cit.

[37] Fruchart D., et al., "United Nations Arms Embargoes: Their Impact on Arms Flows and Target Behaviour", cit.

[38] Erickson J.L., "Stopping the Legal Flow of Weapons", cit..

[39] Thurner P.W., et al., "Network Interdependencies and the Evolution of the International Arms Trade", cit.

[40] *Ivi*, 1739-40.

[41] Roth A., "The Size and Location of Europe's Defence Industry", cit.

8.3. "Race away from Brussels" and intra-EU competition

The EU Common Position, which became legally binding in 2008, replaced the politically binding European Code of Conduct on arms exports that had been developed in the early 1990s. The creation of the Common Position represents the culmination of initial efforts at meetings in Luxembourg and Lisbon in 1992 and 1992, respectively, to develop a set of "central principles" that would guide the EU toward a common foreign and security policy that promoted development, conflict prevention, and respect for human rights in the run-up to the 1993 Maastricht Treaty.[42]

The Common Position that resulted is a "legally binding set of rules" that EU member states must consider when they issue export licenses, with special considerations made for the respect of human rights in the destinations of the arms exports, the preservation of national and regional stability, as well as the compatibility of the arms exports with the development of the destination country.[43] Before the Common Position was adopted in 2008, no legally binding set of rules existed, only politically binding ones from the EU Code of Conduct on arms exports agreed upon in 1998, which was the direct result of meetings from 1991 and 1992 in Luxembourg and Lisbon.[44]

I develop a theory of a "race away from Brussels" to explain why the EU's Common Position on arms exports implemented in 2008 render arms embargoes less effective. I posit that in situations where policy coordination brings *harm* to either business and government, EU member states avoid harmonization and policy coordination and thus "race away from Brussels" by avoiding the divestment of control over a particular policy. Member states reduce potential *harm* by resisting harmonization and maintaining control over a specific policy area.

[42] Cops D., Duquet N., *Reviewing the EU Common Position on Arms Exports: Whither EU Arms Transfer Controls?*, Flemish Peace Institute, 2019, 2, available at https://vlaamsvredesinstituut.eu/wp-content/uploads/2019/12/VI_policy-brief_EU_arms_export_2019highres.pdf.

[43] European Parliament, "EU Arms Exports: Need for More Control and Transparency", September 17, 2020, available at https://www.europarl.europa.eu/news/en/press-room/20200910IPR86831/eu-arms-exports-need-for-more-control-and-transparency.

[44] European Council, "European Union Code of Conduct on Arms Exports", cit.

Figure 8.1. Diagram depicting the "race away from Brussels" or "race to Brussels"

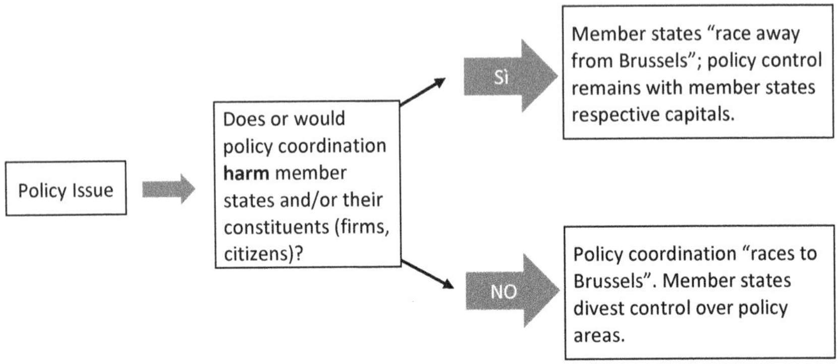

Source: created by the author.

Harm can be defined quite broadly and does not necessarily reflect any threat to the survival of the state or business (although it ostensibly could). I define harm as disproportionate gains on the part of one or more member states or their constituents over other EU member states and their constituents in the EU. When coordinating on a policy leads to harm via disproportionate gains, then member states will "race away from Brussels" and preserve policy control within their respective national governments. Thus, harm may reflect instances where the *relative gains matter* and reflects a classic "relative gains" problem in international relations.[45] When the harm is minimal or at least acceptable or EU policy operates in such a way that mitigates the impact of relative gains, then member states embrace policy coordination and "race to Brussels" as member states divest control over a particular policy area.

The "race to Brussels" is indicative of how member states may be concerned mainly with absolute gains in some policy contexts when policy coordination is successful in mitigating harm.[46] This logic helps to explain the puzzle of why greater information through increased transparency can also undermine cooperation policies. The shift from the EU Code of Conduct

[45] Grieco J., Powell R., Snidal D., "The Relative-Gains Problem for International Cooperation", *American Political Science Review* (September 1993), 87, 3, 727-43, available at https://doi.org/10.2307/2938747; Powell R., "Absolute and Relative Gains in International Relations Theory", *The American Political Science Review* (1991), 85, 4, 1303-20, available at https://doi.org/10.2307/1963947.

[46] Keohane R.O., *Institutional Theory and the Realist Challenge after the Cold War*, in Baldwin D.A. (ed.), *Neorealism and Neoliberalsm: The Contemporary Debate*, Columbia University Press, 1993, 269-300.

to the Common Position on arms exports serves as a crucial case for understanding this dynamic, although areas where member states seek to preserve control has been observed in other policy areas, such as immigration, energy policy (particular energy imports from Russia), and 'vaccine nationalism' during the Covid-19 pandemic.[47]

Both the EU Code of Conduct and Common Position set the stage for greater transparency in the reporting of arms exports even if member states varied in the level of detail and information they initially provided to the European Commission. The Common Position resulted in an increase (on average) in the share of countries providing full reports, making even greater information available on their respective arms exports. Bromley and Bauer and Bromley have described efforts at improving annual reporting by EU member states through better sharing of information.[48] Bromley shows that between 2008-2010, reporting of arms transfers improves relative to the EU Code of Conduct as the share of EU members submitting complete reports increases. Other improvements in transparency can be evidenced by the increase in the length of the reports from just 4 pages in 1999 to over 550 pages by 2018, as member states provide more information on their arms transfers.[49] As the Common Position has made reporting more transparent and competitive pressures already present have intensified,[50] EU member states have been reluctant to give up control over

---

[47] Celi G., et al., "The Asymmetric Impact of War: Resilience, Vulnerability and Implications for EU Policy", *Intereconomics* (May 2022), 57, 3, 141-47, available at https://doi.org/10.1007/s10272-022-1049-2; Lavenex S., *Common Market, Normative Power or Super-State? Conflicting Political Identities in EU Asylum and Immigration Policy*, in Saurugger S., Thatcher M. (eds.), *Constructing the EU's Political Identity*, Springer Nature Switzerland, 2022, 109-26, available at https://doi.org/10.1007/978-3-031-17407-0_7; Evenett S.J., et al., "The Covid-19 Vaccine Production Club: Will Value Chains Temper Nationalism?", Policy Research Working Paper, World Bank, March 2021.

[48] Bauer S., Bromley M., *The European Union Code of Conduct on Arms Exports: Improving the Annual Report*, Stockholm International Peace Research Institute, 2004, available at https://www.sipri.org/publications/2004/sipri-policy-papers/european-union-code-conduct-arms-exports-improving-annual-report; Bromley M., *The Review of the EU Common Position on Arms Exports: Prospects for Strengthened Controls*, Non-Proliferation Papers, EU Non-Proliferation Consortium, 2012.

[49] Bromley M., *The Review of the EU Common Position on Arms Exports: Prospects for Strengthened Controls*, cit., 8; European Union, *Annual Report in Conformity with Operative Provision 8 of the European Union Code of Conduct on Arms Exports (1999/C 315/01)*, European Union, 1999; European Union, *Twenty-First Annual Report According to Article 8(2) of Council Common Position 2008/944/CFSP Defining Common Rules Governing the Control of Exports of Military Technology and Equipment*, European Union, 2019.

[50] Bauer S., Bromley M., *The European Union Code of Conduct on Arms Exports:*

the granting (and denial) of arms export licenses. Arms export harmonization through policies like the Common Code of Conduct and the EU Common Position highlight disparities in how EU member states adhere to these agreements as well as how other member states perceive compliance by competing member states. The coalition agreement created by the Netherlands' new government in 2022, which comprised the People's Party for Freedom and Democracy (VVD); the Democrats 66 (D66); the Christian Democratic Appeal (CDA); and the Christian Union (CU), highlighted an increased focus on international trade and investment, export controls, and sanctions. Of particular note was the coalition's platform on defense, which called for the new coalition "[to pledge] to ensure vital defence sector in the Netherlands and to level the playing field in the EU."[51] Further, a SIPRI report from 2012 also highlighted how "[it] is common practice among national defense industry representatives to complain that the governments of other member states are interpreting the criteria of the EU Common Position less strictly than their own, leading to a loss of competitive advantage."[52] This response to this perceived loss of national competitive advantage of domestic arms industries results in increased competition, and the sharing of information provides governments and their respective constituents with the requisite information to know *when* member states are interpreting the Common Position's criteria less strictly.

The "divergences in governmental 'interpretations'" have often led to the export of arms "in clear contradiction of the fundamental EU Code Criteria" where said arms exports have been used by actors engaging in human rights violations as well as potential violations of international humanitarian law.[53] If the Dutch coalition platform and insights from arms industry representatives discussed above represents the norm among political parties and interest groups within EU member states, then it is likely that the increased transparency, which was meant to increase accountability of arms transfers, has instead generated negative externalities

Improving the Annual Report, cit.; Bromley S., *The Review of the EU Common Position on Arms Exports: Prospects for Strengthened Controls*, cit.

[51] BenninkAmar Advocaten, "New Dutch Government Sworn in: What Does It Mean for International Trade, Export Controls and Sanctions?", 10 January 2022, available at https://batradelaw.com/new-dutch-government-sworn-in-what-does-it-mean-for-international-trade-export-controls-and-sanctions/.

[52] Bromley M., *The Review of the EU Common Position on Arms Exports: Prospects for Strengthened Controls*, cit., 7.

[53] Amnesty International, *Undermining Global Security: The European Union's Arms Exports: A Report*, Amnesty International, 2004.

that often lead to the export of arms to countries outside the parameters of the EU's Common Position on arms exports. To reduce the impact of relative gains and reduce harms caused by policy coordination, EU member states have sought to shift the decision-making locus from Brussels to their respective capitals and undermined the effectiveness of arms embargoes.

8.4. Measuring arms transfers

To measure the transfer of arms, I utilize SIPRI's trend-indicator value (TIV). I construct a data set containing MCW transfers from European countries beginning with the signing of the Treaty of European Union in 1993 through 2018 using data from SIPRI's Arms Transfer Database. The data set contains 26,927 observations across 1040 dyads with each year capturing a potential transfer of arms. I measure arms transfers using SIPRI's trend-indicator value (TIV), and each dyad consists of an EU member state or European country (for those not yet EU members) and arms importing state. Data on multilateral arms embargoes utilizes SIPRI's arm embargo data available on SIPRI's website that captures UN, EU, and other multilateral arms embargoes.[54]

TIV, according to SIPRI methodology, is calculated using the unit production costs of weapons that are commonly sold by arms exporters. It *does not* represent the financial value of the transfer (as is typical with conventional trade flows) but rather "the transfer of military resources."[55] The more arms that are exported from arms producers to importing arms buyers, the greater the transfer of military resources. The TIV may also be adjusted as needed for used weapons or weapons that may have been in service in one country's military and resold later to another. The measurement developed by SIPRI serves as a common unit of measurement to capture the flow of arms from one country to another or from one country to a nonstate actor, such as a rebel group. Several studies on arms embargoes have also utilized SIPRI's TIV as a continuous dependent variable to capture changes in arms transfers between states as well as the effectiveness of arms embargoes.[56]

---

[54] Stockholm International Peace Research Institute (SIPRI), "Arms Embargoes", 2019, available at https://www.sipri.org/databases/embargoes.

[55] Holtom P., Bromley M., Simmel V., *Measuring International Arms Transfers*, SIPRI Fact Sheet, Stockholm International Peace Research Institute, 2012, 2, available at https://www.sipri.org/sites/default/files/files/FS/SIPRIFS1212.pdf.

[56] Erickson J.L., "Stopping the Legal Flow of Weapons", cit.; Moore M., "Arming the Embargoed", cit.

SIPRI's TIV *is not* a measure of the financial value of the arms transfer and "neither reflects the actual price paid for weapons nor represents current dollar values for arms transfers." [57] Instead, the trend-indicator value is a pricing system that captures the volume of deliveries of MCWs and associated components that serves as a common unit of measure. The measure is meant to operationalize military capability rather than a financial value in what SIPRI researchers call a military capability price index. Higher values reflect the transfer of greater military capabilities. [58] SIPRI's TIV has also been utilized by other researchers investigating arms embargoes. [59]

8.5. Harmonization, transparency and arms embargo efficacy

Arms embargoes come in two types: partial and full arms embargoes. The effectiveness of arms embargoes is examined across the two types as both reflect different policy goals and aims. Partial arms embargoes are those in which arms can be exported to an embargoed state but only for specific recipients in a country targeted by the embargo. These arms embargoes permit weapons to recognized governments (as in the case of Somalia) but do not permit the export to other groups in the country. Full arms embargoes are blanket embargoes of all arms transfers to all parties in a region. [60] However, the types of military goods and equipment prohibited is highly dependent upon the language of the embargo itself and often excludes contracts that have already been signed and authorized.

Arms embargoes can change after implementation, as well. The arms embargo initially imposed on Rwanda, for example, cut off all transfers of arms to the entire country but was later relaxed to permit sales of arms to UN-sanctioned governmental entities. Sometimes partial and full arms embargoes can spillover and apply to neighboring countries to restrict the flow of arms to conflict zones to limit the transfer of arms from countries near conflict zones.

---

[57] Holtom P., Bromley M., Simmel V., *Measuring International Arms Transfers*, cit.

[58] *Ivi*, 1-2.

[59] Erickson J.L., "Stopping the Legal Flow of Weapons", cit.; Moore M., "Arming the Embargoed", cit.

[60] Tierney D., "Irrelevant or Malevolent? UN Arms Embargoes in Civil Wars", *Review of International Studies* (2005), 31, 4, 645-64.

Figure 8.2. Mean Trend Indicator Value (TIV) of modern conventional weapons exports by EU member states and Norway to all importing states as reported by SIPRI[61] between 1993-2018

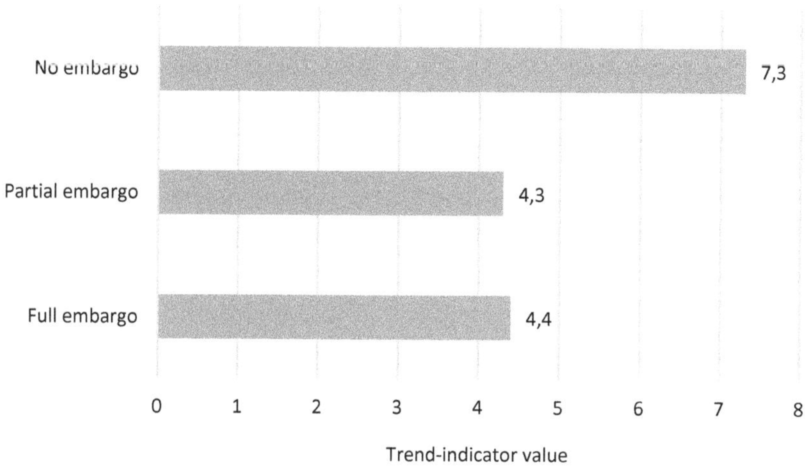

Source: figure created by the author.

On the surface, arms embargoes appear to limit the transfer of MCWs by EU member states between 1993-2018. Figure 8.2 shows the average arms exports measured using SIPRI's TIV across three embargo levels (no embargo, partial, and full arms embargo), and, at first glance, arms embargoes appear effective at reducing trade to embargoed targets. Figure 8.3, on the other hand, shows the average TIV across different embargoes levels across three periods: pre-EU Code of Conduct (1993-1997), EU Code of Conduct (1998-2007), and EU Common Position (2008-2018). When cross-tabulated across these periods (2008-2018), arms to embargoed states nearly doubled compared to the pre-Code of Conduct period. Relative to the EU Code of Conduct, transfers to embargoed states once the EU Common Position is in effect increases 74% compared to the EU Code of Conduct (Figure 8.3a).

The average transfer of MCWs *increases* in the presence of both partial and full arms embargoes *after* the Common Position on arms exports enters into force. What accounts for the increase in the average TIV across levels of arms embargoes? Kranz has argued that normative developments have been unsuccessful at overcoming the required consen-

[61] Stockholm International Peace Research Institute (SIPRI), *SIPRI Arms Transfers Database*, cit.

sus within the CFSP. These normative developments embodied in both the EU Code of Conduct and the Common Position[62] have sought to place human rights and development front and center in evaluating whether arms export licenses are warranted. While the inability of these normative developments at reducing the flow of arms is a necessary cause, it is insufficient in explaining why the average arms transfers (TIV) to embargoed states have *increased* since the Common Position went into force in 2008.

Figure 8.3a. Mean trend-indicator value (TIV) of modern conventional weapons exports by EU members and Norway as reported by SIPRI (1993-2018) to embargoed states

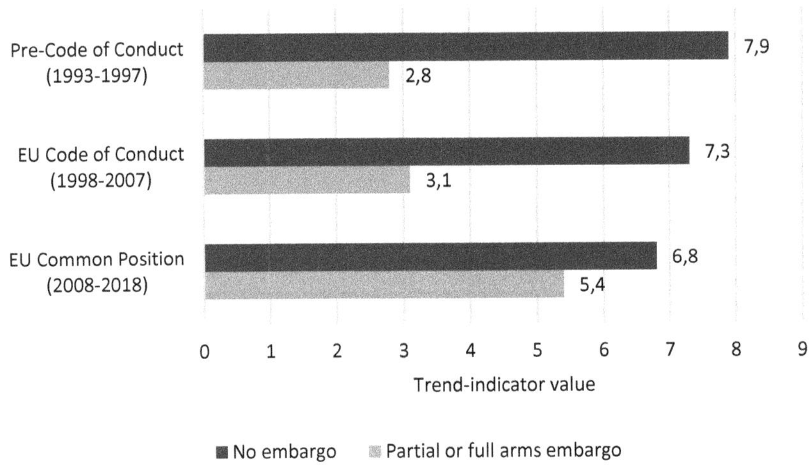

Source: figure created by the author.

[62] European Council, "European Union Code of Conduct on Arms Exports", cit.; Council of the European Union, "Council Common Position 2008/944/CESP of December 8 2008 Defining Common Rules Governing Control of Exports of Military Technology and Equipment", L 3 35/99 § (2008).

Figure 8.3b. Mean trend-indicator value (TIV) of modern conventional weapons exports by EU members and Norway as reported by SIPRI (1993-2018) across partial and full embargoes

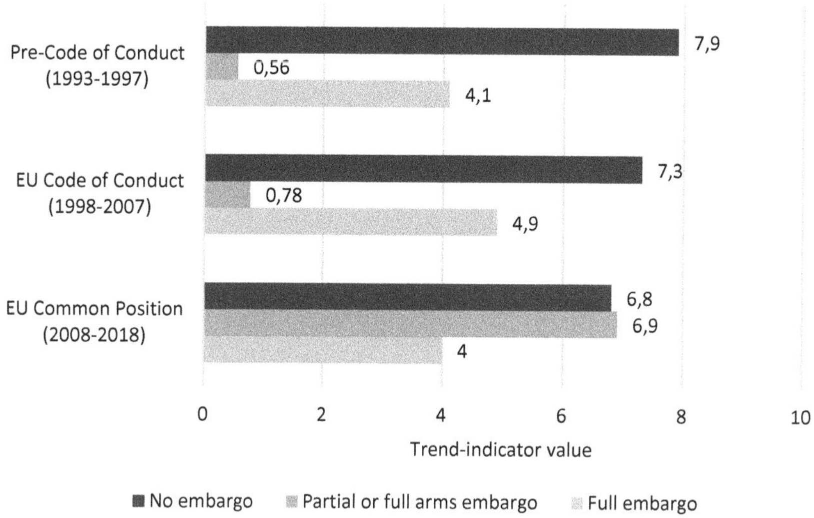

Source: figure constructed by the author.

Disaggregating trade across embargoed states provides a more complete picture of the impact of the Common Position (Figure 8.3b). Full arms embargoes are more often targeted on state actors to slow or halt interstate aggression or to restrict the flows of weapons to state and non-state actors operating in a particular region. For example, the arms embargo imposed on Rwanda first targeted not only the territory of Rwanda but later also targeted neighboring states. The average transfer during the Common Position to fully embargoed targets decreases by 900,000 TIV (0.9) or 18% from the prior period, reversing an 18% increase in trade to fully embargoed targets during the period of the EU Code of Conduct This modest decrease may reflect how member states interpret arms embargoes or even the definition of what constitutes "arms" in different ways to circumvent the prohibition against such transfers. The presence of arms embargoes may allow European manufacturers to seek better terms of trade, thus reaping higher prices for modern conventional weapons despite the "buyers' market" [63] – a dynamic more pronounced under a full embargo where the political costs of fulfilling orders and transfer-

[63] Yanik L.K., "Guns and Human Rights: Major Powers, Global Arms Transfers, and Human Rights Violations", *Human Rights Quarterly*, 2006, 28, 2, 357-88.

ring arms are much higher and riskier. This slight increase in the TIV may indicate that only states well-positioned to absorb the political and economic costs can successfully violate a full embargo against another state actor.

The partial arms embargo creates new commercial opportunities as legitimate sales to support the government or local police may be permitted, which may explain why there is a significantly larger increase in arms export during partial embargoes versus full arms embargoes. Figure 8.3b shows that the increase in arms transfers in the Common Position period is largely driven by transfers to partially embargoed target states, which increased eightfold since the EU Code of Conduct was replaced by the Common Position. Partial arms embargoes permit transfers of some military equipment and not others. Thus, arms manufacturers may push to capitalize on the increased demand for transfers that *are permitted*, especially if they seek to head off the competition and work to avoid being cornered out of such markets made more lucrative by the imposition of the embargo. The huge increase in the average TIV for partial embargoes *after* the imposition of the Common Position (Figure 8.3b) may reflect two trends. First, partial arms embargoes may be easier to implement and may be the more preferred policy choice by EU member states, especially if unanimity among European members is required. Partial arms embargoes may provide more opportunities to exploit and create loopholes in these sanctions. Second, the implementation of partial arms embargoes has become the more common form of arms embargo over time.

The competition among arms manufacturers in Europe is driven both by the type of instrument employed – whether the embargo is full or partial – as well as by the institutional EU efforts to limit arms transfers. Evidence at the national level has demonstrated a discontinuity in the arms export control processes in the EU.[64] An unintended consequence of the Common Position has been an increase of arms transfers to embargoed targets and further discontinuity with the EU's CFSP, reflecting a lack of cohesion among EU member states when economic and political incentives dominate.

---

[64] Maletta G., *Legal Challenges to EU Member States' Arms Exports to Saudi Arabia: Current Status and Potential Implications*, Commentary/Backgrounders, Stockholm International Peace Research Institute, 2019, available at https://www.sipri.org/commentary/topical-backgrounder/2019/legal-challenges-eu-member-states-arms-exports-saudi-arabia-current-status-and-potential; Maletta G., "Seeking a Responsible Arms Trade to Reduce Human Suffering in Yemen", *The International Spectator*, 2 January 2021, 56, 1, 73-91, available at https://doi.org/10.1080/03932729.2021.1876862.

8.6. Conclusion

There is a significant disconnect in the practice[65] of setting "high common standards" and strengthening efforts "to prevent the export of military technology and equipment, which might be used for internal repression or international aggression or contribute to regional instability."[66] Media reports profiling how arms exports by European companies destabilize Libya and other conflict zones provide strong empirical evidence of the Common Position's impact. The Common Position enables European and EU member states to exploit loopholes in the common position and take advantage of the commercial opportunities arms embargoes have created in the highly competitive EU arms market.

Much more needs to be done to harmonize EU efforts at both reining in arms manufacturers while simultaneously supporting the "...wish of Member States to maintain a defence industry as part of their industrial base."[67] Increasing the quantity and quality of information on the arms exports conducted throughout the EU potentially exacerbates the relative gains problem and may accelerate a drive away from a centralized EU policy on arms exports. The Common Position of 2008 with its contradictory support for export control while simultaneously privileging robust arms industries may also explain the lack of enforcement mechanisms to bind members to a single supranational policy. Further, the lack of competences at the supranational level means that each member state is responsible for assessing export license applications on a case-by-case basis, but these assessments may be unduly influenced by the increasing quality and quantity of information available through annual reporting.

The lack of policy congruence between the EU and its member states in this area has allowed member states to prioritize the competitiveness of their respective arms industries as they "race away from Brussels." While both the EU Code of Conduct and the EU's Common Position had annual reporting requirements, reporting requirements since 2008 have resulted in significantly greater transparency. While EU member states are pledged not to use the data they share to improve their competitive positions, the Exports Director of the Defence Manufacturer's Association and Secretary

---

[65] Rettman A., "Why Do EU Arms End up in Libya despite UN Ban?", cit. Trevisan, "Revealed: Loopholes Letting EU firms 'break' arms embargoes", cit.

[66] Council of the European Union, Council Common Position 2008/944/CESP of December 8 2008 defining common rules governing control of exports of military technology and equipment.

[67] Council of the European Union, 335/99.

of the Export Group for Aerospace and Defense, in testimony given before the UK's House of Commons in 2006, noted that "there are always going to be discrepancies in decision making between the national governments on export license applications which they receive from their companies." [68]

These discrepancies may reflect the perception of lost markets and customers, furthering "a race away from Brussels" as member states privilege their own arms industries and market position to preserve a key economic sector while undermining cohesion in this critical common CFSP area. Further, these discrepancies may further demonstrate an example of a policy area in which an international institution, with its reliable and near "perfect" information, may undermine both cooperation and the perceived effectiveness of arms embargoes.

[68] Bromley M., *The Review of the EU Common Position on Arms Exports: Prospects for Strengthened Controls*, see note 53, specifically the reference to Salzman B, "Exports Director of the Defence Manufacturer's Association and Secretary of the Export Group for Aerospace and Defence, Evidence before the British House of Commons Quadripartite Select Committee", 31 January 2006.

Chapter 9

DEMOCRATIC SANCTIONS IN AFRICA. A REASSESSMENT OF THEIR SELECTIVE AND INCONSISTENT USE ACROSS MULTIPLE SENDERS

Tiziana Corda

ABSTRACT: *When it comes to sanctions, Africa plays a major, albeit often overlooked, role. Not only is it a primary target of these measures, but it is also a primary sender of them. African regimes have been frequently targeted by unilateral as well as multilateral sanctions even since before the latter became in higher demand after the end of the Cold War. Since the early 2000s, they have also become active senders in their own region, as several African regional organizations began imposing democratic sanctions against local regimes. While such developments have been largely praised, the recently growing inconsistencies in their application at a time of a return of coups and close authoritarianism across the continent demand a reassessment of their use. Looking at all the democratic sanctions imposed in Africa by regional and extra-regional actors since the 1990s, this chapter aims to examine the factors that influence their imposition in the region, exposing variations in their selective use across senders, and reflecting on the causes of recent inconsistencies.*

9.1. Introduction

Why are democratic sanctions imposed on some African autocrats but not on others? Is this selective use on the rise, with what consequences on Africa's democracy? This chapter contributes to the literature on the selective targeting of democratic sanctions and on regional organizations by examining the factors that influence the imposition of these sanctions in Africa across multiple senders. Differently from most existing works on selective targeting, this chapter's contribution aims to expand the spectrum of the senders under investigation also to intra-regional organizations in addition to traditional extra-regional senders. Africa is evidently an interesting object of such analysis not only for being one of the least democratic regions in the world with a rising number of episodes of autocratization,[1] but also for hosting both intra-regional and extra-regional senders of democratic sanctions aiming at promoting democratic processes in the region.

This inclusion allows us not only to examine whether Africa confirms the literature's theoretical expectations about the selective targeting of democratic sanctions, an issue relevant also for discussions on sanction success,[2] but also to test additional hypotheses related to the potentially different behaviour of intra-regional senders, thus providing this literature with original comparative insights on how selectivity varies across different senders. As further explained below, we should expect intra-regional senders to be more attentive to norm violations in their own region than extra-regional ones, thus intervening more consistently and less selectively. However, in a region still rife with autocratic rulers such as Africa, we should also assume that such democratic norm violations they are more attentive to are only those which subscribe to a minimalist definition of democracy. On top of this, the international context remains relevant, with the rise of global authoritarian powers creating costs to democratic sanctions imposition, including in Africa, with possible effects on both extra- and intra-regional actors' behaviour.

The chapter explores these expectations with a systematic analysis of thirty years of democratic sanction imposition in Africa. Overall, the results of the analysis confirm some expectations but also provide some original insights. The visibility of democratic violations remains a significant trigger for any sender, with the strongest effect for an intra-regional actor such as the African Union. The analysis also shows this response has certainly manifested growing inconsistencies after 2014. This practice is argued to be due to some limits and ambiguities in the AU's normative framework and to an international environment increasingly more averse to the promotion of democratic norms. Although the analysis shows these inconsistencies are not yet significantly different from the period before 2014, major concerns remain regarding their effects on Africa's democracy on the longer term.

The rest of the chapter proceeds as follows. The next section situates this contribution in the literatures on selective imposition and on regional

---

[1] After years of decline, scholars registered ten new coups in 2017-22 globally, all but one taking place in Africa. Cf. Powell J., Thyne C.L., "Global instances of coups from 1950 to 2010: A new dataset", *Journal of Peace Research* (2011), 48, 2, 249-259 (data version "V2022.11.07").

[2] Nooruddin I., "Modeling Selection Bias in Studies of Sanctions Efficacy", *International Interactions* (2002), 28, 1, 59-75.

organizations. On this basis, it formulates the hypotheses applied to the African context. Next, using one of the most up-to-date sanction datasets available, it first maps the different senders active in Africa for democracy-related objectives. Then, it systematically compares the factors that may affect the likelihood of democratic sanction imposition in Africa across these different senders, with a distinctive focus on intra-regional ones, most notably the African Union. The discussion of the results reflects on the causes of selective imposition and of recent inconsistences, both in light of limits set by intra-regional senders' legal frameworks and of evolving features of the international environment. The conclusions highlight some ongoing sanctions-related reforms in African regional organizations which can improve selectivity and inconsistency issues alike.

9.2. Contribution to the literatures on selective imposition and regional organizations

Scholars have long discussed the internal and external causes of the global third wave of democratization, which finally reached large swathes of the African continent in the 1990s.[3] Among them was the role of foreign pressure and sanctions that extra-regional actors – mostly Western ones – imposed more and more frequently after the end of the Cold War to promote democratic principles.[4] Over the 1990s, the use of democratic sanctions to counter authoritarianism has in fact grown across the whole world. However, "there [was] a general suspicion [...] that Western leaders use them selectively" given that "some of the most autocratic regimes with the poorest human rights records have escaped international sanctions, whereas several more competitive and liberal regimes have been subjected to repeated sanction episodes".[5] To solve this puzzle, von Soest and Wahman (2015) investigated the selective targeting of US and EU democratic sanctions on authoritarian regimes globally, to find that the likelihood of these Western senders' coercive response was influenced by the highly disruptive nature of the violations of democratic norms, as well as by the vulnerability

[3] Schraeder P.J., "Understanding the "Third Wave" of Democratization in Africa", *The Journal of Politics* (1995), 57, 4, 1160-1168.

[4] Escribà-Folch A., Wright, J., "Dealing with tyranny: International sanctions and the survival of authoritarian rulers", *International studies quarterly* (2010), 54, 2, 335-359.

[5] von Soest C., Wahman M., "Not all dictators are equal: Coups, fraudulent elections, and the selective targeting of democratic sanctions", *Journal of Peace Research* (2015), 52, 1, 17-31.

of the target and the lack of strong political and economic links between the latter and the senders.

As their study and other works on selective targeting largely focused only on Western senders,[6] there are some aspects of this research strand that remain to be addressed. One is precisely a comparative analysis inclusive of intra-regional senders. The broader literature on sanctions has long overlooked these actors, except for the EU, a sui-generis regional organization which imposes sanctions also on non-member targets. Over the past few decades, many regional organizations (ROs) across the world – such as the African Union in Africa but also the Organization of American States in Latin America, among others[7] – have developed legal frameworks and coercive instruments such as sanctions to react to their members' norm violations, including democratic ones. Certainly, African regional organizations' leading role in this did not remain unnoticed and, in recent past, has rather captured growing scholarly attention investigating the different legitimacy bases and logics behind the African Union's use of sanctions.[8] What is

---

[6] In addition to von von Soest C., Wahman M., *op. cit.*, see for instance on Africa also Del Biondo K., "Donor Interests or Developmental Performance? Explaining Sanctions in EU Democracy Promotion in Sub-Saharan Africa", *World Development* (2015), 75, 74-84; Saltnes J.D., "The European Union's human rights policy: Is the EU's use of the human rights clause inconsistent?", *Global Affairs* (2018), 4 (2-3), 277-89. Other works which do include regional organizations do so in relation to UN sanctions only; see for instance von Borzyskowski I., Portela C., "Global Governance From Below: Regional Sanctions as Drivers of UN Sanctions", *Journal of Conflict Resolution* (2023), 0(0), available at https://doi.org/10.1177/00220027231153565.

[7] von Borzyskowski I., Portela C., *Sanctions Cooperation and Regional Organizations*, in Aris S., Snetkov A., Wenger A. (eds.), *Interorganizational Relations in International Security*, Routledge, 2018, 240-261; Hellquist E., Palestini S., "Regional sanctions and the struggle for democracy: Introduction to the special issue", *International Political Science Review* (2021), 42, 4, 437-45; Hohlstein F., *Regional Organizations and their Responses to Coups,* Bristol University Press, 2022.

[8] Eriksson M., *Supporting Democracy in Africa - African Union's use of Targeted Sanctions to deal with Unconstitutional Changes of Government*, FOI, Swedish Defence Research Agency, 2010; Omorogbe E.Y., "A club of incumbents? The African Union and *coups d'état*", *Vanderbilt Journal of Transnational Law* (2011), 44, 123-54; Charron A., *Sanctions and Africa: United Nations and regional responses*, in Boulden J., *Responding to conflict in Africa*, Palgrave Macmillan, 2013, 77-98; Witt A., "Convergence on Whose Terms? Reacting to Coups d'État in Guinea and Madagascar", *African Security* (2013), 6, 3-4, 257-275; Souaré I.K., "The African Union as a norm entrepreneur on military coups d'état in Africa (1952-2012): an empirical assessment", *The Journal of Modern African Studies* (2014), 52, 1, 69-94; Charron A., Portela, C., "The UN, regional sanctions and Africa", *International Affairs* (2015), 91, 6, 1369-1385; Nathan L., *A survey of mediation in African coups*, African Peacebuilding Network, APN Working Papers no 15, 2017; Hellquist E., "Regional sanctions as peer review: The African Union against Egypt (2013) and Sudan (2019)", *International Political Science Review* (2021), 42, 4,

missing, though, is a comparative assessment of the factors that, across the multiple senders active in Africa, influence their imposition. This chapter aims precisely to bring together these two strands of the sanction literature, on selective imposition and on regional organizations, to systematically compare selectivity and inconsistency issues in the imposition of democratic sanctions in Africa across regional and extra-regional senders.

9.3. African peculiarities and the role of regional organizations: hypotheses and research design

When thinking of selectivity issues across regional and extra-regional senders in Africa, two major considerations come to mind. The first concerns the target, namely the consideration that the marginalization of Africa on the global stage may influence selectivity issues in a different way than other more central regions; the second concerns senders and, most notably, the fact that reactions of intra-regional and external senders active in the region may be influenced by different triggers to varying extents. The following paragraphs elaborate one hypothesis for each consideration, with an additional third hypothesis related to the role of the international context.

First of all, the African region stands out for some structural conditions that may influence the imposition of democratic sanctions more than elsewhere: rhetoric aside, most African regimes remain marginal in global powers' strategies, economically weak, and institutionally fragile. As these conditions are generally expected to increase their political and economic vulnerability to external pressure,[9] while decreasing the costs for the senders, we should expect a higher likelihood of democratic sanctions imposition especially from Western democratic senders such as the EU and US, certainly for highly-visible democratic violations, as inaction before such events would generate high audience costs, but also for more discreet violations because of the little costs they would incur, hence challenging some of the literature's previous findings.[10] As a result, we can expect that:

> **H1:** *In Africa, even less visible violations of democratic norms are likely to positively influence the imposition of democratic sanctions, especially in the case of Western senders.*

451-468; Hellquist E., *The African Union in a World of Sanctions,* in Charron A., Portela C., *Multilateral Sanctions Revisited,* McGill-Queen's University Press, 2022.

[9] Levitsky S., Way L., "Linkage versus leverage: rethinking the international dimension of regime change", *Comparative Politics* (2006), 38, 4, 379-400.

[10] von Soest C., Wahman M., "Not all dictators are equal", cit.

Today, African regional organizations are also endowed with the ability to impose sanctions against member states. The creation of the African Union in 2000-2002 radically changed Africa's ability to promote democracy and good governance on the continent through coercive means.[11] Its predecessor the Organization of African Unity (OAU) had largely remained indifferent to democratic violations in Africa. The only sanctions imposed by the OAU were those against *apartheid* regimes in South Africa and Rhodesia, which were also those very two single cases that the UN was ever able to target during the Cold War worldwide. Only the creation of a new organization (precisely the African Union in 2000-2002) with new legal frameworks eventually changed the continent's ability to impose sanctions, including those to sustain democratic norms.[12]

Upon and following the creation of the African Union (AU), African states adopted four key legal instruments which are generally considered the basis for AU's sanctioning behaviour: the 2000 Constitutive Act; the 2000 Lomé Declaration; the 2002 Protocol Relating to the Establishment of the Peace and Security Council (PSC) of the African Union; the 2007 African Charter on Democracy, Elections and Governance (ACDEG, or Addis Charter).[13] These documents authorise the AU assembly or, since 2004, also the more agile, 15-member-strong PSC to suspend or sanction with further measures state authorities, and those who supported them, who violated the constitutional order of their countries. The violations listed in these documents are not extensively detailed (more on this in the discussion) but broadly speaking concern the replacement of elected governments by violent means, including coups, as well as the refusal of incumbents to relinquish power to the winning party after free and fair elections, and constitutional manipulations, potentially including also those related to term limits. Given these developments, the African Union is the most important intra-regional actor on the continent as long as democratic sanctions are concerned.

Regarding the behaviour of such a major intra-regional actor, we can expect that its proximity to African targets and the higher level of legitimacy it enjoys to the eyes of member states compared to extra-regional ones should make this intra-regional sender more attentive to democratic viola-

[11] Powell J., Lasley T., Schiel R., "Combating Coups d'état in Africa, 1950-2014", *Studies in Comparative International Development* (2016), 51, 4, 482-502; Nathan L., *op. cit.*; Djinnit S., *The Case for updating the African Union Policy on Unconstitutional Changes of Government*, ACCORD, 2021, 54.

[12] Udombana N.J., "The institutional structure of the African Union: A legal analysis", *California Western International Law* (2002), 33, 69.

[13] All available at https://au.int/en/treaties.

tions happening in their own region than distant senders.[14] In other words, their community-derived authority on the matter should make them intervene more consistently over time and less selectively across norm violations they were given authority on, even if this were to entail costly interventions. At the same time, however, as intra-regional senders are both "rule-makers and enforcers"[15] in a region rife with autocratic rulers, we should also assume that, overall, such attention would eventually focus only on a more minimalist, some would say fallacious,[16] conception of democracy limited to how power is obtained. As a result, we should expect this thin, procedural sense of democratic norms also influences African regional organizations' sanction imposition. This would mean that highly-visible democratic violations related to how governments change, such as coups, are likely to trigger a strong effect, even stronger than distant democratic senders. By contrast, discreet violations such as civil liberties restrictions should remain neglected. Expectations related to election-related irregularities remain more ambiguous, but, according to some interpretations, those responsible for fraudulent elections do infringe principles of democratic changes of government, and thus should be treated similarly to those responsible for unconstitutional changes of government.[17]

H2: *The probability of democratic sanction imposition in Africa is stronger for intra-regional than for extra-regional senders, but only against highly-visible, 'procedural' democratic violations.*

Selectivity aside, charges of inconsistent uses of democratic sanctions in Africa over time have recently been moved against both the AU and extra-regional actors, because of their recent (lack of) responses to the most dramatic of such violations, coups d'état.[18] Inconsistency in such cases refers not to the selective targeting of some autocrats instead of others because of more or less visible violations, but to different reactions over time to the

[14] Duursma A., "African Solutions to African Challenges: The Role of Legitimacy in Mediating Civil Wars in Africa", *International Organization* (2020), 74, 2, 295-330; Hellquist E., "Regional sanctions as peer review", cit.

[15] Hellquist E., *The African Union in a World of Sanctions,* cit., 107.

[16] Diamond L., "Is the Third Wave Over?", *Journal of Democracy* (1996), 7, 3, 22.

[17] Vandeginste S., "The African Union, Constitutionalism and Power-Sharing", *Journal of African Law* (2013), 57, 1, 23.

[18] Phakathi M., "An analysis of the Responses of the African Union to the coup in Burkina Faso (2015) and Zimbabwe (2017)", *Journal of African Union Studies* (2018), 7(3), 129-145; Stocker S., Quirk P., "The False Tradeoff: Revisiting the Democracy vs Security Paradigm in Africa", *Democracy in Africa* (blog) (2022); Singh N., "The Myth of the Coup Contagion", *Journal of Democracy* (2022), 33, 4, 74-88.

same kind of violation. Reactions to coups seem to have become all the more erratic as of late. When in Chad, in 2021, Mahamat Déby Itno replaced his father at the presidency through an unconstitutional transfer of power, no regional or international actor imposed any measure. Chad was not an exception, though. Over the past ten years, the AU did not impose, or delayed, sanctions against at least three other coup plotters besides Chad 2021 (Burkina 2014; Zimbabwe 2017; Sudan 2019; and according to some interpretations also Tunisia 2021), while in all such cases extra-regional actors acted in neither coordinated nor consistent fashion. If a year needs to be selected to mark the beginning of a period of growing inconsistency, then 2014 is a valid candidate for several reasons. On a regional level, that year, in October, the AU and ECOWAS failed to suspend Burkina Faso after the overthrow of President Blaise Compaoré and the junta's unwillingness to transfer power to a civilian authority.[19] Inconsistencies of this kind, with the AU failing to suspend and sanction coup-born regimes, only intensified later in 2017-2022. On the international level, in 2014 Russia challenged the democratic norms-based international order by violating the territorial integrity of Crimea[20] while in the same year China launched its Belt and Road Initiative, a medium of power projection in the world that has since contributed to expand and reinforce its authoritarian practices abroad.[21] We can therefore hypothesize that a combination of local and international factors has engendered a scenario more conducive to authoritarian rule and unfavourable to democratic responses, so that:

> **H3**: *The probability to react to even highly visible democratic violations has decreased as of late, across all senders, due to growing regional ambiguities and international fragmentation.*

To systematically test these hypotheses, the chapter adopts the following research design. First, it draws on the latest and most-updated dataset on sanctions, the third edition of the Global Sanctions Data Base (GSDB),[22] to map the multiple senders active on the African continent in 1990-2022.

[19] BBC, "Burkina Faso's Isaac Zida dismisses African Union intervention", 2014 available at https://www.bbc.com/news/world-africa-29948773; Nathan L., *op. cit.*, 21.

[20] Walker C., "Authoritarianism Goes Global", *Journal of Democracy* (2015), 26, 4.

[21] Gurol J., "The authoritarian narrator: China's power projection and its reception in the Gulf", *International Affairs* (2023),99, 2, 687-705.

[22] Syropoulos C., Felbermayr G., Kirilakha A., Yalcin E., Yotov Y., *The Global Sanctions Data Base - Release 3: COVID-19, Russia, and Multilateral Sanctions*, School of Economics Working Paper Series 2022-11, LeBow College of Business, Drexel University, 2022.

Although the GSDB is most suitable for trade-related analyses of sanctions, it was selected for this analysis because it was, as of late 2022, the most up-to-date global sanctions database inclusive of regional sanctions.[23] Then, it tests empirically which factors effectively affected the likelihood of democratic sanctions imposition in Africa over the past three decades. This is done through different probabilistic statistical models to reveal differences between intra-regional and extra-regional senders.

9.4. Sanctions in Africa 1990-2022: multiple senders and objectives

Over the past three decades Africa was the most sanctioned region in the world. According to the newly updated sanction data of the GSDB, more than 350 democratic sanction cases[24] were recorded against African countries for the period 1990-2022 (35 were already ongoing as of 1990, mostly related to South Africa and Libya). As shown in Table 9.1, only 12% of these cases were multilateral UN sanctions, mostly imposed on targets already subject to non-democratic sanction regimes. 20% were those imposed by the EU, 32% by the US, 9% by African regional organizations, 28% by others (of which 6% by other African individual states or ad-hoc coalitions). Only a small share of UN's Africa sanctions explicitly sought democracy support or promotion (13%), while the percentage increases for the other senders.

Table 9.1. Overview of sanctions imposed in 1990-2022 against African targets, by most-frequent senders.

	African ROs	UN	EU	US
Share of all Africa sanctions, per sender	9%	12%	20%	32%
% of which are democratic sanctions	76%	13%	44%	37%

Source: GSDB data (Syropoulos C., et al, *op. cit.*) integrated by the author.

---

[23] This notwithstanding, GSDB v3 still misses some well-known African ROs' sanctions. As a result, the following were integrated by the author: AU-Comoros 2007-08; AU-Sudan 2019-ongoing; AU-Mali 2020-ongoing, ECOWAS-Mali 2020-ongoing.

[24] Cf. Felbermayr G., Kirilakha A., Syropoulos C., Yalcin E., Yotov Y., "The global sanctions data base", *European Economic Review* (2020), 129, for their definition of a sanction case. Instead of using episodes, GSDB codes different cases when objectives and instruments employed against the same target change over time. The dataset used in this analysis is made of a total of 351 cases, inclusive of author's above-mentioned integrations.

The different share of democratic sanctions per sender reflects the different legal instruments each sender can use to intervene in Africa or elsewhere. The UN has the lowest share considering that, historically, in the region the UNSC managed to impose sanctions primarily on cases of civil or interstate wars, proliferation of weapons, including those of mass destruction, and terrorism.[25] Although the UN does support democratic objectives, its Charter makes no explicit provision about intervening to protect democratic rule in case of violations of democratic norms.[26] This is a fundamentally different approach from the one of the EU, here already presented as a sui-generis regional organization which is entitled to impose sanctions also against non-member states through its Common Foreign and Security Policy (since 1993, but also able to do so earlier as a European Community)[27] and through the conditionality clauses introduced in its trade agreements in case of democratic violations.[28] As Table 9.1 shows, differently from the UN, democracy promotion has certainly been a major focus of EU's foreign policy, including towards Africa.

This was also the case for the United States (US), the single-most active user of sanctions with an oft-neglected soft spot for Africa, as one third of all its post-1990 sanctions cases have been on African targets. Although the post-9/11 war on terror has given security and terrorism a prominent focus, democracy has remained a priority in its Africa policy.[29] Just like the EU, Washington can suspend states from commercial agreements (most notably, for African states, from AGOA) in case of human rights violations (see the case of Ethiopia in 2021) and unconstitutional changes of government (see the cases of Guinea and Mali in 2021).[30]

The previous sections already described the primary legal instruments

---

[25] Biersteker T., Eckert S., Tourinho M. (eds.), *Targeted Sanctions: The Impacts and Effectiveness of United Nations Action*, Cambridge University Press, 2016.

[26] Donno D., *Defending democratic norms: international actors and the politics of eleectoral misconduct,* Oxford University Press, 2013.

[27] Giumelli F., Hoffmann F., Książczaková A., "The when, what, where and why of European Union sanctions", *European Security* (2021), 30, 1, 1-23.

[28] Portela C., "Where and why does the EU impose sanctions?", *Politique européenne* (2005), 3, 83-111.

[29] White House, *US Strategy towards Sub-Saharan Africa,* 2022, available at https://www.whitehouse.gov/wp-content/uploads/2022/08/U.S.-Strategy-Toward-Sub-Saharan-Africa-FINAL.pdf.

[30] Office of the United States Trade Representative, *Statement From Ambassador Katherine Tai*, 2021, available at https://ustr.gov/about-us/policy-offices/press-office/press-releases/2021/november/statement-ambassador-katherine-tai-african-growth-and-opportunity-act-eligibility-review.

the African Union has adopted to address democratic violations, including through sanctions. The African Union is not the only intra-regional organization endowed with the power to impose democratic sanctions on the continent. Certainly, most of Africa's sub-regional organizations, such as major Regional Economic Communities (RECs) like Eastern Africa's IGAD and EAC, Southern Africa's SADC, and West Africa's ECOWAS, have remained development-focused, thus neglecting sanctions imposition and other forms of direct intervention in member states, except for ECOWAS (and more marginally SADC, with only one sanction case registered, Madagascar 2009). ECOWAS adopted a Protocol on Democracy and Good Governance in December 2001, ensuring it could deal specifically with unconstitutional violations of power with an automatic mechanism similar to that of AU's PSC for membership suspensions, while other types of sanctions are agreed with unanimity.[31] Most interestingly, ECOWAS is the African RO which is most convincingly driving for stronger enforcement and for an expansion of the scope of democratic sanctions in Africa, to better address presidential term limits violations and electoral law manipulations.[32]

9.5. Empirical test

To systematically test what factors have affected the likelihood of democratic sanctions imposition in Africa over the past three decades[33] across the various senders active in the region, this section uses a series of logistic regressions whose unit of analysis is the African country-year. Three binary dependent variables are used, one for each sender under examination, dichotomously capturing whether democratic sanctions were imposed on that African target in any given year, given no democratic sanctions were already in place at t–1 by the same actor. The senders analysed in the empirical test are the African Union (AU), the European Union (EU), and the (US). The UN is excluded because the very limited number of UN *demo-*

[31] Cowell F., "The Impact of the ECOWAS Protocol on Good Governance and Democracy", *African Journal of International and Comparative Law* (2011), 19, 2, 331-342.

[32] Vanguard, *ECOWAS urged to adopt proposed amendment to protocol on democracy, good governance*, 4 July 2022, available at https://www.vanguardngr.com/2022/07/ecowas-urged-to-adopt-proposed-amendment-to-protocol-on-democracy-good-governance/.

[33] Although the dataset covers 1990-2022, the effective sample of the test covers only 1995-2021 due to missing data concerning the years 1990-1994 and 2022.

cratic sanctions imposed in Africa does not allow for a thorough statistical test. Differently from von Soest and Wahman (2015), this test does not reduce the sample to non-democratic targets only, because Africa's recent history shows even democratic regimes experience autocratization events that lead to democratic sanction imposition (i.e., Burkina 2022).[34] Because sanction imposition is a relatively rare event, especially in models where sanctions are imposed by a specific sender only, this empirical test uses rare-events Firth logit models with cubic polynomials modelling time dependence.[35]

The factors which are tested as potential triggers of the imposition of democratic sanctions in Africa in 1990-2022 largely build on von Soest and Wahman (2015).[36] To capture highly-visible violations, the models include a dichotomous variable for successful coups, drawn from Powell and Thyne's dataset,[37] and another for fraudulent and controversial elections, drawn from the NELDA dataset,[38] tracking the presence of quite visible democratic violations such as opposition harassment by the government during elections. The latter operationalisation is preferred to von Soest and Wahman (2015)'s focus on allegations of fraud by Western electoral monitors because the latter is ill-suited to this chapter's broader focus inclusive of non-Western senders. To capture less visible democratic triggers, the models also include a measure of the year-on-year decrease in an African country's civil liberties score, drawn from V-Dem's Civil Liberties Index.[39] Here V-Dem data is preferred to Freedom House because captures more variation across countries and years, leading to more precise estimates.[40] Because of this choice, no 'democracy' variable (sourced from the same da-

---

[34] Carter D., Signorino C., "Back to the Future: Modeling Time Dependence in Binary Data", *Political Analysis* (2010), 18, 3, 271-292. As a robustness check, a replication of these tests was done on a non-democratic sample which excludes Africa's very few democratic countries. The results do not change.

[35] Nonetheless, running the analyses as logit models (clustered with robust standard errors at the target level) does not alter the results substantially.

[36] The codebook of the data used in their article is available at https://ink.library.smu.edu.sg/cgi/viewcontent.cgi?article=3233&context=soss_research.

[37] Powell and Thyne (2011), *op. cit.*

[38] Variable 15 in Hyde S.D., Marinov N., "Which Elections Can Be Lost?", *Political Analysis* (2012), 20, 2, 191-201.

[39] Values previously reversed and rescaled between 0 and 100. Coppedge M., Gerring J., Knutsen C.H., et al., *V-Dem [Country-Year/Country-Date] Dataset v12*, Varieties of Democracy (V-Dem) Project, 2022, available at https://doi.org/10.23696/vdemds22.

[40] Vaccaro A., "Comparing measures of democracy: statistical properties, convergence, and interchangeability", *European Political Science* (2021), 20, 666-684.

taset) is included to control for the absolute level of democracy of the target because of high correlation between the two. Finally, the lagged variable of the imposition of non-democratic sanctions (by any sender) is also included to account for the role that existing non-democratic sanctions (such as those imposed for conflicts, terrorism, or other issues) may have in facilitating the subsequent imposition of democratic sanctions.

Additional controls are included to account for the role of the ties between senders and targets as plausible alternative explanations conventionally used in the literature.[41] Specifically, they consist of a dichotomous measure of security-political instability capturing ongoing conflict in the target state, drawn from the UCDP/PRIO armed conflict dataset.[42] To operationalise the target's economic weakness, there are measures of GDP per capita growth and inflation, both sourced from the World Bank's World Development Indicators (WDI) dataset.[43] As a possible counterbalance of target's vulnerability, in all models a 'black knights' variable is also included to capture external authoritarian support, by coding dichotomously whether the target had strong political ties with Russia and China.[44] Especially Western powers are expected to be less inclined to impose sanctions on targets aligned with global authoritarian powers who can help them offset the economic and political impacts of such measures.

Moving onto the costs for the senders, the models include the natural log of the GDP per capita (PPP) of the target and variables about net inflows of foreign direct investments and oil production (the latter two are measured as percentages of the target state's GDP), all drawn from the WDI dataset. Absolute values of dyadic trade flows between the target and the sender (all member states if ROs) are also included.[45] In addition to

---

[41] McLean E.V., Whang T., "Friends or foes? Major trading partners and the success of economic sanctions" *International Studies Quarterly* (2010), 54, 2, 427-447; Lektzian D., Biglaiser G., "The effect of foreign direct investment on the use and success of US sanctions", *Conflict Management and Peace Science* (2014), 31, 1, 70-93.

[42] Gleditsch K., Petter N., Wallensteen P., et al., "Armed Conflict 1946-2001: A New Dataset", *Journal of Peace Research* (2002), 39, 5; Davies S., Pettersson T., Öberg M., "Organized violence 1989-2021 and drone warfare", *Journal of Peace Research* (2022), 59, 4.

[43] World Bank, *World Development Indicators*, 2022, available at https://data.worldbank.org/.

[44] If the dyadic voting similarity for UN General Assembly votes is above 0.8 (on a 0-1 scale), the target is coded as having black knight ties. Voeten E., *Data and Analyses of Voting in the UN General Assembly*, in Reinalda B., *Routledge Handbook of International Organization*, Routledge, 2013.

[45] UNCTAD, *Bilateral Merchandise Trade Matrix*, 2022, available at http://unctadstat.unctad.org/. Values reported in billion USD (constant 2020).

these economic costs, to measure the political costs of imposition for the senders, some model specifications, namely those regarding US and EU sanctions, also include the variable of dyadic voting similarity for UN General Assembly votes between the targets and themselves.[46] All these controls are lagged by one year to ensure temporal precedence with regard to the imposition of sanctions, except for the variables of ongoing instability and trade flows.[47] Finally, all these models include a dichotomous variable referring to post-2014 country-years to test whether recently there has been a significant relaxation of the application of regional and international norms against democratic violations, as hypothesised in H3.

9.5.1. Results

Table 9.2 reports the results of the empirical test on the likelihood to impose democratic sanctions in Africa. As logistic regression coefficients are more difficult to interpret than linear models,[48] the discussion below summarises the major insights focusing on the sign and significance of the estimated effects.

Starting from EU and US models (1-2), the results confirm the overall selective nature of democratic sanctions imposition on the basis of the way norms are violated: the higher their visibility (i.e., coups or controversial elections), the higher the likelihood for an African country to be targeted by Western democratic sanctions. Partly defying Africa-specific expectations (H1), more discreet violations such as yearly declines in civil liberties are not found to systematically increase the likelihood of being targeted by sanctions, except for the EU. An insignificant effect is also found regarding the role of the target's economic vulnerability. On the contrary, the political closeness between the target and the sender has a significant constraining effect on sanction imposition, albeit only for the EU. It is not significant for the US which, however, is negatively influenced by global authoritarian powers' support to the target. A recent case in point of authoritarian black knights' deterrent effect on Washington's decision to impose democratic sanctions was the US reluctance to sanction Equatorial Guinea's President

[46] Voeten E., *op. cit.* EU-related values are mean indices computed on the data of the four most important European powers in African affairs, namely France, Germany, Italy, and the UK until Brexit.

[47] As in von Soest C., Wahman M., "Not all dictators are equal", cit.

[48] The coefficients are not reported in odd ratios. Thus, for numeric predictor variables (hence non-categorical variables), they describe a difference in the log odds for one unit change in the predictor.

Obiang because of his growing ties with China despite credible allegations of major irregularities during the November 2022 elections.[49]

Table 9.2. Factors influencing the imposition of democratic sanctions in Africa. Coefficients are estimated with Firth Logits. Standard errors in parentheses. Time-related cubic polynomials not displayed in the table

DV: Democratic sanctions imposition in Africa	(1) By EU	(2) By US	(3) By AU
Coups	2.972***	3.923***	5.465***
	(0.643)	(0.607)	(0.706)
Controversial elections	1.617**	1.277**	-0.758
	(0.693)	(0.609)	(1.844)
Worsening civil liberties	0.118**	0.0477	0.0934
	(0.0594)	(0.0716)	(0.0770)
Non-democratic sanctions $_{t-1}$	0.196	0.432	1.652**
	(0.597)	(0.482)	(0.763)
Ongoing instability	0.539	0.605	0.0305
	(0.581)	(0.466)	(0.806)
Black knight ties $_{t-1}$	0.402	-1.225**	0.457
	(0.936)	(0.521)	(0.995)
Inflation $_{t-1}$	0.000537	0.000639	0.000122*
	(0.000455)	(0.000695)	(7.37e-05)
FDI dependence $_{t-1}$	0.0201	-0.102	0.0169
	(0.0205)	(0.0923)	(0.0146)
GDP pc PPP (thousands) (log) $_{t-1}$	-0.206	-0.0937	0.0841
	(0.404)	(0.328)	(0.559)
GDP pc growth $_{t-1}$	-0.0364	-0.00448	0.0296
	(0.0454)	(0.0382)	(0.0256)
Oil dependence $_{t-1}$	0.00556	0.00252	-0.0144
	(0.0258)	(0.0267)	(0.0505)
Trade ties (billions) (log)	0.0361	0.0322	-0.0717
	(0.175)	(0.120)	(0.189)
Political ties (bilateral) $_{t-1}$	-0.0674**	-0.0184	
	(0.0306)	(0.0183)	
Post-2014	-1.752*	-0.316	-0.210
	(1.032)	(0.628)	(1.196)
Constant	1.071	-0.735	-4.616*
	(2.390)	(1.096)	(2.426)
Observations	1,151	1,154	1,297

Notes: ***p < 0.01, **p < 0.05, *p < 0.1

Source: author's own elaboration.

Regarding the behaviour of an intra-regional sender such as the AU, the analysis largely confirms H2. Across all senders, the predicted probability change generated by democratic norms violations is the strongest for the AU, yet only for the most visible ones, coups (.331 vs .163 and .225),[50] re-

[49] Gramer R., Mackinnon A., Detsch J., "Biden Plays Nice With Equatorial Guinea to Spoil China's Atlantic Ambitions", *Foreign Policy* (2022), available at https://foreignpolicy.com/2022/12/12/biden-equatorial-guinea-china-atlantic-base-us-africa-leaders-summit/.

[50] This is calculated only for the coup variable on three simpler models excluding all

flecting its 20-year-long efforts to create an anti-coup norm on the continent. More discreet violations do not play a significant role in triggering AU sanctions instead, as only Western actors are more likely to react to them. This latter specification confirms the AU's recent practice: despite its normative framework does provide legal space for such interventions, the "ambiguous wording" [51] of some provisions has so far created obstacles to their effective implementation. [52]

Overall, the above-mentioned results confirm the selective nature of democratic sanction imposition in Africa, as highly-visible democratic violations are more likely to trigger sanctions than any other violation, especially in countries not aligned with the EU and not politically close to China and Russia. It remains to verify whether this selective behaviour has become also more inconsistent in recent years, as hypothesised in H3. To do so, a post-2014 dichotomous variable was introduced in all the models. The results show mixed support. A negative effect is found across all models, but with statistical, albeit weak, significance only for the EU. Overall, this confirms today's looser implementation of democratic violations, most notably of the anti-coup norm, but not yet in a significantly different way from the past. If this is good news in the short term, because it means that despite today's more inconsistent response to democratic violations than in the past this is not a systematic behaviour yet, it still raises concerns in the longer term as this inconsistent application of rules risks setting a precedent for tomorrow's norm violators who may think, with good reason, they can violate them with fewer consequences.

9.6. Conclusions

This chapter aimed to shed light on the use of democratic sanctions in Africa, uncovering possible selectivity and inconsistency issues across multiple senders. Given a global sanction environment in which regional organizations are taking a more active role against democratic norms violations, a primary focus of the analysis was placed precisely on the behaviour of African regional organizations. The creation of the African Union in 2000-02 put an end to the traditional indifference of African regional

---

economic and political controls, holding civil liberties at their means and the other dichotomous variables at zero.

[51] Djinnit S., *op. cit.*

[52] Wiebusch M., Aniekwe C.C., Oette L., Vandeginste S., "The African Charter on Democracy, Elections and Governance: Trends, Challenges and Perspectives", *Africa Spectrum* (2019), 54, 2, 95-105.

organizations (i.e., AU's predecessor, the OAU) towards local regimes' domestic politics. It endowed itself with the ability to impose sanctions against member states violating democratic norms, most notably those related to the constitutionality of governmental changes. Its response to the latter was remarkably consistent for most of the time, but lately a growing number of inconsistencies have demanded a reassessment of the use of such measures.

Building on the seminal work by von Soest and Wahman (2015), this analysis provided both expected and surprising insights regarding the main factors influencing their use in Africa. The analysis confirmed a selective use insofar as highly visible democratic violations remain those most likely to trigger sanctions, while more discreet violations only pique the attention of the EU. The analysis also found that intra-regional senders are indeed more sensitive than extra-regional powers to democratic violations taking place in their region, but only in relation to a procedural conception of democracy. The analysis also showed evidence of growing inconsistencies across most senders, but, to date, only in the case of the EU these inconsistencies have had a significantly different effect on sanction imposition than in the past.

The long-awaited activation of a sanction sub-committee[53] at the AU's Political Affairs, Peace and Security (PAPS) and the establishment of a PSC sub-committee on unconstitutional changes of government to monitor potential violations can help address both these issues.[54] Indeed, not only can they make democratic sanction imposition more consistent because better monitored, but also less selective, by dealing with some of those contradictions which are inherent to the AU's logic of mediation which is part of its sanction policy but often ends up legitimizing the interlocutor and offering concessions which dilute democracy's essence.[55]

The international environment also remains key in this, as the rise of global authoritarian powers providing political protection if not economic support to African autocrats risks offsetting the benefits of these ongoing

[53] The creation of a sanctions sub-committee was endorsed in the 2009 Ezulwini framework, yet never operationalised. The AU's 16th Extraordinary Summit held in Malabo in May 2022 called for its reactivation and asked the AU Commission to develop guidelines for this.

[54] Woldemichael S., *Africa's security depends on action – not just commitment*, *ISS Africa* (2022), available at https://issafrica.org/iss-today/africas-security-depends-on-action-not-just-commitment.

[55] See the above-mentioned case of Burkina 2014 in which ad-hoc mediators set arbitrary criteria to evaluate the situation. Nathan L., *op. cit.*

intra-regional reforms. Certainly, Western powers do not have an unblemished record either, as they also often act selectively and inconsistently with political allies, in the name of an often-fallacious democracy-security tradeoff. A topic of interest for future research concerns not only the evolution of such AU reforms, but precisely also the intended and unintended external constraints to these developments.

Chapter 10

HUMAN RIGHTS-SPECIFIC SANCTIONS' CONTRIBUTION TO HUMAN RIGHTS

Annalisa Ciampi

ABSTRACT: *While the down of the XX century coincided with a profound crisis for human rights, the new century seems to be characterized by a renew centrality for the latter – with the adoption by Western States of a set of new measures designed to ensure respect for human rights. The author focuses on the so called Global Magnisky Legislation – named after the US Global Magnisky Human Rights Accountability Act of 2016 – which allows to target individual persons and entities (including state actors) for human rights abuses, without any relevant action being taken against the state of origin of the alleged violations. By examining the relevant practice – most notably in response to serious abuses against the Uyghur minority in the Xinjiang (China) – the author finds that human rights-specific sanctions do not necessarily result in the cessation of the violations which triggered their imposition in the first place. They are, however, impactful in many different ways and do ultimately contribute to making human rights more effective worldwide.*

10.1. Introduction

Since the modern human rights movement was born in the 60s and for the past 60 years, the central collective strategy to promote respect for, and observance of, human rights has been the development of international legal rules: new treaties, declarations, and resolutions. [1]

---

[1] As is well known, the international movement for the affirmation of human rights draws inspiration from the Charter of the United Nations (UN) and the Universal Declaration of Human Rights proclaimed by the General Assembly in 1948. With the 1975 Helsinki Agreements, in exchange for the recognition of the inviolability of national borders and respect for territorial integrity, the former Soviet Union accepted the principle of respect for human rights. In the same years, two universal international treaties entered into force: the Covenant on Civil and Political Rights and the Covenant on Economic, Social and Cultural Rights, both ratified today by over 170 States. Since then, the centrality of international human rights norms has established itself in rela-

A development in isolation from other domains of global governance such as trade, investment, and development. [2]

While States and NGOs continue to feel a need for such international instruments covering certain areas of human rights, this traditional strategy was seriously put into question at the down of the last century, with visions of human rights at their Twilight, the End Times or as the Last Utopia. [3]

Things have started to change in the second, and most prominently the third, decade of this century, with the adoption of a series of new unilateral measures by Western States, in order to ensure respect for human rights around the world.

One of such measures, to which this Chapter is devoted, are *human rights-specific sanction regimes* under the so called Global Magnitsky Legislation. These regimes allow States to unilaterally target individual persons and entities (including state actors) for human rights abuses, without any relevant action being taken against the state of origin of the alleged violations. Other measures consist of *bans on the import of goods* suspected of having been produced with forced labour or as a result of other human rights violations. New tools to address human rights violations worldwide are also the requirements of *corporate sustainability due diligence*, which aim to foster responsible corporate behaviour and to anchor human rights in companies' operations and corporate governance, by ensuring that they address adverse impacts of their actions.

These developments correspond to a more general return of human rights to the center of international politics and the public debate in various parts of the world, including the European Union (EU). In this respect, therefore, they are a welcomed development. By focusing on the recently

---

tions between East and West and beyond. The European Convention for the Protection of Human Rights and Fundamental Freedoms concluded within the framework of the Council of Europe in 1950 – which after the expulsion of the Russian Federation in 2022, brings together 46 member States – is still considered worldwide the most advanced instrument for human rights protection. Within an immense bibliography on the subject, see for example Shelton D.L., *Advanced Introduction to International Human Rights Law*, 2nd ed., Edward Elgar Publishing, 2020; Jensen L.B. Steven, *The Making of International Human Rights*, Cambridge University Press, 2016; Tomuschat C., *Human Rights Between Idealism and Realism*, 3rd ed., Oxford University Press, 2014.

[2] Ciampi A., "The Divide between Human Rights, International Trade, Investment and Development Law", *German Yearbook of International Law* (2018), vol. 61, 251-293; Id., *History, Isolation and the Effectiveness of Human Rights*, in Ciampi A., *History and International law: An Intertwined Relationship*, Edward Elgar Publishing, 2019, 44-81.

[3] Hopgood S., *The Endtimes of Human Rights*, Cornell University Press, 2013; Moyn S., *The Last Utopia. Human Rights in History*, Harvard University Press, 2010, 11-43; Posner E.A., *The Twilight of Human Rights Law*, Oxford University Press, 2014.

established and implemented human rights-specific sanctions regimes, this Chapter inquiries into whether they are also a sign of the emergence of a new set of human rights enforcement mechanisms.

The fundamental assumption, to be tested, is that human rights-specific sanctions carry a distinct blaming and shaming effect – ensuing from the allegation of human rights violations which triggered their imposition. In this, they produce a stigma different from other sanctions and similar to findings of human rights courts and monitoring bodies.

Following an outline of the legal framework of Global Magnitsky Legislation Acts worldwide (par. 10.2), the Chapter examines the new EU Global Human Rights Sanctions Regimes (EUGHRSR, also known as the European Magnitsky Act) and its early practice (par. 10.3). It then focuses on Western measures adopted in response to the serious human rights violations and abuses against the Uyghur minority in the Xinjiang (China) and the chain of reactions and counter-reactions triggered by them (par. 10.4). It further elaborates on the internal political objectives and the geopolitical foreign policy goals pursued by the imposers of sanctions under these new regimes (par. 10.5). It concludes with a general appraisal of the new centrality of human rights in international relations and the contribution of human rights-specific sanctions to the enforcement and/or effectiveness of human rights worldwide (par. 10.6).

10.2. The legal framework

Sanctions as a tool of foreign policy have been around for almost a century.

As is well known, the Security Council can take action to maintain or restore international peace and security under Chapter VII of the UN Charter. Sanctions measures, under Article 41, encompass a broad range of enforcement options that do not involve the use of armed force.

They can take a number of different forms, ranging from comprehensive economic and trade sanctions to more targeted measures such as arms embargoes, travel bans, and financial or commodity restrictions. Traditional economic sanctions – typically import and/or export restrictions – have been questioned in relation to their effectiveness, (sometimes devastating) humanitarian impact on the population, legitimacy and morality. Financial measures, asset freezes, travel bans, and arms embargos are examples of so-called targeted (or smart) sanctions – measures tailored to maximize the target regime's costs of non-compliance while minimizing the target population's suffering. The Security Council has applied sanctions in pursuit of a variety of goals: to support peaceful transitions, deter non-constitutional changes, constrain terrorism, promote non-proliferation and protect human rights.[4]

But States have also resorted to unilateral sanctions in the ordinary course of their foreign policy, either individually or collectively, for a range of objectives, including human rights, most recently against Russia following its annexation of Crimea in 2014, first, and later the outbreak of a full-scale armed conflict with Ukraine, in 2022 – when unilateral sanctions of unprecedented scale were adopted in tandem by the United States (US), the EU, the United Kingdom, Canada, Australia, but also Switzerland, Japan and others.[5]

The new human rights-specific sanctions regimes do not fall under the realm of UN-led sanctions but are established by States individually on the basis of their respective national legislations. They differ, however, from pre-existing regimes because they *specifically* allow sanctions (typically, asset freeze and travel bans) against individuals and entities (including state actors) allegedly responsible for human rights violations and abuses specifically – outside the framework of a UN Security Council resolution and without any relevant action being taken against the state of origin of the human rights violations.

The US led in this effort through the adoption of the *Global Magnitsky Human Rights Accountability Act* (*Global Magnitsky Act*), which was signed into law on December 23, 2016[6] and implemented by the Executive order issued by the President on December 20, 2017. Developing human rights-specific sanction regimes is now a widespread legal trend among most Western democracies.

Canada[7] and the United Kingdom[8] have enacted similar legislation in 2017 and 2020, respectively.

The EU established its own *Global Human Rights Sanctions Regime*

---

[4] An updated list of ongoing sanctions regimes imposed by the UN Security Council is available at https://www.un.org/securitycouncil/sanctions/information.

[5] For an updated list of sanctions adopted by the EU, UK, Japan and Australia against Russia, see *Russia Sanctions Tracker*, ASHURST, available at https://www.ashurst.com/en/news-and-insights/hubs/sanctions-tracker. On US sanctions against Russia, Welt C., Archick K., Nelson R.M., Rennack D.E., Cong. Res. Serv., *U.S. Sanctions on Russia*, 2022, R45415.

[6] *Global Magnitsky Act*, Public Law 114-328, Subtitle F. available at https://www.state.gov/global-magnitsky-act/.

[7] *Canada Justice for Victims of Corrupt Foreign Officials Act (Sergei Magnitsky Law)*, S.C. 2017, c. 21, available at https://laws.justice.gc.ca/eng/acts/J-2.3/FullText.html.

[8] *UK Global Human Rights Sanctions Regulations*, statutory Instrument No. 680 of 2020, available at https://www.legislation.gov.uk/uksi/2020/680/contents/made.

(EUGHRSR or *European Magnitsky Act*) on 7 December 2020. It is made up of two elements: Council Decision (CFSP) 2020/1999 and Council Regulation (EU) 2020/1998.[9]

Australia adopted its own version of the Global Magnitsky Act through reforms to the Autonomous Sanctions Act 2011 and Autonomous Sanctions Regulations 2011, which constitute Australia's sanctions framework. The *Autonomous Sanctions Amendment (Magnitsky-style and Other Thematic Sanctions) Regulations 2021* of 16 December 2021,[10] now addresses human rights violations through sanctions allowing the imposition of sanctions on individuals and entities identified as being involved in certain thematic categories of conduct, including human rights violations.

Kosovo, Latvia, and Lithuania all have their own versions of the Global Magnitsky law, while others such as Japan are considering whether to initiate legislative processes to adopt regulations addressing human rights violations through targeted sanctions.

Each regime has its own legislative history, adoption procedure and legal basis under national (including constitutional) law. The new regimes, however, share some common features.[11]

From a *substantive* point of view, each piece of legislation identifies the human rights abuses and violations which may trigger the adoption of human rights-specific sanctions. The sanctions consist of restrictive measures against natural or legal persons, including state officials and public bodies, but not against a state as a whole. These measures are the typical targeted sanctions: assets freeze and travel bans. Formally viewed as non-criminal measures, they are normally imposed based on permissive evidential standards.

Procedurally, while each national legislation defines who decides and with what procedure, human rights-specific sanctions are generally imposed through a faster and more flexible process than the one available for ordinary unilateral sanctions.

---

[9] The consolidated text of Decision (CFSP) 2020/1999 and Regulation (EU) 2020/1998, is available at https://eur-lex.europa.eu/legal-content/EN/TXT/?uri=CELEX%3A02020R1998-20211213.

[10] *Autonomous Sanctions Amendment (Magnitsky-style and Other Thematic Sanctions) Regulations 2021*, 16 December 2021, available at https://www.legislation.gov.au/Details/F2021L01855.

[11] For a useful overview see the Briefing of the European Parliament, *Global human rights sanctions. Mapping Magnitsky laws: The US, Canadian, UK and EU approach*, November 2021, available at: Global human rights sanctions (europa.eu). See also the document prepared by the Law Library of Congress, *Worldwide Global Magnitsky Act Legislation. Australia. Canada. Estonia. European Union. Gibraltar. Jersey. Latvia. Lithuania. United Kingdom*, Washington, D.C., July 2022, available at https://www.europarl.europa.eu/thinktank/en/document/EPRS_BRI(2021)698791.

The US President's Executive Order that implemented the Global Magnitsky Act, for example, declares a national emergency with respect to serious human rights abuses and corruption globally, identifying these issues as threats to the national security, foreign policy, and economy of the US. Under this national emergency, the President can invoke the authorities provided by the *International Emergency Economic Powers Act* to impose financial sanctions (delegated to the Secretary of the Treasury, in consultation with the Secretary of state and the Attorney General) and visa restrictions (delegated to the Secretary of state) on persons determined, among other things, to be responsible for or complicit in, or to have directly or indirectly engaged in, certain human rights abuses or corrupt acts anywhere in the world. As a result of designations pursuant to the Executive Order, all of the property and interests in property within US jurisdiction of the designated individuals and entities are blocked, and US persons are generally prohibited from engaging in transactions with them.

Moreover, previous unilateral sanctions, except those imposed on the basis of terrorism lists, were all state-based sanctions. In contrast, the new human rights-specific sanctions are individual-based.

As is well known, state-based sanctions may induce a deterrent effect on countries guilty of human rights violations. They may, however, unintendedly affect the social rights and the quality of life of innocent civilians living in the targeted state. For example, a trade ban targeted at a third country can significantly disrupt the distribution of food and sanitation supplies to vulnerable groups such as the poor or women, but the oppressive elites in the targeted state may be able to maintain their quality of life as they usually enjoy considerable wealth. This may also diminish the effectiveness of sanctions as the elites may be unaffected by them. Therefore, a sanction regime targeting individuals instead of States can avoid the unintended adverse impact on innocent civilians, while also being more effective in applying pressure to those responsible for the human rights violations.

The structural novelty and common feature of human rights-specific sanctions is that unlike previous sanctions imposed for human rights violations, they establish a gap between the imposition of such sanctions and the context in which the violations occur.

The new regimes provide for the possibility to sanction individuals in cases where it is difficult for economic and political reasons to find unanimity to target States or regions. In principle, therefore, they *could* lead to the imposition of sanctions against individuals and entities without any relevant action being taken regarding the critical geopolitical issues that are strongly linked to the violations.

10.3. The European Magnisky Act

EU restrictive measures against serious human rights violations and abuses are the result of a long process aimed at introducing a specific regime that would allow the EU to target individuals and entities for human rights violations, separately from the EU's political and economic strategy toward their States of origin.

In the past, the EU had issued several sanctions lists targeting, among others, human rights violations. Such initiatives, however, were part of a broader policy aimed at countering political and economic crises in specific States or regions. With the purposes of avoiding their unintended negative effect, the EU felt it urgent to develop a specific approach toward human rights violations.

In March 2019, the European Parliament adopted a resolution calling "for the swift establishment of an autonomous, flexible, and reactive EU-wide sanctions regime." On 9 December 2019, the Council welcomed the launch by the High Representative of the EU for Foreign Affairs and Security Policy of preparatory work to establish a horizontal EU sanctions regime against serious human rights violations and abuses. On 17 November 2020, the Council approved conclusions on the EU Action Plan on Human Rights and Democracy 2020-2024, which set out the EU's level of ambition and priorities in this field in its relations with all third countries. On 7 December 2020, it finally adopted both Decision (CFSP) 2020/1999 and Regulation (EU) 2020/1998, establishing for the first time a European Magnitsky Legislation, which now enables the EU to target individuals, entities and bodies – including state and non-state actors – responsible for, involved in or associated with serious human rights violations and abuses worldwide, no matter where they occurred. [12]

The EU Global Human Rights Sanctions Regime applies to acts such as genocide, crimes against humanity and other serious human rights violations or abuses. Other human rights violations or abuses can also fall under its scope, if they are widespread, systematic or otherwise of serious concern as regards the objectives of the EU's common foreign and security policy.

The restrictive measures consist of travel bans, which apply to individuals, and freezing of funds applying to both individuals and entities. In addition, when the assets of the listed persons and entities are frozen, it is also

---

[12] For one of the first analysis of the new regime, see Beaucillon C., "Lutte contre l'impunité ou alternative à la justice? À propos des mesures restrictives de l'Union européenne en réaction aux violations des droits de l'homme", *Revue trimestrelle des droits de l'homme* (2021), 127, 551-571.

prohibited to make any funds or assets directly or indirectly available to them by all EU persons and entities. Derogations to the restrictive measures are possible, including for the delivery of humanitarian aid.

The general procedure required to impose an EU sanction on an individual is complex and long, and it is thus usually only utilized when a major event involving violent conflict or democratic backsliding occurred. [13] In contrast, the new sanctions framework provides a simpler procedure to blacklist human right violators without having to adopt a new legislation every time. Under the European Magnitsky Legislation, where the Council decides to target a natural or legal person, entity or body, it can do so by way of a simplified procedure of amendment of Regulation (EU) 2020/1998, rather than the ordinary legislative procedure.

Council Decision (CFSP) 2020/1999, which establishes the framework for targeted restrictive measures to address serious human rights violations and abuses worldwide, provides that the Council, acting by unanimity upon a proposal from a Member state or from the High Representative, shall establish and amend the lists set out in Annex I to Regulation (EU) 2020/1998: section A ("Natural persons") and section B ("Legal persons, entities and bodies"). It is further provided that the list shall be reviewed at regular intervals and at least every 12 months and the Commission shall be empowered to amend it "on the basis of information supplied by Member states." No formal role is provided for the European Parliament.

The Decision provides, however, for the involvement of the interested persons. [14] The Council shall communicate the decision of listing, including the grounds for listing, to the natural or legal person, entity or body concerned (either directly, if the address is known, or through the publication of a notice), providing that natural or legal person, entity or body with an opportunity to present observations. Where observations are submitted, or where substantial new evidence is presented, the Council shall review the decision and inform the natural or legal person, entity or body concerned accordingly.

Since its adoption, Council Decision (CFSP) 2020/1999 and Regulation (EU) 2020/1998 have been implemented, hence amended, seven times –

---

[13] Under Article 75 of the Treaty on the Functioning of the EU concerning terrorism, any measures of freezing funds or assets must be adopted by the Council and the European Parliament through the normal legislative procedure.

[14] In principle, only minimum due process guarantees apply, following a number of European court cases where sanctions withstood judicial challenges on the basis of being non-criminal, non-punitive, preventive and temporary. For an appraisal, see Alì A., *Examining the legality of restrictive measures on the Russian Federation: the information gathering Process in sanction imposition*, Chapter 2 above.

most recently on March 7, 2023, in relation to sexual and gender-based violence against women committed in Afghanistan, Russia, Ukraine, South Sudan, Myanmar, Iran and Syria.

The EU *first* resorted to the new sanctions' regime on March 2, 2021, in relation to the case of the Russian opposition politician Alexei Navalny. Condemning the detention of Navalny upon his rcturn to Moscow on 17 January 2021 and calling for his immediate release, Council Decision (CFSP) 2021/372 of 2 March 2021 amended Decision (CFSP) 2020/1999 concerning restrictive, natural and legal persons, entities and bodies subject to restrictive measures, to include four individuals: the Director of the Russian Federal Penitentiary Service (FSIN), the Chairman of the Investigative Committee of the Russian Federation, the Prosecutor General of the Russian Federation and the Director of the Federal Service of National Guard Troops of the Russian Federation (Rosgvardia). The Council Decision states for each individual, in addition to the names and identifying information, the reasons for the designation. The measures applied are the usual asset freezes and restrictions on admission: all assets of the listed persons should be frozen. It is also prohibited to make any funds or assets directly or indirectly available to them and member States shall enforce travel restrictions on them.

The *second* and to date most relevant act of implementation of the EUHRSGR was adopted less than three weeks later, on March 22, 2021, when the Council decided to impose restrictive measures on further eleven individuals and four entities for "serious human rights violations […] committed […] in China, the Democratic People's Republic of Korea (DPRK), Libya, Eritrea, South Sudan and Russia".

Regarding the DPRK, the Council listed two individuals – the Minister of state Security since 2017 and the Minister of Social Security since January 2021 (as well as former Chief of the General staff of the Korean People's Army between 2018 and January 2021) – and one entity: the DPRK Office of the Prosecutor. Concerning Libya, the Council designated the Head and a key member of the Kaniyat Militia – a Libyan armed militia, which exercised control in the Libyan town of Tarhuna between 2015 and June 2020, allegedly responsible for serious human rights abuses therein, in particular extrajudicial killings, and enforced disappearances of persons. Another listed entity is the National Security Office of Eritrea, allegedly responsible for serious human rights violations in Eritrea, in particular arbitrary arrests, extrajudicial killings, enforced disappearances of persons and torture committed by its agents. For the abduction and execution of three officers of the Sudan People's Liberation Army in Opposition (SPLA-IO) in May 2020, the Council designated the Major General of the South Sudan

People's Defense Forces (SSPDF) as the person that ordered the operation. Council Decision (CFSP) 2021/481 of 22 March 2021 also added two new entries to the list of natural persons of Russian nationality for the widespread and systematic persecutions in Chechnya, which began in 2017: the Head of Department of the Ministry of Internal Affairs of the Russian Federation in the city of Argun in the Chechen Republic and the Commander of the Special Rapid-Response Unit (SOBR) Team "Terek", Deputy Prime Minister of the Chechen Republic, unofficial bodyguard of the Head of the Chechen Republic Ramzan Kadyrov.

While a detailed examination of these and subsequent episodes of human rights-specific sanctions would exceed the scope of this paper, [15] the analysis will concentrate on sanctions adopted under the new regime against China. At least two reasons concur to make the latter a particularly suitable case-study. First of all, this is the West's first full-format imposition of significant sanctions against China over human rights issues since the Tiananmen events in 1989. Second and perhaps most importantly, because of the magnitude of China's reaction, which in turn led to further counter-sanctions by the EU – with effects, in terms of both costs and benefits for all actors involved, still ongoing at the time of writing and largely unknown. [16]

10.4. Western human rights-specific sanctions for violations against the Uyghur minority in the Xinjiang (China)

Regarding China, Decision (CFSP) 2021/481 of March 22, 2021 amended Decision (CFSP) 2020/1999 concerning restrictive measures against serious human rights violations and abuses to include four new entries to the list of natural persons in Annex A and one legal person in Annex B.

The sanctions were adopted in response to alleged violations and abuses

---

[15] The full – and updated – list of sanctions adopted under the European Magnitsky Legislation can be extracted from the official website of EU sanctions, under the heading "Human Rights", available at https://sanctionsmap.eu/#/main.

[16] It may seem preposterous to write about the effects of the HR sanctions currently in effect against China since the process is not yet completed: we do not know how it will all end, and primary sources material of crucial nature is not yet available. But the purpose of this paper in more in the direction of a general appraisal, using the case of human rights specific sanctions against China as a source of examples and illustrations of the new centrality of human rights in international relations and the public debate. The supporting material included here consists of a few secondary sources, such as articles and blogs, and some primary sources, such as legislations and other available documents.

of human rights of the Uyghur people and other Muslim minorities in the Xinjiang Autonomous Region in northwest China.

The EU imposed travel restrictions and asset freezes on a Chinese public company – the Xinjiang Production and Construction Corps (XPCC) Public Security Bureau – and four senior Chinese officials, including the Director of the XPCC Public Security Bureau.

The serious human rights violations they are held responsible for are: large-scale surveillance, arbitrary detentions, indoctrination and degrading treatment inflicted upon Uyghurs and people from other Muslim ethnic minorities, their systematic use as a forced workforce, in particular in cotton fields, as well as systematic violations of their freedom of religion or belief.

The sanctions by the 27 EU member States were synchronized with those of other Western States. On the same day, the UK, the US and Canada announced restrictive measures against the same targets. It was the second time this was happening, in the now almost half a century old history of the Western response to human rights conditions in China.

As mentioned at the end of the previous paragraph, the first occurrence was at the end of the 80's, when the Soviet Union was in the throes of its collapse with the fall of the Berlin Wall just a few months away, in response to two events with serious human rights implications: the Chinese Government's armed repression of the political unrest in Tibet in 1987-1989 and the violent suppression of the pro-democracy movement at Tiananmen Square in June 1989. Western countries imposed severe economic sanctions and arms embargoes on Chinese entities and officials, which led in turn to a spiral of harsher measures of suppression of other protests around China and heavier condemnation by the West.

Initially, the US adopted strong measures against the Chinese government, including the suspension of military sales, the cancellation of high-level visits and regular meetings between the two countries, a request to stop all new loans from the International Monetary Fund and the World Bank, the revocation of China's most favoured nation status and the connection of the issue of human rights with trade.

The US bilateral monitoring' of Chinese human rights conditions, however, officially ended in 1994, when the Clinton administration decided not to link these two issues. The EU arms embargo is still in place, but even the EU had not sanctioned China significantly since 1989 for human rights violations.

With the human rights-specific sanctions of March 2021, for the first time, the West is re-establishing a link between respect for human rights and its economic relations with China. This is an important policy change worth careful reflection, regardless of the validity and gravity of the accusations made against the Chinese authorities in relation to the Uyghur minorities in Xinjiang or elsewhere.

And it comes at a particular historical moment – with the war on tariffs triggered by Trump's US presidency in 2018 about to end, and the world on the path to recovery from the most serious health and economic crisis since the Second World War, generated by the Covid-19 pandemic. China has shown to have the numbers to come out of it better and before others, including the EU. Today China is the EU's second largest trading partner after the US, and it is both a large market and an important investor for Europe and the rest of the world. [17]

In *response* to the Western human rights sanctions – which at the time of writing are still in place – China denied the alleged violations and abuses in the Xinjiang region, claiming that its camps provide vocational training and are necessary to combat extremism, and urging the EU to "correct its mistake" and to not interfere in China's internal affairs. [18]

But on the same day when the EU took the decision to make use of the EUGHRSR in order to address serious human rights violations in the Xinjiang Uyghur Autonomous Region, China also reacted by imposing its own targeted sanctions against five members of the European Parliament, three members of EU national parliaments, two EU committees (including the main foreign policy decision-making body known as the Political and Security Committee), and a number of European think tanks and experts on China (including the non-profit Alliance of Democracies Foundation, founded by former NATO Secretary General Anders Fogh Rasmussen). As a result, the individuals concerned and their families are prohibited from entering the mainland, Hong Kong and Macao, while they and the companies and institutions associated with them are also restricted from doing business with China.

This reaction is of particular significant importance for at least two reasons.

First of all, the Chinese counter-sanctions constituted a precedent. Just over a month later, on April 30, 2021, the Russian authorities decided to impose sanctions against eight EU nationals, including the past President

[17] In this context, the old relationship between trade and human rights could even be reversed: it is not Sino-Western economic relations that are conditioned to the respect of human rights in China, but the issue of human rights could become a tool to curb China's economic development. This would be a completely new relationship, the implications of which, only sketched out here, are far from obvious.

[18] Robert S.R., *The War on the Uyghurs: China's Internal Campaign against a Muslim Minority*, Princeton University Press, 2020.

of the European Parliament, David Sassoli, and Vice-President of the Commission, Věra Jourová, as a response to the first set of European human rights sanctions against Russian officials for the detention of political opponent Alexei Navalny, on March 2, 2021.

Second and perhaps most importantly, the EU responded in turn to the Chinese counter sanctions, with a further move.

On May 20, 2021, the European Parliament suspended the ratification of the EU-China Comprehensive Agreement on Investment (CAI). It also called the European Commission to use the debate around the CAI as a leverage to improve the protection of human rights in Xinjiang and other places, including Hong Kong and Tibet. For it considered the lifting of sanctions against the Members of the European Parliament and EU institutions as an inevitable precondition for the European Parliament and its committees to proceed with any deliberations regarding the ratification of the CAI.

This call froze any reasonable prospect of entry into force in the short term of the CAI, the negotiations of which between the EU and China lasted seven years and were concluded after 35 rounds at the end of 2020. There is little doubt that the EU has traditionally been much more open than China to foreign investment. While ultimately beneficial to both sides, therefore, the Agreement primarily aimed to rebalance EU-China economic relationship through China's commitments to open up to the EU in a number of key sectors and to ensure fair treatment for European companies.

As it is always the case with sanctions (of any kind), the impact of human rights specific sanctions ought to be measured at the macrolevel, so to say, of the States concerned, but also in relation to specific private activities, economic sectors or even individual corporations and enterprises, which bear the costs thereof (and/or may benefit therefrom).

In this case, one ought to take into account the impact of Western sanctions as well as of Chinese counter-sanctions and responses thereto, on China, Europe, and the rest of the world.

Also, to this interplay of formal sanctions and counter-sanctions, one should add China's instruments of pressure and mobilization of an informal nature, such as, for example, the invitation to its citizens not to travel as tourists to a certain country, not to be consumers of the products of a particular country or company, and not to participate as students in the education programs of other countries.

The effectiveness of these communications by the Chinese government and the size of the Chinese population mean that such invitations can be true instruments of economic coercion that can have an impact in many different ways.

While an economic analysis of the costs and benefits of formal and informal measures and countermeasures originating in the new human rights-specific sanctions regimes is beyond the scope of this paper, the considerations above do set the stage for their legal and political appraisal as instruments for human rights enforcement – to which we now turn.

10.5. Internal political objectives, foreign policies and geopolitical goals

According to the prevailing view, which considers sanctions a foreign policy tool aimed at inducing a change in the target's actions, it is natural to maintain that the effectiveness of sanctions can only be assessed by reference to such "behavioural change".

This model, however, sits uneasily with the reality of human rights-specific sanctions. Measured against this benchmark, the effectiveness of Western restrictive measures in relation to their stated goal in China (or elsewhere) would be close to zero. For there has been no change in the human rights situation of the Muslim minority in the Xinjiang (or other places where alleged human rights violations and abuses are addressed through targeted sanctions under the new regimes). To posit that human rights-specific sanctions primarily aim solely or primarily to change the alleged perpetrators' behaviour, therefore, is to postulate an unworkable criterion.

The effectiveness of human rights-specific sanctions ought to be assessed, instead, more broadly, taking into account that sanctions are a foreign policy tool aimed at achieving various, often multiple, policy goals – beyond the desired change in the behaviour of the individuals and entities directly targeted by the restrictive measures.

First of all, the very existence and operationalization of human rights-specific sanction regimes serve the interests of *domestic pressure groups* of various nature. One interest that clearly stands out is the need for the political branch to respond to the nigh-inevitable calls by the public opinion to sanction those involved in alleged human rights abuses, irrespective of the actual possibility of realization. But other domestic factors may also play a role: from a government's demonstration of resolve to the need to assert a moral stance that would help enhance its legitimacy – as was probably the case for the EU's decision to impose sanctions under the EUGHRSR in relation to China.

These are moral and psychological factors that are hard to document and impossible to quantify. Yet, domestic considerations may even outweigh the international concerns of the imposer of human rights sanctions, in addition to the stated aim of prevention, cessation and punishment of the alleged violations and abuses.

Moreover, albeit targeted, human rights sanctions have an impact beyond the listed individuals and entities, as they affect the *reputation*, and may trigger the reaction, of the state of origin of the violations. This is particularly obvious where the measures are targeted against state officials, state organs and institutions, state-owned economic enterprises, or military organizations.

Unlike counter-terrorism sanctions, where individuals and entities may be listed irrespective to a connection to a specific country, the human rights violations and abuses at the origin of the imposition of sanctions are always linked to a state (most often, but not necessarily the territorial state).

The reputational cost for the state may be high, therefore, precisely because of the stigma which ensues from the allegation of serious human rights violations and abuses, and it reverberates over the attractiveness of its institutions, industries and people. The infliction of this reputational cost can, and often does, constitute a foreign policy objective pursued by the imposer of the sanctions. When measured against such objective, human rights sanctions prove, more often than not, effective.

In this perspective, human rights-specific sanctions may also be seen as adopted in pursuance of the imposer's broader *geopolitical goals*, such as for the EU antagonizing an economic rival in the case of China and altering the economic competition between their respective businesses and industries.[19]

It is not easy to disentangle the economic and more broadly political motivations which play a role in the implementation of Global Magnitsky Legislation. There is little doubt, however, that the new regimes do serve interests which go beyond their stated aim of monitoring human rights compliance worldwide and putting an end to the breaches that triggered their implementation. If measured against these other objectives – whether consciously pursued or otherwise resulting from their imposition – sanctions can be considered effective, even when they do not achieve an improvement in the human rights conditions in the situation concerned.

In the light of the policy and geopolitical objectives of the imposer, one can also explain why human rights sanctions are capable of triggering the reaction of the state of origin of the violations, especially where this is a powerful state like China, which in turn may produce a counterreaction by

[19] See our remarks *supra*, note 17.

the imposer of the sanctions – such as the EU response to China's counter-sanctions described above.

The new regimes give the imposer the opportunity to sanction individuals and entities in cases where it is difficult for economic and political reasons to find the political will to directly target the state of origin of the violation. In principle, they can lead to imposing sanctions against individuals without any relevant action regarding critical geopolitical issues that are strongly linked to the violations. As a matter of fact, the contrary is true. For Global Magnitsky Legislations are only theoretically meant to be used separately from the imposer's political and economic strategy toward the state of origin of the human rights violations. In reality, they are intrinsically connected to the economic and political context of the relations of the imposer with the state concerned and part of its broader national and international policy and politics agenda.

10.6. Conclusions

As is well known, international human rights law is relatively weak compared to the regime of international trade or direct investment abroad. Traditionally, no competitive market forces push countries towards compliance, nor are States generally consistent in their application of human rights standards to their foreign policy, or traditionally employ political, economic, military, or other sanctions to coerce other countries to improve their human rights situation. This is because, contrary to trade openness or the protection of foreign investments, a state and its citizens are generally considered as hardly affected, where the human rights of citizens of other countries are violated in the territory of their home state.

This is the conundrum and the eternal dilemma of human rights, respect for which should be imposed in the name of the international society as a whole, but which in fact are generally enforced only when specific national interests are at stake.

And without powerful States taking a strong interest in the effectiveness of human rights, it generally costs little or nothing for countries with a poor human rights reputation to ratify human rights treaties as a symbolic gesture of goodwill, without changing their own practices in reality.

Historically, a number of developments have led to the particular evolution of international human rights law as a separate branch of international law, distinct from trade and investment law as well as international development law.

I previously held that one of the causes of the ineffectiveness of international human rights law lies in its relative isolation from these other realms of international law and international relations more broadly, and I argued for the desirability to overcome such a separation. [20]

The new human rights-specific sanctions regimes, which following the US Global Magnitsky Act of 2016, have been adopted in most Western countries, have now been implemented in relation to human rights breaches in/by China and Russia and many other non-democratic States. More instances of implementation are expected in the near future.

It is submitted that this is a welcome development. Not only because it contributes to put human rights back at the centre of international politics and the public debate. Also, because it helps to reconnect human rights with other domains of global governance, most notably trade and investment, thereby contributing to their enforcement worldwide.

The paragraphs above have attempted to demonstrate the hypothesis that human rights-specific sanctions regimes – both their very existence and their implementation in practice – serve interests which go beyond the stated aim of monitoring and putting an end to human rights violations around the world. They do not necessarily achieve an improvement of the human rights conditions in the situation concerned but may trigger a chain of reactions the magnitude and scope of which will depend on the military, political, economic and/or technological might of the state of origin of the violations.

The incident of Western human rights-specific sanctions for violations against the Uyghur minority in the Xinjiang (China) provides evidence that the blaming and shaming ensuing from the imposition of human rights sanctions produces a stigma, which alters the economic competition between the players concerned and may result in the achievement of the imposer's internal politics objectives and/or broader geopolitical goals.

Human rights-specific sanctions do offer a concrete prospect of bridging the gap between human rights and other domains of global governance such as trade and investment, which is both at the origin of human rights' inherent weakness and one of the causes of their lack of effectiveness in many parts of the world.

In this respect, they are a welcome development also with a view to their stated goal to enhance compliance, and hence to ultimately contribute to the enforcement, of human rights.

[20] *Supra*, note 1.

Chapter 11
CONCLUSIONS

Mirko Sossai, Francesco Giumelli, Clara Portela

ABSTRACT: *In recent years the literature on sanctions has exploded in quantity and scope. But interdisciplinary dialogue has been limited or it mainly resulted in recognizing the existence of a stark contrast in the ways the disciplines of Law, Economics and Political Science view and analyse sanctions.*
The cacophony produced by a debate where the same concepts mean different things is one of the main drivers that led to the preparation of this collective and interdisciplinary effort. The work done in this volume is to highlight the differences and, wherever possible, to initiate an interdisciplinary dialogue, even though a lot is yet to be done in this direction. It would be already a considerable improvement if the three disciplines would agree on a common vocabulary to discuss sanctions.

11.1. The added value of interdisciplinary collaboration

The various rounds of sanctions imposed on the Russian Federation, while exceptionally robust and severe, do not offer new content, in many respects. They consist of a combination of 'targeted sanctions' directed at individuals and government elites, along with a more comprehensive set of measures of a commercial and financial nature that affect Russia as a whole and its principal ally, Belarus. What is new, however, is the current debate not only within academic circles but also in the mass media and among the general public. Questions are being raised about the effectiveness of these measures in bringing about a change in the target State. Furthermore, there is a growing discussion on how the issue of legitimacy impacts their effectiveness, the relationship between economic effects and specific political goals, and how sanctions can be enforced beyond the borders of the States imposing them.

The intensity and the multiplicity of measures adopted by governments have profound and widespread legal, political, and economic implications that have not been adequately considered. This occurred despite the fact that the increasing utilization of sanctions had been scrutinized by legal scholars, who warned about the legal challenges, by political scientists, who assessed the impact on the targets, and by economists, who pointed at the structure of international markets to show the limitations of targeted sanctions.

In recent years the literature on sanctions has proliferated in quantity and scope. Nevertheless, interdisciplinary dialogue has remained limited or it mainly resulted in recognizing the existence of a stark contrast in the ways the disciplines of Law, Economics and Political Science view and analyse sanctions. The added value of bringing scholars of different backgrounds together is to better understand the impact of sanctions because of the "shared interest in how the drivers, mechanisms, and processes of change – internal and external to the law – interact[1]". This would leave apart theoretical discussions on the (relative) autonomy of the disciplines and the question of methodology: it is not a matter of integration, like in the ambitious projects of some scholars back in the nineties, but a pragmatic approach in which authors share data, insights, and methods. In other words, if there is an advantage in studying the phenomenon of sanctions from different perspectives, it could be already a considerable improvement if the three disciplines would agree on a common vocabulary to discuss sanctions. These concluding remarks are the expression of a joint writing effort aimed at highlighting, if possible, certain paths of constructive dialogue among disciplines.

11.1.1. A comparative approach

One added value of this collaboration has been to agree on the utilization of a comparative approach in relation to the measures adopted autonomously by States and by regional organizations. With the exception of the United Nations, the attention on sanctions has focused mainly on the case of the United States, while the debate on regional sanctions has been dominated for a long time by the restrictive measures taken by the European Union (EU) against individuals as well as third States. This has represented a methodological challenge for the risk of European hegemonism,[2] which might lead to a sort of misconception as for what regional sanctions are.

[1] Krieger H., Liese A., *Introduction: Value Change in the International Legal Order*, in Krieger H. and Liese A. (eds.), *Tracing Value Change in the International Legal Order: Perspectives from Legal and Political Science*, OUP, 2023, 1-22, at 4.

[2] See Riegner M., *Global Governance and Regionalism: Legal Perspectives*, in Rüland J., Carrapatoso A. (eds.), *A Handbook on Global Governance and Regionalism*, Elgar, 2022, 85-100, at 89.

In recent years, the issue of international sanctions has become a research theme through the prism of comparative regionalism. The increasing interest in the use of sanctions by regional and sub-regional organizations, particularly in Africa and in the Americas, has allowed for a better understating of the relational nature of such measures based on membership. A comparative approach has emphasized that regional sanctions are institutional reactions to violations of fundamental common values committed by member States and non-state actors, particularly against democracy and the rule of law.[3] Moreover, regional sanctions are characterized by the rupture of the normal relations between the members and the organization, which takes place through alterations in the substance of membership.[4]

The focus on the United States has also overshadowed the emerging role played by non-western States in the realm of sanctions. For instance, the Russian Federation and China have developed sanctions policies and practiced the imposition of restrictive measures on the model established by the United Nations and replicated by other western States and its allies. These new sanctions players, also operating withing competing legal frameworks, represent a novelty that ought to be investigated by and pose challenges to be addressed jointly by legal, political and economic scholars.

11.1.2. The need for reliable data

The advancement of knowledge in the field of sanctions is related to the availability, reliability and management of large amounts of data. This is an emerging field of analysis in international law, particularly with respect to decisions of international courts and tribunals as well as acts of international organizations.[5]

Recent years have seen the judicialization of sanctions, particularly with respect to the case law of the Court of Justice. The defining feature of the EU action is the existence of a full and effective judicial review: indeed, since 2014, various targeted persons have challenged the validity of the restrictive measures before the Court of Justice of the EU, mostly in the framework of actions for annulment. It follows that the Court has already developed a conspicuous case-law on 'sanctions' against the Russian Feder-

---

[3] See Sossai M., *UN Sanctions and Regional Organizations: an analytical framework*, in Herik L. van den (ed.), *Research Handbook on UN Sanctions and International Law*, Elgar, 2017, 395-417.

[4] See Chapter by T. Corda.

[5] Shaffer G., Ginsburg T., "The Empirical Turn in International Legal Scholarship", *American Journal of International Law* (2012), 105, 1-46.

ation, that has contributed to elucidate the principles underpinning the exercise of this power by the EU, including the nature of the measures, the motivation, and the criteria for designation of targeted persons.[6] After the imposition of the new packages of EU restrictive measures, a significant amount of annulment actions has been brought,[7] with an increasing number of requests for preliminary rulings. It goes without saying that recourse to databases is essential in order to chart the practice of domestic courts, which are facing additional challenges in applying EU sanctions as well, because of the new types of restrictions imposed against Russia and the potential risks of circumvention.

By contrast, in the realm of Political Science, and even more in the domain of Economics, research has long been dominated by either the resort to databases (e.g. the Global Sanctions Database – GSDB, the Threat and Imposition of Economic Sanctions – TIES, the Targeted Sanctions Consortium – TSC) or to a few case studies. This situation is not without risks: on the one hand, the availability of dataset "homogenizes" the research field, given that different sets of researchers test their models and theoretical assumptions on the same empirical material. The definitions used in the design of the database circumscribe the universe of sanctions we investigate, which influences the research questions that are looked into. This is often done without paying close attention to the choices that were made in the preparation of the data, which may also have an impact on the interpretation, and therefore the accuracy of the results.[8] Some critical reflections on the implications of dataset configuration would help us to better understand existing findings. More granular data is absolutely necessary as existing datasets rarely distinguish for type of sanctions and, even more importantly, if possible, for sectors affected by sanctions. Moreover, the construction of new databases that include previously excluded sanctions exercises, such as that employed in the chapter on Africa authored by Tiziana Corda, is instrumental in advancing our knowledge.[9] On the other hand, there has been a number of single or few case studies, which cannot provide the breath needed to reach wider conclusions on questions related to sanctions, their utilization and impact.

---

[6] See the Chapter by A. Alì.

[7] According to the judicial statistics of the General Court, cases involving restrictive measures, totalling 103 new cases, represented 11.4% of all new cases brought in 2022.

[8] Portela C., Charron A., "The Evolution of Databases in the Age of Targeted Sanctions", *International Studies Review* (2023), 25, 1-20.

[9] See Chapter by T. Corda.

11.2. A common vocabulary

International sanctions and their recent targeted version are subjects of studies of multiple disciplines, which reason and speak with different concepts and analytical categories that resonate within disciplinary boundaries. The cacophony produced by a debate where the same words mean different things is one of the main drivers that led to the preparation of this collective and interdisciplinary effort. As noted by Andrea Bianchi,[10] certain concepts and categories have entered into the language of international lawyers, IR scholars, and even some research in Economics. Some concepts that are used across the disciplines with respect to sanctions, are: legitimacy, compliance/implementation, effectiveness, and last but not least, the binary opposition between multilateral and unilateral sanctions.

The work done in this volume was to highlight the differences and, wherever possible, to initiate an interdisciplinary dialogue even though a lot is yet to be done in this direction.

11.2.1. Legitimacy (and legality)

The issue of legitimacy of (unilateral) sanctions is still the elephant in the room as it stands at the centre of any discussion. The politics of (de)legitimation involves four distinct problems: the identity of the sender; the choice of the measure; the procedure followed for its adoption; the status of the norm breached by the target.[11]

The question of the identity of the sending entity remains particularly divisive: when deadlock prevents UN Security Council action, the main rift is on whether States individually, or in the context of regional organizations, are empowered/authorized to act in the name of the international community for the protection of certain general interests. A further aspect concerns the choice of means regarding a crisis. Indeed, sanctions are often considered to be the instrument of the strong against the weak. Alternatively, they are seen as an instrument of coercion that is not appropriate to address conflicts and crises that require mediation, aid, and more positive incentives.

The legal debate has clarified a number of issues regarding the 'legality' of this instrument. First, the distinction between sanctions *stricto sensu*, a category including only measures decided by the UN Security Council, and

---

[10] Bianchi A., *International Law Theories: An Inquiry into Different Ways of Thinking*, OUP, 2016, 131.

[11] See the Chapter by S. Palestini.

countermeasures, a category referring to decentralized reactions by individual States or regional organizations for the purpose of protecting general interests of the international community, has gained acceptance in the 'estern' literature. In order to be legal, countermeasures must respect the principle of proportionality and shall not entail the use of armed force. Moreover, the aim underlying the adoption of countermeasures is not that of inflicting a punishment; rather, it is to put pressure on the targeted State, with the aim of inducing it to take responsibility, and hence to re-establish a situation of adherence to international law. However, the use of targeted measures, particularly in the context of thematic or horizontal regimes seems to challenge the adequacy of the notion of countermeasure to capture these developments, although authors tend to disagree on the further consequences of this. [12]

What emerges from a wider perspective is that a large number of States, including China, South-East Asia States and the member States of the African Union, remain sceptical or even strongly oppose this view. These States support the position whereby the only legitimate sanctions are those adopted by the UN Security Council and unilateral coercive measures are always in violation of the principle of sovereign equality of States and an unlawful intervention in the internal affairs of the targeted State.

The prohibition of intervention is a well-established rule of customary international law: in the *Nicaragua* case, the International Court of Justice considered coercion as the "very essence [13]" of prohibited intervention, but it did not provide for any specific definition of the notion. It is a shared view among lawyers that sanctions could indeed constitute unlawful coercion, to the extent that they intervene in the *domaine réservé* of a target State by interfering with its freedom of choice of a political, economic, social, and cultural system. But the point has been made that coercion would not be prohibited so long as it is strictly confined to compelling the target State's compliance with its international obligations. This contributes to explain why the topic of coercion has been related to the issue of the existence of a norm on democratic governance. [14] As a growing number of sanctions have been imposed for the purpose of safeguarding democracy and the rule of law, it has been debated whether

---

[12] See the Chapters by Ventura D. and Hofer A.

[13] *Military and Paramilitary Activities in and against Nicaragua (Nicaragua* v. *United States of America)*, Merits, Judgment of 27 June 1986, [1986] ICJ Rep 14, at 108, para. 205.

[14] See GC, 13 September 2023, *Venezuela* v. *Council*, T-65/18 RENV, ECLI:EU:T:2023:52, § 92: although the General Court rejected the arguments relied on by Venezuela alleging that the restrictive measures were unlawful countermeasures, it did not take the chance to discuss whether the measures in question constituted an interference with the internal affairs of the targeted country.

there exists a legal obligation with respect to democracy[15] and whether the form of government remains, in any case, part of the reserved domain.

Other disciplines have determined different boundaries for what constitutes a legitimate intervention, justifying the imposition of sanctions. For instance, the norm of non-proliferation is widely considered a good reason to resort to sanctions, therefore sanctions in this regard would be more likely to be considered legitimate than sanctions on civil wars, which assume knowledge on who to target and why. Economists have considered sanctions legitimate insofar as they do not violate WTO and other trade regulations, but there is more resistance to accept measures that clearly violate contracts and/or are seen as abusive of the security clauses embedded in trade treaties.

Finally, the issue of economic coercion becomes relevant also with respect to the effect of the so-called extraterritorial (secondary) sanctions,[16] to the extent that they are aimed at limiting third States' sovereignty to freely conduct their external economic relations with other States. In this regard, the issue of extraterritoriality is also related to the legitimacy not only of the content of the measures but also of the sender: if collective action is not a viable solution and to the extent that no State has the power to bind other States to impose sanctions, the question is whether a State would be justified in trying to enmesh other States and actors by including an extraterritorial element in unilateral measures imposed on a target State.[17]

Consequently, if the process is inclusive, it involves the UN Security Council and it involves the consideration/utilization of all other alternatives before resorting to sanctions, then the adoption of restrictive measures could be seen as more legitimate. Instead, when the process is unclear and untransparent, when some actors may jump ahead and resort to sanctions also with extra-territorial implications, *de facto* forcing the decision upon others as well, then sanctions may be seen as illegitimate. This may happen also when decisions of the UN Security Council are used to adopt further measures, the so-called "floor versus ceiling" debate. This scenario occurs when the Security Council agrees on a set of measures, but while some actors think of it as the "ceiling" (i.e. no sanctions beyond the ones adopted can be imposed), others see it as a "floor" (i.e. further sanctions can be imposed at the discretion of the sender).

---

[15] The debate on the existence of a norm of international law on democracy emerged at the beginning of the 1990s: see Franck T., "The Emerging Right to Democratic Governance", *American Journal of International Law* (1992), 86, 46-91.

[16] See the Chapter by F. Rodriguez Silvestre.

[17] See White N., "Autonomous and Collective Sanctions in the International Legal Order", *Italian Yearbook of International Law* (2018), 27, 1-32, at 14.

11.2.2. A divergence: unilateral *versus* multilateral sanctions

Closely linked to the issue of legitimacy is therefore the distinction between multilateral and unilateral (also autonomous) sanctions. The use of terms that bridge this divide, like "plurilateral",[18] remains scarce outside the realm of WTO law. This is perhaps one of the most pronounced points of divergence between Political Science and Law.

In Political Science, "multilateral" designates any sanctions exercise including multiple senders, while unilateral refers to only one sender. By contrast, from a legal point of view, multilateral is generally reserved for sanctions imposed by the UN Security Council.[19] The sharp distinction between sanctions emanating from the UN, on the one hand, and from any other actor, collectively or individually, on the other, obviously places international organizations in an uncomfortable grey area. A most interesting finding of our authors is that sanctions by regional entities are perceived as more legitimate than similar measures by individual States, at least in Latin America and Africa.[20] The reason could be that regional measures against member States are provided for by the constituent instrument of the relevant organization (and, therefore, covered by consent) and that the degree of legitimacy would be different in case of sanctions *vis-à-vis* third States. Whether this situation will eventually find legal reflection of any sort remains to be seen.

11.2.3. Compliance/full implementation

The implementation and compliance of international sanctions involve a complex web of actions and considerations at the international, regional, and national as well as at the non-state actor levels. Understanding the dynamics of sanctions requires a multi-faceted analysis that takes into account different levels of authority, overlapping jurisdictions, and varying sanctions regimes adopted by different actors.

First, sanctions can be adopted by international organization, regional organizations and States. In the first two cases, decision-making and implementation are split and carried out by different institutions (e.g. it is the UN Security Council that makes a decision to impose sanctions, but it is

---

[18] See foreword by A. Bultrini.

[19] Barber R., "An Exploration of the General Assembly's Troubled Relationship with Unilateral Sanctions", *International & Comparative Law Quarterly* (2021), 70, 343-378.

[20] See Chapters by S. Palestini and T. Corda respectively.

the member States who are responsible for implementing the Resolution), but this gap narrows down the closer we get to autonomous sanctions. Implementation at the international and regional level can be challenging as it involves coordination among numerous countries, each with its own interests and priorities. States must align their domestic laws with the UN obligations and guidance to ensure effective implementation. Firms and companies need to comply with national legislation delegating implementing functions to them and cooperate with public authorities.

National implementation of sanctions requires each country to translate international or regional sanctions into domestic laws and regulations. However, complications can arise due to differing interpretations or varying domestic priorities. In some cases, overlapping authorities among different government agencies can lead to inconsistent enforcement, affecting the overall effectiveness of sanctions. Additionally, certain countries may choose to impose secondary sanctions, targeting individuals or entities in other jurisdictions that engage in transactions with the sanctioned parties. This can create further complexities and compliance challenges, as entities operating internationally must navigate multiple sets of sanctions regulations. Furthermore, different actors such as the United States, China, Russia, and other major players may adopt their own sanctions regimes in response to specific geopolitical situations. These unilateral actions can create further complexities, as they may not align with broader international consensus or may have extraterritorial effects, impacting entities and individuals beyond their borders.

Drawing conclusions on the sources of noncompliance is crucial to refine and improve the implementation of international sanctions. Lack of capacity within national institutions can hinder the proper enforcement of sanctions. The cross-border nature of international trade that sanctions attempt to limit is also at the core of the problem as it limits the jurisdiction of enforcement authorities to national borders. Failure to coordinate with private sectors might result in unintended loopholes or inadequate impact.[21] Indeterminate and ambiguous language in sanctioning decisions can lead to confusion and loopholes in compliance. Moreover, indifference driven by self-interest or deliberate defiance of the sanctions can undermine the entire efficacy of these measures.

In conclusion, the implementation and compliance of international sanctions require comprehensive analysis at various levels. Navigating the intricate web of overlapping authorities and different sanctions regimes is

[21] Giumelli F., Onderco M., "States, Firms, and Security: How Private Actors Implement Sanctions, Lessons Learned from the Netherlands", *European Journal of International Security* (2021), 6, 190-209.

essential to ensure effectiveness and adherence to the intended objectives. Harmonizing efforts among States, regions, and international bodies is vital in creating a coherent and unified approach to address global challenges and promote responsible behaviour in the international community.

11.2.4. Functions and purpose

Already at a definitional level, both Political Science and Law underline behavioural change as the ultimate objective of the sanctions exercise. In the legal field, this has major consequences, given that the persistence of sanctions, and their duration in general, is made conditional on the continuation of the wrongdoing to which they respond: an idea that is also reflected in case-law.[22] In other words, a continuation of the sanctions beyond the termination of the objectionable action is unwarranted and can become an illegal act in itself in case of continuation. For the assessment of the efficacy of the measures, the question of their purpose is of paramount importance: it is necessary to first determine the objectives of the sanctions in order to be able to evaluate whether they are effective or otherwise.[23]

In contrast to Law, Political Science has so far displayed more openness to the idea that sanctions may follow more than one objective, and that compliance may not even be the most important among them.[24] Nossal mentioned the role of punishment as in itself the objective of sanctions, Lindsay listed six main goals motivating the utilization of sanctions.[25] There is a consensus on the fact that sanctions can do more than one thing, but what these functions are remains to be debated. Some scholars have opted for a tripartite definition of 'purposes' that sanctions would achieve: to coerce, to constrain and to signal. Understanding the different roles sanctions play – coercive, constraining, and signalling – is essential in comprehending their impact on the global stage.[26]

---

[22] Miadzvetskaya Y., Challet C., "Are EU Restrictive Measures Really Targeted, Temporary and Preventive? The Case of Belarus", *Europe in the World: A Law Review* (2022), 6, 1-20.

[23] See the approach adopted by P.A.G. van Bergeijk and S.F. Dizaji as well as K.A. Preble in their Chapters in this volume.

[24] Jones L., Portela C., "Evaluating the Success of International Sanctions: A New Research Agenda", *Revista CIDOB d'Afers Internacionals* (2020), 39-60.

[25] Lindsay J.M., "Trade Sanctions as Policy Instruments: A Re-Examination", *International Studies Quarterly* (1986), 30, 153-173.

[26] Giumelli F., *Coercing, Constraining and Signalling. Explaining UN and EU sanctions after the Cold War*, ECPR Press, 2011.

Coercive sanctions are designed to force a targeted country or entity to alter its behaviour by inflicting economic, political, or diplomatic pressure. By imposing restrictions on trade, financial transactions, or access to resources, coercive sanctions aim to create economic hardships and induce the target to comply with certain demands or change objectionable practices. The intention is to make the cost of non-compliance higher than the benefits, pushing the target towards desired behaviour or policy shifts.

Constraining sanctions, on the other hand, are primarily focused on limiting the actions or capabilities of a targeted actor without necessarily seeking a specific change in behaviour. These sanctions are aimed at preventing certain actions or activities rather than forcing a shift in policy. For example, arms embargoes can be considered constraining sanctions, as they restrict the flow of weaponry to specific regions or countries, aiming to prevent escalation of conflicts or violence. Sanctions can also serve as signals of disapproval or support from the international community. By imposing sanctions, countries can demonstrate their opposition to certain actions, policies, or behaviours, expressing their displeasure through diplomatic means. On the flip side, lifting sanctions can signal approval or recognition of positive changes in the behaviour of the target country. These signals can be important for shaping perceptions and aligning international actions with shared values and principles.

In general terms, the practice of sanctions has shown the frequent application of constructive ambiguities in the place of very specific actions that targets should embark on to have sanctions removed. This approach consists in leaving a range of options at the disposal of both targets and senders that would justify the removal of sanctions in the course of crisis. This dynamic understanding of sanctions is yet to be fully comprehended by both legal scholars and economists.

In conclusion, sanctions are versatile instruments with the capacity to coerce, constrain, and signal on the global stage. Coercive sanctions apply pressure to compel behavioural changes, constraining sanctions restrict specific actions or capabilities, while signalling sanctions express disapproval or support for certain actions or policies. Understanding these different roles allows policymakers to craft effective and targeted sanction regimes that align with broader foreign policy objectives and contribute to promoting peace, stability, and adherence to international norms.

11.3. An emerging interdisciplinary avenue

The contributions in our volume hint at intriguing avenues for interdisciplinary dialogue. Keith Preble's chapter highlights how the export controls may not only fail to reduce transfers, but may actually display the opposite effect, a question as interesting to economists and political scientists as to lawyers, or to anyone involved in regulation. The chapter by Peter van Bergeijk and Sajjad Dizaji highlights how, even within Economics, the evaluation of sanctions' impact takes different forms and remains open to innovation, a methodological issue with implications across the board.

Both the chapters by Tabasom Djourabi-Asadabadi and Annalisa Ciampi emphasize the complex interaction between sanctions and human rights, for instance with respect to the impact of trade and financial restrictions on economic and social rights. Moreover, further discussion is needed on the implications of horizontal *Magnitsky*-style regimes, with respect to possible overlaps with country-label regimes as well as the pursuance of individual criminal accountability.

The contributions by Tiziana Corda and Stefano Palestini draw attention to the sanctions adopted by regional organizations, a neglected practice enjoying an unusually high degree of legitimacy, a notion of interest to legal scholars as much as to anyone studying norms in international society.

An enhanced dialogue between the disciplines on these emerging research issues with a view to establishing a common language would be highly useful. Our hope is that the promising contributions in the present collection can mark a first step in this direction.

INDEX

www.ingramcontent.com/pod-product-compliance
Ingram Content Group UK Ltd.
Pitfield, Milton Keynes, MK11 3LW, UK
UKHW020009200926
475702UK00015B/2553
9781032481340